GENDER
in a Globalized World
IDENTITIES

GENDER

in a Globalized World

IDENTITIES

Edited by
ANA MARTA GONZÁLEZ
VICTOR J. SEIDLER

Humanity
Books

an imprint of Prometheus Books
59 John Glenn Drive, Amherst, New York 14228-2119

Published 2008 by Humanity Books, an imprint of Prometheus Books

Inquiries should be addressed to
Humanity Books
59 John Glenn Drive
Amherst, New York 14228–2119
VOICE: 716–691–0133, ext. 210
FAX: 716–691–0137
WWW.PROMETHEUSBOOKS.COM

12 11 10 9 08   5 4 3 2 1

Library of Congress Cataloging-in-Publication Data

Gender identities in a globalized world / edited by Ana Marta González and Victor J. Seidler.
 p. cm.
Includes bibliographical references.
ISBN 978–1–59102–674–7
1. Gender identity—Congresses. 2. Sex role—Congresses. 3. Sex differences (Psychology)—Congresses. 4. Globalization—Social aspects—Congresses. I. González, Ana Marta, 1969– II. Seidler, Victor J., 1945–

HQ1075.G373 2008
305.309—dc22

2008030590

Printed in the United States on acid-free paper

CONTENTS

MASCULINITIES IN A GLOBALIZED WORLD

GENDER GLOBALIZATION AND AN ETHICS OF CARE

PREFACE

The Social Trends Institute (STI) is an international research center dedicated to the analysis of globally significant social trends.

STI aims to assess the long-term social impact of these trends and to suggest alternative ways of approaching social phenomena. To this end, the Institute holds a series of Experts Meetings that bring together experts on given topics to present papers and discuss their findings. The institute disseminates the results of these Experts Meetings by publishing books, through a variety of events, and through the media.

As the social phenomena under consideration are too complex to be properly understood by any single academic discipline, STI takes a multidisciplinary approach. It works with leading international experts from such diverse fields as sociology, economics, psychology, communication, anthropology, technology, ethics, law, medicine, and politics, among others.

STI chose to arrange a conference on the subject of gender identities out of a growing concern that traditional gender roles and norms are in the process of breaking down across many societies, and no convincing alternative is yet in view. Indeed, while de-institutionalization of traditional gender-roles all around the world can be regarded as entailing many positive consequences, it also brings uncertainties and serious ethical challenges of a global dimension. People's beliefs about what the respective gender roles of male and female should entail have an obvious impact on social life and structures, beginning with institutions such as marriage and family. Hence, cultural and social trends regarding gender identity deserve serious reflection. STI approaches issues from a Judeo-Christian worldview. Therefore, it does not endorse every viewpoint within the field of gender studies. With this framework in mind, however, STI encourages conversation with gender experts of any and all persuasions, in hopes of contributing to the greater conversation about gender.

STI is a non-profit foundation registered in New York and runs its operations from New York and Barcelona.

ABOUT THE CONTRIBUTORS

Chris Beasley is Reader in Politics at the University of Adelaide, South Australia. She has lectured in a number of disciplinary/interdisciplinary areas, particularly Women's Studies, Sociology, Aboriginal Studies, and Cultural Studies. Her most recent book is *Gender & Sexuality: Critical Theories, Critical Thinkers* (2005).

Ana Marta González is deputy chair of the Department of Philosophy and Professor of Moral Philosophy at the University of Navarra, Spain. She is co-editor, along with Alejandro García, of *Moda y distinción social* (2007).

Carol Gould is Professor of Philosophy and Political Science, and Director of the Center for Global Ethics and Politics at Temple University, Pennsylvania, USA. She is editor of the *Journal of Social Philosophy* and President of the American Section of the International Society for Philosophy of Law and Social Philosophy. Her most recent book is *Globalizing Democracy and Human Rights* (2004).

Michael S. Kimmel is Professor of Sociology at State University of New York, Stony Brook, New York, USA. He is the founder and Editor of *Men and Masculinities*, Spokesperson for the National Organization for Men Against Sexism (NOMAS), and the author of numerous books.

Emanuela Mora is Professor of Sociology and Culture at Università Cattolica del Sacro Cuore, Milan, Italy. She is the author of *Culture metropolitane* (2001).

Melissa Moschella is a Graduate Student in the Department of Philosophy at Princeton University, New Jersey, USA. She is writing her thesis on personal identity, the body, and social structures as seen in the work of Margaret Archer.

Lucia Ruggerone is Professor of Sociology at Università Cattolica del Sacro Cuore, Milan, Italy. Her main research interests are in urban and popular culture, gender studies, the sociology of fashion and the body, and qualitative methodologies.

Victor Jeleniewski Seidler is Professor of Social Theory in the Department of Sociology, Goldsmiths, University of London, UK. He has written in the areas of social theory, ethics and gender, particularly in relation to men and masculinities. His most recent book is *Urban Fears and Global Terrors: Citizenship, Multicultures and Belongings After 7/7* (2007).

Shelley Wilcox is Associate Professor of Philosophy at San Francisco State University, USA. She has published several articles in the areas of social and political philosophy, feminist philosophy, and applied ethics. Her current research explores citizenship theory and its applications to immigration and urban environmental issues.

Nira Yuval-Davis is Professor and Post-Graduate Studies Leader in Gender, Sexuality and Ethnic Studies, in the School of Social Studies, Media and Cultural Studies, University of East London, UK. Her book *Gender and Nation* (1997) has been translated into seven different languages.

INTRODUCTION

Chapter 1

GENDER IDENTITIES IN A GLOBALIZED WORLD

Ana Marta González

This book brings together a number of contributions that several scholars prepared for the interdisciplinary and international Experts Meeting on "Gender Identity In a Globalized Society," organized by the *Social Trends Institute* in Barcelona in October 2006. For two days, sociologists, philosophers, feminists, and masculinity scholars discussed the relationship between gender identity and globalization.

In spite of the increasing attention paid to the influence of gender inequality on issues such as economic development[1] or conflict resolution,[2] the relationship between gender identity and globalization remains largely unexplored.[3] The cause of this neglect may be that we lack sufficient perspective and perhaps the requisite conceptual tools to engage in a rigorous analysis of this topic. The difficulties have partly to do with the intrinsic complexity of approaching both the ideas of gender identity and globalization in the same "breath." However, to the extent that globalization does have an impact on our entire lives and hence on matters of identity, pioneering studies along these lines are likely to be welcomed, or so I hope.

ON GENDER IDENTITY

By gender identity, we usually mean the self-identification (or others' identification of one given individual) as a man or a woman, where "man" and "woman" do not merely designate a perceived biological difference,[4] but also a set of social roles and expectations—language, clothing, behavior . . .—constituting a symbolic order associated with that difference.[5] Thus, individuals develop their gender identity through experience and practice of what is socially assumed as being a man or a woman, that is, by entering in that symbolic order, and by reflecting upon their meeting the social standards represented in it. Likewise, we can say that people express and reinforce their own gender identity—that is their own self-identification as a man or a woman— insofar as they assume and perform those roles, which are usually associated with a certain gender. In this way, social structures and the cultural norms pertaining to the *symbolic order* work together towards the reproduction of gender roles.

As we know, the concept of gender was first introduced by psychiatrist and psychoanalyst Robert Stoller, who in his work *Sex and Gender* employed this term to characterize one's sense of femaleness or maleness.[6] This distinction was then borrowed by British sociologist Ann Oakley to challenge the traditional view that most social differences between men and women were based in nature.[7] From then on a basic point of feminist critique has been to show that most of those peacefully accepted "natural" differences were in fact the product of socialization processes, which entailed the systematic subordination of women to men.[8]

In introducing the term "gender" to convey the social elaboration of the feminine, feminists were giving words to the idea already conveyed by Simone de Beauvoir in 1949: "one is not born, but rather becomes a woman," but, most importantly, they coined a conceptual tool apt to unveil the relations of power disguised in ordinary practices and assumptions. Ever since, gender has become a *lens* through which we can view society, and discover the practical incoherence of sustaining a universalistic discourse on human rights and dignity while accepting discriminatory practices or customs as something "natural." Likewise, the "gendered lens" has made suspect of ideology every discourse remotely resembling the justification of the *status quo*.

In doing so, feminist thought has obviously incorporated crucial elements of Marxism, but has also departed from it. For, while Marxism applied the master-slave dialectic mainly to the public sphere, feminists started to apply it to intra-family relationships. This meant that they mainly approached gender relations from the perspective of domination—an approach which involved a challenge to the Parsonian view of families as harmonious units, organized around the supposedly unproblematic complementarities of the sexes.

However, the feminist critique did not remain within the boundaries of the private realm: it soon involved a challenge also to the inherited view of social stratification merely in terms of class difference. The adoption of the gendered lens, indeed, allowed feminists to show how the labor market was in fact segregated according to gender, and not merely according to racial or class standards. In this way, they made apparent to what extent the liberal distinction between the public and the private sphere, according to which gender issues were a private matter, disguised the existence of a hierarchical gender divide which went far beyond the private realm.

The latter discovery has been rich in consequences: on the one hand, it has led to ask for the gendered dimension of institutions, values, and symbols; on the other, it has led to ask whether things happening in the domestic realm—such as domestic violence—could actually be regarded as merely a private matter. More generally, it has shown the potential of a critical approach to inherited structures and cultural norms, insofar as they may be incorporating silent relations of power.

Now, to the extent that not every human relationship is adequately understandable in terms of power, feminist thought has a theoretical challenge ahead: it has yet to find the epistemological resources to discriminate relations marked by power from other sorts of relations. After all, even within oppressive structures and institutions we are able to distinguish between oppressive relations and non-oppressive ones. This means that we cannot dispense with the immediacy of moral perception. Miserable structural conditions certainly favor miserable behaviors, but they are often the occasion for generous ones, which unveil new moral possibilities.

In my view, those are questions which still need to be addressed if we are to be able to deal with matters of "gender identity" in a way that does not necessarily involve its dissolution. Indeed, to the extent that we view gender merely as a social construction to be explained from the perspective of power, and we regard power merely from the master-slave perspective, the logical aim is the complete abolition of gender difference, for the simple reason that nobody wants to be dominated. From this perspective, the emergence of the women's movement, and hence women's identity, would be merely a transitory phase in social history. As Frank notes "women are to appear only to disappear. They are to be present as women only to efface themselves as women in particular. They are to emphasize difference as a consequence of sin, only to seek its ultimate eradication in a new order of complete equality."[9] Yet, if this is the aim to be pursued and achieved, all talk about "gender identity" might be an undesirable postponement of the goal. For identity somehow points at the stabilization of certain difference, but what is the difference that one may legitimately desire to stabilize, if every difference is supposed to emerge in opposition to domination?

In asking this question we are pointing at the heart of the debate not just on gender identity, but on identity in general. How are we to think of identity at all? How are we to think of difference? While an account of the contemporary philosophical debate on identity exceeds the scope of this book, its relevance for subsequent developments in feminist thought, as well as for understanding its connection to globalization, is undeniable.

As Eli Zaretsky has observed:

> Before the 1960s, when Marxism was the dominant critical outlook, there was a tacit division of labor between Marxism and psychoanalysis. This division was based on an assumed division between the "public" and the "private," where the "public" was understood by Marxists as the capitalist economic realm and the "private" was the realm of gender relations, sexuality and the family. But, in

another sense, the "private" realm also referred to ethnicity, culture and national, racial or religious identity.
Psychoanalysis developed theories that applied to both
meanings of the private realm. It did so by reducing both
of them to the question of how individuals construct their
identity. . . . After 1968 it was as if what had heretofore
been private became public. The issues that Freud had
described as intra-psychic and familial were acted out on
a social scale and on a political stage.[10]

Social inequalities, which had remained hidden behind
formal political equality, came out into the public space. At
first it was merely the difference between *bourgeois* and *prole-
tarian* under the common mark of *citoyen* (or citizen). As
pointed out above, in the 1970s feminist thought started to
question the difference between men and women within the
family, which Marxism had overlooked. At this point, it
resorted to psychoanalysis, and issues of gender came to the
fore. In *The Reproduction of Mothering*, Nancy Chodorow
developed one of the first feminist readings of Freud. While
she expressly rejected an essentialist account of gender,[11] her
approach nevertheless admitted a basic duality in the sex-
gender system, since the term "gender" was used to characterize men and women in terms of *different* psychic structure.
Yet in the 1980s, some strands of feminist thought began
to develop a non-dual assertion of gender identity. In this
way, they converged with the more general strand of identity
politics, which advocated non relational and particularistic
identity forms: not only gender identity, but also ethnic,
national, or linguistic identities were seen as positive sources
of meaning, and as such claimed for recognition in the
public sphere. In this way, identity politics were drawing

conclusions from the 1960s: they were ultimately challenging the modern liberal split between the private and the public spheres. In doing so, they also gave a new reality to the intermediate sphere of culture.

Inspired by de-construction, later approaches such as "queer theory" have tended more to disrupt than to reinforce identity claims; more to emphasize marginal difference than institutionalized identity. Diana Fuss and Eve Kosofksy Sedgwick's works are relevant in this context. In different ways, both authors have criticized any attempt to confine individuals among socially prefixed categories. Particularly, they called into question the oppressive fusion of gender, sex, and sexuality at the level of the self.[12] By developing genealogical accounts of the formation of sexualities, queer theory has provided us with analytical tools to recognize the interrelations between gender and other identitarian discourses.[13] As Anthony Elliot observes:

> Queer theory represents a sexual politics sensitive to our new era of transnational capital, globalized technology, and postmodern culture. The social and historical forces influencing the shift from identity to queer politics are located in the fragmentation of social identities and political alignments associated with globalization. Queer politics is pluralistic, multidimensional, and open-ended, especially at the level of addressing experience of the self and sexuality.[14]

While gaining respect for the individual beyond any prefixed stereotypes is a desirable goal, strategies of de-construction of those very stereotypes merely through transgression or subversion always runs the risk of becoming a further stereotype. In all these cases it is uncritically assumed that respect and dignity is gained through dialectically self-assertive behaviors. But is this really so? While self-assertion may denote self-confidence, it very often indicates the opposite. This is perhaps best shown in the paradoxes and uncertainties around masculinity.

Masculinity studies, indeed, have acquired prominence in very recent years, and this not without reason. A couple of decades ago, Nancy Chodorow argued, from a psychoanalytic perspective, that masculine core gender identity is more fragile than feminine core gender identity.[15] A similar point had been made at the beginning of the twentieth century by Georg Simmel, as he noted that women were more able to play with fashion, because their identity was not so linked to the surface, whereas men feel the need for more *stabile* conventions. While this point could be easily contested in a variety of ways—for instance, by showing men's affinity for fashion at other times and places in history, the implication is that masculine identity relies more heavily on social and cultural conventions. We could convey this by saying that, in the definition of their own subjectivities, women find solid ground in themselves, while men look more at the periphery. This would explain why masculine identity is proving particularly vulnerable to the fading of those conventions that, throughout modernity, served as the social differentiation of gender,[16] so that very often the only "distinctive mark" presently left seems to be a pathological resort to violence.

Self-assertion through violence is a mark of fragility. Now, masculine identity has proven to be particularly fragile to social change: changes in the social roles of women have deeply affected men's self-conceptions. As Holden points out, "Any discussion of masculinity cannot ignore the social position of and the representation of women."[17] Accordingly, if the twentieth century has witnessed the liberation of women, and their assimilation of traditionally masculine roles, this could not leave masculine identities unaffected. The radical social changes undergone by women in the past century have been followed by the most radical cultural changes undergone by men's self-conceptions.

As Bauman has noted, contemporary individuals can find their image in Ulrich, the so often quoted hero of Musil's novel, *Der Mann ohne Eigenschaften* ("The Man Without Qualities"): "Having no qualities of his own, whether inherited or acquired once and for all and unde-tachable, Ulrich had to compose whatever quality he might have wished to have by his own effort, using his own wits and acumen; but none of these qualities were guaranteed to last indefinitely in a world full of confusing signals, prone to change fast and in a way no one expected."[18]

This is perhaps best shown as we think of the cultural construction and/or de-construction of gender identities in a global context.

GENDER IDENTITY FROM A GLOBAL PERSPECTIVE

The problems surrounding the recognition of particular identities—among them gender identity—in the public sphere are implicit in the more general debate between uni-versalism and cultural relativism. In her paper on "Women's Human Rights as Equality through Difference," Carol Gould confronts exactly this problem: How can one advocate human rights abroad, very often opposing the self-understanding of people born within different cultures, while waging local efforts to recognize cultural difference within our western societies? After noting how cultural diversity can certainly help, but also hinder the recognition of the equal dignity of women, Gould introduces the distinction between abstract and concrete universality, helpful to the purpose of promoting human rights from within particular cultures, and creating networks of transnational solidarities. In this regard, she notes that the permeability to universal notions of dignity and individual human rights does not merely depend on local cultural diversity but also on structural social conditions which may or may not favor a sense of one's individuality beyond the communal bonds institutionalized by kinship or communal ties. That this approach does not remain merely in the realm of ideas but has very practical consequences is shown by Shelley Wilcox, who with her contribution makes clear to what extent some sort of double moral standard is a daily matter. She points namely at the paradox involved in the fact that the freedom enjoyed by contemporary western women in matters of gender—particularly their supposedly generalized access to the market labor previously confined to men—depends on the sacrifice of immigrant women employed to do their domestic labor, very often in precarious conditions.

This certainly raises a number of interesting questions about the proper way of promoting gender equality in a globalized world. Recent research has called our attention on the increasing demand for childcare and domestic work within European and American countries, a need which is usually filled by immigrant women.[19] While we can keep fighting for gender equality in the workplace all around the world, this is bound to remain an unrealistic goal as long as the issue of domestic care is not adequately solved. And, as it seems, this requires both political and cultural changes, so that domestic work definitely acquires the social recognition which it presently still lacks, in spite of being the basis of family life and hence the basis of work-life.

The practical relevance of this problem, however, should not lead us to forget the most basic question that we posed above: Is there any way to unveil some relationships which are constitutive of gender difference and yet are not adequately described in terms of power? A proper answer to this question requires an effort to make our moral way through ordinary experience, so that we can appreciate the complexities of the interplay between structure and agency.

While the ways to do so remain a theoretical challenge, some of the contributions here collected may provide useful hints to work in that direction: thus, while Melissa Moschella's contribution represents a seminal attempt to rework the concept of gender through the Aristotelian—as opposed to the Marxian—concept of praxis, Lucia Ruggerone resorts to phenomenology as a way to voice the requirements of our embodied existence, and retaining a critical stance against the disciplining strategies of patriarchal society—very often summarized in stereotypical accounts of femininity.

In fact, gender identity is bound to remain an ambivalent reality to the extent that claims to identity very often incorporate, as something natural, elements which are the result of socialization processes embedded in hierarchical relations of power. While critical thinking may help recognize those elements, it cannot provide us with the tools necessary to recognize whether gender *identity* might have, after all, a positive meaning, beyond the social roles it can incorporate: a meaning which, beyond all domination, can really lead the process of self-construction and individuation. Ruggerone's phenomenological approach constitutes an attempt in that direction.

Likewise, Victor Jeleniewski Seidler's contribution represents a particularly insightful attempt to work out the complexity of human experience through a narrative recreation of the meaningful contexts of interaction in which gender identity comes into play not merely in terms of dialectical relations of power, but rather as something to be discovered through experience and reflection.

Seidler's reflection on gender deals directly with the uncertainties and ambiguities surrounding masculinity in the contemporary world, marked as it is by the de-institutionalization of traditional role-expectations, and the insecurities of a global society: "Where do men belong?"—a question all the more relevant as the traditional identification of men with the public sphere and impartial authority has lost its former stronghold. While Seidler insists on the danger of elaborating universal accounts of the masculine irrespective of the particular forms it can adopt in men belonging to different cultures and ages, he is aware of the emergence of a new form of "global corporate masculinity."

Indeed, as Michael Kimmel shows in his paper, globalization is actually framing a new hegemonic masculinity: "You can see him sitting in first-class waiting rooms in airports, or in elegant business hotels the world over, wearing a designer business suit, speaking English, eating 'continental' cuisine, talking on his cell phone, his laptop computer plugged into any electrical outlet, while he watches CNN International on TV. Temperamentally, he is increasingly cosmopolitan, with liberal tastes in consumption (and sexuality) and conservative political ideas of limited government control of the economy." But, as Kimmel points out, this global masculinity is also fuelling local reactions, such as nationalist, racial, or fundamentalist movements—which also have a gendered factor built into them.

Taking into account the local declinations of the global, Chris Beasley argues in her paper that the very concept of "hegemonic masculinity," first introduced by Robert Connell in 1979, needs to be de-massified. Accordingly, she tries to discern three different meanings collapsed into it: hegemonic masculinity as a political tool for legitimating power, dominant masculinity as the most powerful or widespread form of masculinity, and finally the empirically dominant form of masculinity, as comprised by actual men. The relevance of her analysis is shown as we start thinking of a global gender order, requiring the re-articulation of national hegemonic masculinities in the global arena. An example of this might be found in Emanuela Mora's analysis of the relationship between masculine identity and Italian fashion.

GLOBALIZATION AND IDENTITY

In suggesting this more nuanced approach to the concept of "hegemonic masculinity," Beasley and Mora's papers somehow echo Roland Robertson's argument for "glocalisation." As it is known, Robertson coined the term to designate

a middle way between those theorists who approached globalization from a macro-perspective which favored some sort
of world-system, marked by a more or less lineal development, and those who favored a particularist approach, disconnected from any talk of homogeneous or parallel development. In contrast to the systematic confrontation of
global processes and anti-global reactions, Robertson's concept of "glocalisation" was meant to designate the global creation of locality, that is, the generation of some sorts of local
movements under the conditions of globalization.[20]

Indeed, since it first appeared in the early 1990s the concept of globalization has come to designate a multifaceted
general trend, resulting from the coincidence of a variety of
processes, such as the liberalization of the markets or the
development of communication technologies, which, taken
together, tend to foster an increasing sense of deterritorial-
ization and interconnectedness. A conspicuous result of
these processes has been the increasing acceleration of
human life, which, in turn, has deeply impacted on the social
perception of time and space,[21] and hence, on the totality of
social experience.

The visible side of those transformations is quite
apparent. As we all witness, because of these economic and
technological transformations, travelling has become an ordinary matter; migratory movements have increased, global
flows influence our lives even more than national events. Facts
like these show that the scope of individual deliberations has
been enlarged, and people feel more prone to make decisions
they would not have made if they were confined to the
horizon of a pre-globalized world. As a result, cultural
exchanges increase, and so does cultural hybridization.[22]

While economic theorists see globalization mainly as an economic process, in continuity with modern capitalism, cultural theorists tend to view this process as an opportunity to redefine individual identities. What is clear by now is that global changes have not entailed the complete irrelevance of the local, but rather its reconstruction through the lens of global relationships.[23] This, however, should not prevent us from noting the continuity between globalization and the process of modernization.[24] While this perspective, first introduced by Giddens, may be regarded too unilateral,[25] it is nevertheless particularly helpful in order to explain the often dialectical relationship between globalization and identity.

To the extent that globalization represents a continuation of the process of modernization, it incorporates some of the features of this latter process, most notably, its rational, individualistic, and abstract character. Now, while all these characteristics account for the efficiency of modern economy and politics, they are insufficient as sources of meaning. This is why modernity has so often fuelled romantic reactions, which reflectively emphasize traditional identities, as different ways of capturing what is resistant to change, and, at the same time, as ways of recognizing those aspects of oneself which cannot be adequately conveyed by abstract rationality.

Identity was not a problem in the pre-modern world because in that world, one's position in life was largely determined by tradition, and face-to-face communities provided an immediate context for self-recognition. Identity only becomes a problem in the modern era, precisely because of the acceleration of social change, which entails the disruption of tradition, and individualizing trends, which eroded communitarian life. As a result, modern individuals are increasingly confronted with the titanic task of negotiating with others their own individual identities, in the light of a plurality of standards. As Bauman writes,

> Modernity, which invented and proudly promoted individualism, also spawned nationalism, communism, and fascism. All in equal measure were its legitimate children; all were equally at home in the family house of modernity, as were the elites and the masses, which modern society sedimented at its poles. . . . Individualism and collectivist ideologies alike were responses to the modern identity crisis. All offered identity as a choice; individualism offered it to the minority who could choose; the ideologies of "belonging" offered it, as a sort of consolation prize, to the majority that could not. There was a constant demand for both kinds and offers.[26]

In the case of gender identity, the 1960s were a particularly critical period, insofar as those years constituted a Marxist and Freudian reading of romantic ideals of authenticity and self-creation.[27] Some decades later, we observe that in modern democratic societies, activities and attitudes formerly regarded as typically masculine or feminine are increasingly at the disposal of everyone, regardless of whether they are men or women.[28] Although many forms of inequality still persist, it is also true that the fact of being a man or woman is increasingly perceived as socially unimportant—unless, of course, you, as an *individual* human being, freely *choose* to develop certain roles and features traditionally linked to gender.

It is from this latter perspective that an observer of

modern individualization such as Lipovetsky can understand and even legitimize the rather spontaneous affinity
between many contemporary women and domestic life: not
as some sort of natural destiny but rather as an option experienced as a source of meaning and even power. After taking
note of this fact, Lipovetsky concludes:

> Democratic dynamics does not arrive until its last conse-
> quences. Although it works to reduce gender oppositions,
> it does not prepare its confluence: sexual identities recom-
> pose more than crumble, and the economy of the mascu-
> line and the feminine is not invalidated by the course of
> equality.[29]

Lipovetsky's words reflect a perceived reality: while de-
institutionalization of traditional identities—among them
gender identity—is inextricably bound up with a new sense
of freedom and equality, the freedom thus acquired does not
necessarily subvert traditional gender expectations, rather it
very often just develops them under new and unexpected
forms.

One might perhaps be willing to qualify this latter
thought, pointing at the persistence, even within contemporary western democracies, of closed societies, which, confronted with the increasing fluidity of gender roles, develop
reactive responses: societies which, instead of recognizing in
that fluidity an opportunity for personal development, tend
to reinforce former social roles, by invoking cultural traditions impermeable to reason. Societies embracing religious
fundamentalism are the most obvious example. Religious
fundamentalism, indeed, represents a *cultural* reaction

against the risks and uncertainties following the expansion of a highly individualistic western culture. Because of this reactive character, it cannot simply be equated with traditional religion. As Zygmunt Bauman has observed, it rather represents another aspect of the multifaceted contemporary-society:

> With the market-induced agony of solitude and abandonment as its only alternative, fundamentalism, religious or otherwise, can count on an ever growing constituency. Whatever the quality of the answers it supplies, the questions, which it answers, are genuine. The problem is not how to dismiss the gravity of the questions, but how to find answers free from totalitarian genes.[30]

As some of the contributions here reflect, issues about gender identity are at the core of those problems. Indeed, while these contributions cannot possibly address all the issues involved in current social changes, they certainly detect some crucial problems concerning gender identity in our globalized societies. At any rate, since the present collection of essays does not exhaust the topic, either from a thematic or from a methodological perspective, we sincerely hope that these reflections will find a continuation in the near future.

GENDER IDENTITIES IN A CULTURALLY DIVERSE WORLD

Chapter 2

WOMEN'S HUMAN RIGHTS AS EQUALITY THROUGH DIFFERENCE[1]

Carol C. Gould

INTRODUCTION

In a provocative article for the journal *Foreign Policy*, Ronald Inglehart and Pippa Norris argue that the true "clash of civilizations" between the Muslim world and the west does not concern democracy, as Huntington and others supposed, but rather gender identity, that is, attitudes to gender equality, divorce, abortion, gay rights, etc. On the basis of surveys of values in these different cultural contexts, Inglehart and Norris conclude that there is by now wide agreement among Muslim and western populations on the value of democracy. But such agreement is very much missing in regard to women's equality or what they call other "self-expressive" values such as tolerance for a variety of sexual lifestyles.[2]

In fact, the analysis that these authors offer poses troubling issues of research methodology, especially concerning how these culturally defined values are interpreted and more generally constructed, and how the various terms such as equality are used. But it is not my concern here to dispute their empirical results. Rather, granting that there remain significant differences in the valuation of women's equality and the perception of appropriate gender identities in diverse cultural contexts, I want to consider the appropriate *normative attitude* that one can take to these differences, in light of our commitment to the value of women's equality.

Specifically, I want to return to the much-discussed issue of the approach we can take to differently constructed gender identities in various cultures, and to interrogate the significance of women's human rights as an appropriate set of norms in this context. I will argue that these human rights need to be reinterpreted in important ways. Further, I will briefly suggest how they can usefully be supplemented by new norms of solidarity, taken in a feminist sense, such that both human rights themselves and our solidarity with others at a distance become relevant to contemporary transnational, if not fully globalized, interrelationships of people and cultures.

WOMEN, GLOBALIZATION, AND GENDER IDENTITY

Gender identity has been treated by feminist theorists in the globalization literature in many ways, which can only be pointed to here. First of all, these analyses propose that globalization processes should be understood as "global restructuring," because they entail the neoliberal control of economies by transnational actors, most especially, global corporations, with attendant demands for cheap labor, often combined with a diminution of social services. It is frequently noted that women tend to be disproportionately employed in these forms of manufacturing (because of their supposedly "nimble fingers") or in the provision of services because they are less often organized and more subject to exploitation. Yet, these powerful globalization processes themselves are held to be masculinized, as revealed at a symbolic level and often in practice as well, in the priority given to the masculine spaces "of finance capital over manufacturing, finance ministries over social welfare ministries, the market over the state, the global over the local, and consumers over citizens."[3]

Beyond this, it has been argued by Chandra Mohanty and others that these globalization processes are in fact racialized, in that black women may be least able to participate in this sort of modernization or may be most profoundly oppressed by it.[4] Other theorists have emphasized the rise in the migration of women that has characterized these processes, whether as domestic care workers in "global care chains,"[5] or in a quite different (and wholly uncaring) context, through sex trafficking.[6] Resistances to these various dimensions of globalization have themselves become more transnational, in the form of women-led social movements or in more local manifestations.[7] Interestingly, the development of such locally organized programs has not diminished with globalization but has perhaps increased in this period.

At the same time, the new information and communication technologies, and global media more generally, have increased awareness of, and brought heightened attention to, practices that can only be anathema to believers in gender equality. These include the aforementioned sex trafficking in young girls, and also of course female genital cutting, which has received considerable critical attention in recent years. Needless to say, this does not exhaust the list: While sati and dowry killings have diminished, female infanticide and sex-selective abortions continue to contribute to millions of missing females, as Amartya Sen has written.[8] Yet it is not only men who participate in these practices, but sometimes women support them as well and this poses a problem for the feminist critique, which I will consider in the next section.

It is perhaps important to stress, on the positive side, that the globalization of communications not only has made these oppressive practices more widely known but also has brought new appreciation of the diversity of cultures and has contributed to the emergence of so-called world cultures in several domains (perhaps most notably "world music"). The interaction of cultures has led to the scrutiny of gender practices both in post-industrialized societies and in more traditionally oriented ones (though not fully reciprocally), and there has been some sharing of perspectives in both directions.

PARADOXES OF EQUALITY AND THE CHALLENGE FOR FEMINIST THEORIES

The persistence of practices like genital cutting that are inconsistent with women's equality continues to pose difficult problems for feminist theorists. To the degree that we wish to be respectful of cultural differences and are aware of the negative consequences of imperialist impositions or even judgments from the position of another culture, we may be hesitant to criticize the practices of others, whom we regard as equal in their differences. Yet, to the degree that we are committed to equality for women, we feel that we cannot tolerate these practices.

This deep tension, which constitutes a paradoxical feature of a commitment to universal human equality, presents difficulties for both theory and practice. It applies most sharply to traditional practices of the objectionable sort described above, but in a different way it applies as well to many instances of women's work in the context of economic globalization, for example, where the work is routine and endlessly repetitive. In that context too, feminists who want to be attuned to the different perspectives of others may well be unwilling to criticize the situation of women who appear satisfied by the new—though unequal—opportunities opened up by global corporations and free trade. Yet, these feminists remain explicitly critical of the functioning of the capitalist economy that has contributed to providing only these sorts of work opportunities and that retains a strong preference for male workers in its reward structure.

In this case the conflict is perhaps not as stark, because we can appreciate that the situation may be relatively better than the previous ones the women had to endure. Nonetheless, the problem of a discrepancy in point of view and the idea that the subjects of criticism may not share the evaluation of their situation applies here as well. These various tensions pose the difficulty for feminism of expressing criticism and working for change even when some of those who are in the putatively oppressed situation do not recognize it to be such.

But there is a second paradox of equality that deserves mention here. This concerns the contrasting implications of a commitment to equality, first in regard to tolerating the divergent modes of behavior of individuals within a multi-cultural nation-state and second, in regard to tolerant attitudes towards different cultural traditions across nation-states. Liberal-minded egalitarians are very likely to argue for extending tolerance towards people with highly unconventional lifestyles within a given country. But when faced with problematic cultural practices in other cultures or nation-states, these attitudes of tolerance are replaced with fundamental critique and efforts to eliminate the objectionable practices. How is it that people committed to universal human equality can apply the norm so differently in each context? Is this a true paradox of equality exposing an inconsistency at the heart of the concept and in the attitudes of those committed to its realization? Or is there another way to explain this divergence?

FEMINIST PERSPECTIVES ON DIVERSE CULTURAL PRACTICES AFFECTING WOMEN

In her essay "Global Responsibility and Western Feminism," Alison Jaggar gives a good summary of the existing positions in the feminist literature and offers her own critique of them.[9] While sympathizing with the critique of violence and discrimination toward women that has been offered by liberal feminists, Jaggar shares the concern of post-colonial feminist theorists to avoid imposing western values on women of the global south and to avoid also an assumption of western women's superiority. She is also sympathetic to the need, stressed by liberal feminists, to steer clear of the cultural relativism that has marked some postcolonial perspectives. Jaggar's main recommendation, though, is for theorists to examine western complicity in the oppression that is often experienced by women of the global south, whether it has operated through military or economic coercion or other more indirect sorts of imposition; in this way, she recommends that feminists engage in self-critique first and foremost. Although she recognizes that nonintervention or isolationism is no longer a possible posture, she advises that any interventions be cooperative and respectful, and undertaken with an awareness (and critique) of the power differential that is often involved.[10] I think that these points are very well-taken. And they are coupled in Jaggar's analysis with a helpful emphasis on meeting the economic needs of women (and men) in the global south.

Yet I would suggest that the examination of western complicity in poverty and oppression needs to be supplemented with a positive account of the human rights of women. These rights can provide some guidance for actions and policies that can help to alleviate violence, poverty, and entrenched forms of discrimination. In the remainder of this paper, I will turn to these human rights and consider in general outline how they can be interpreted such that they are understood as neither imposed on other cultures nor simply regarded as relative to them. I will conclude with a brief discussion of the ideas of care and solidarity in relation to these human rights.

THEORETICAL STATUS OF WOMEN'S HUMAN RIGHTS AND THEIR APPLICATION

The recognition that "Human Rights are Men's Rights," as Hilary Charlesworth has put it,[11] has led to an extensive revisioning of human rights beyond their traditional role as constraints on the public domain of the state and its actors. Feminist theorists have shown how such rights need to be reinterpreted to apply to the so-called private sphere in order to prohibit domestic violence against women and to prevent other violations of their bodily integrity, health, and well-being (such as genital cutting and other practices).[12] Rhonda Copelon has argued for reinterpreting the basic prohibition against torture to apply to rape and domestic violence,[13] while other theorists have urged a focus on "bringing rights home" and on their applicability to nonstate actors more generally.[14]

The attention to women's human rights has also led to an important emphasis on social and economic human rights (so-called second stage rights) as modalities for advancing women's equality. These rights have been taken both in general terms, as in the work of Sen and Nussbaum,[15] and recently also in specific ways that highlight women's labor outside and within the home.[16] This emphasizes the ways in which access to means of subsistence, or meaningful work, along with access to education, can contribute to the diminution of oppressive practices, in that they become less effective. Along somewhat similar lines, some theorists have advocated addressing genital cutting through the implementation of a right to health and to adequate health care. And it is clear that such social and economic rights in fact have wide purchase across quite diverse societies (although not the United States!).

A focus on human rights can help us with the earlier puzzles that I presented concerning the requirement of equality. Although it does not fully resolve the paradoxes of equality, it does suggest that human rights can serve as a legitimate constraint on the toleration of cultural practices, that is, that such practices can be tolerated if they do not violate human rights. In this respect, the toleration for unconventional sexual lifestyles within a given society is not incompatible with the critique of any practices in cultural groups that violate the bodily integrity of women. So, as I have argued elsewhere, the test becomes whether the practice in question violates human rights.[17]

Nonetheless, for this reliance on human rights to avoid simply being an imposition of preferred western mores, it has to meet certain other criteria: A crucial one is that the human rights standards have to be applied to criticize the situation in the United States and other post-industrial societies, as well as elsewhere. It cannot be used one-sidedly to criticize only cultural practices within the global south. Moreover, as the anthropologist Sally Merry has argued, it is not as though the United States and other societies that strongly advocate for human rights are themselves culture free. Culture, if it is to be a viable concept, has to be seen as applying not only to so-called traditional cultures but to so-called modern ones as well, in that cultures consist of everyday practices, mores, and relatively stable expectations of actions and roles across the range of societies.[18]

We can propose too that any human rights critique of cultural practices needs to be coupled with a social, political, and economic analysis and critique of the conditions that have given rise to or contributed to the practices in question. Indeed, as Merry also points out, not all objectionable cultural practices are ancient, and current political and economic conditions can at the very least exacerbate them, as in the case of battering that is aggravated by war and violence.[19] Further, the idea that these practices are entirely due to individuals in the "other" culture absolves western societies and neo-liberal economics of any role in aggravating them.

An additional factor to be kept in view in understanding the normative acceptability of cultural practices is summed up in the question "Who speaks for the culture?," as several feminist theorists have observed.[20] It is important that women be among the spokespeople, and not only the rulers who are likely to be the ones benefiting from the status quo and accordingly interested in its perpetuation. Indeed, too often the representations of cultural and religious norms that are proffered by rulers and other elites are taken as definitive where a more open and democratic reading of the variety of cultural practices would be more illuminating and perhaps also more accurate.[21] And as has been frequently noted, cultures are not homogeneous entities but rather incorporate differentiated groups within them. The practices in question may well violate basic mores within the given cultural tradition and may in fact be viewed critically for the most part (e.g., widow immolation or sati). In such cases it is a mistake to lump together such practices with others that are more fully supported by the cultural group in question. Finally, we need to keep in mind that, from the standpoint of both contemporary anthropology and social philosophy, cultures are appropriately conceived as relatively dynamic and changing, even though these transformations are some-times slow and not very evident. And even relatively isolated cultures normally have some interaction with cultures and perspectives external to them.

SOME DIFFICULT NORMATIVE ISSUES REGARDING WOMEN'S HUMAN RIGHTS

It is clear, then, that social critique and self-criticism play an important role in the interpretation and application of women's human rights. In a complementary way, Brooke Ackerly proposes starting from women's activist networks and cases of cross-cultural dialogue in order to construct an account of human rights, which she understands as based in a universalist reciprocity of rights.[22] In this she follows An-Naim who writes ". . . human rights are those that a person would claim for herself or himself and must therefore be conceded to all other human beings."[23] Political philoso-phers will recognize here a view similar to that developed by Alan Gewirth, who derives human rights to freedom and well-being from an account of what an individual agent must claim as the necessary conditions of his or her action, where universalizability requires extending such rights to all other human beings.[24]

My own account of rights is somewhat different. I have characterized it as quasi-foundational since it is based on a *social ontology* of individuals-in-relations, which is not meta-physical in the classical sense. Briefly, these individuals, as equally agents and as fundamentally interdependent, neces-sarily and from the first make claims on each other for the fulfillment of the conditions of their agency. This sort of claiming is not originally legal, but rather social, manifesting people's ties with others. While the claims are in the first place particularly directed to members of one's own family or social group, they are in principle extensible to all others.

The universality of human rights as an abstraction explicitly recognizes the freedom and dignity of these social individuals. In this account, freedom is understood as self-transformation, whether individual or collective, and thus not simply as autonomy (even when understood as relational). To use a rather archaic terminology, freedom in this sense is ingredient in and emergent from people's agency. Crucially, and here the positive freedom idea comes clearly into view, agency presupposes a web of social relations, and is developed and transformed over time by means of access to the conditions specified in basic human rights.[25] The dignity dimension of human rights, widely shared cross-culturally, articulates not only the respect due human beings but also their shared neediness with respect to both recognition and the material conditions of life.

Yet there is inevitably a tension between the abstractly universal recognition of equal agency with its basic conditions, and the concrete social interrelationships that this entails, which vary culturally and evolve historically. In previous work, dating from my 1974 article on the "woman question,"[26] I have discussed these two features of norms in terms of the ideas of *abstract and concrete universality*.[27] Whereas abstract universality specifies a norm common to all humans (in my view, a conception of recognition of equal agency itself understood as individual or collective and the various conditions specified in human rights that it requires for its development), concrete universality brings into focus the emergence of networks of increasingly universalistic or many-sided interrelationships and capacities, where these are also concretely differentiated in time and place. We can say that although the bare recognition of equal agency as a transformative power of change ingredient in human action is essential, such agency always takes concrete form in differentiated ways that are themselves partly constitutive of the human and that also give specification to the conditions needed for the development of these agential powers.

The two sorts of norms—abstract and concrete—can to a degree be understood as in dialectical relation to each other. Thus, the abstract recognition of universal human equality (of agency) acts as an inclusive principle (at least as far as human beings go) and can provide some guidance in people's evaluations of practices that make a claim to instantiate such agency in various contexts. Conversely, the concreteness of the differentiated and historical expressions of such transformative agency are partly constitutive of what it is in fact, and specify the particular social and historical conditions necessary for the development of capacities. Thus each form of universality can at least in principle serve as a corrective to the other and our conceptions of them likewise evolve in interrelation with each other.

In this connection, we can point to the ways in which women's human rights as conceived here acknowledge and indeed call for equality through difference, or perhaps a differentiated equality. Here I would draw again on my 1974 paper on concrete universality, understood as universality through differences, where these differences are understood as socially and historically constituted through practices and specific forms of relationships.[28] First, then, recognizing women's human rights presupposes the critique of oppression and of lesser forms of discrimination, and this is indeed central in CEDAW and its formulations, although CEDAW does not yet have teeth within international law. The equality entailed in the critique of domination or oppression is one that emphasizes the process of overcoming obstacles to people's development and the elimination of unfair disadvantages. A second aspect of differentiated equality comes from the idea of equal positive freedom, which argues for equal access to a range of different conditions depending partly on people's social and historical circumstances. In this way, the account of needs for basic conditions of human life, including the three types I have suggested in previous work, namely, material needs, the need for recognition, and the need for relationships, are themselves appropriately differentiated socially and culturally despite the commonalities they point to. Even the historically and culturally variable understandings of the line between public and private can be accommodated to a significant degree while also counseling the preservation of women's security and bodily integrity as matters of human rights. Finally, and centrally, this view sees human rights as partly constituted in their meanings by ongoing processes of intercultural dialogue and as open to reasonably wide interpretations within a diversity of cultural localities. The arguments I have given require, however, that women have to be able to play a large role in these discursive processes and that dialogues need to incorporate socially critical perspectives.

We may briefly take note of a second difficult normative issue that comes from a somewhat different direction. Certain feminist theorists have criticized the human rights project itself from the standpoint of the ethic of care. In a recent article, for example, Fiona Robinson argues that a rights framework such as that offered by Thomas Pogge is necessarily individualist and disregards the requirements of care that are so essential for a more ethical form of globalization.[29] She holds that feminist care ethics instead presupposes a "relational moral ontology," which places everyone's need for care at the center of its consideration. Care perspectives would take a critical view of globalization not so much in terms of failure to respect and provide for people's human rights, but by pointing to the denial of the possibilities of care worldwide, for children, women, the ill, workers, and indeed everyone who needs it.

I agree with Robinson's trenchant critique of globalization and indeed the centrality she and others give to care. Nonetheless, I think that her portrayal of human rights as necessarily individualistic and legalistic, and in some sense standing in opposition to care, is misguided. In my view, human rights and care are essentially interconnected in important ways (in a sense analogous to the relation of justice and care for which I argued in a 1990 article, "Philosophical Dichomities and Feminist Thought: Towards a Critical Feminism").[30] Here, I would only stress that rights are in fact relational and that they manifest the interdependence of each human's claims on others for the conditions of agency. As already intimated, "claiming" is not to be understood in the sense of making legal claims but rather social, practical, and indeed moral, ones on others. And aside from the possibility that there may indeed be human rights to care itself in some senses, we can observe that the recognition of human rights is based not only in our abstract reasoning about human equality but on the growth of care about each other, in widening circles (or so we hope).

NETWORK SOLIDARITY

A crucial element in the extension of both care and human rights to those at a distance is the development of new forms of transnational solidarity that I have elsewhere called "network solidarities."[31] This conception of solidarity differs from the traditional use in which it denotes the close and mutual relations of concern and aid among the members of a particular group. The new conception proposes that it is possible to stand with people who are oppressed or suffering, even if they are not members of one's local community or nation-state, and act to help them if they wish such aid. However, like the traditional concept, in this use solidarity remains limited to particular people or groups and associations (in relation to each other). It thus is not to be identified with the notion of general human solidarity, though the latter can serve as a limit notion. Since, on this revised conception, solidarity can be extended across different people and groups, which may overlap with each other, it can be described as a set of networks of solidarity relations, rather than as a unitary relation among all the members of a group.

This conception partly emerges from a reflection on some recent social movements, especially resistance movements that are women led, especially in Latin America.[32] It attempts to capture some of the diversity of cultural contexts that are linked by such networks, and at the theoretical level it may be said to reflect a feminist relational social ontology.[33] For my purposes, transnational solidarities can serve to unite care with respect for human rights because of the centrality they give to a common commitment to justice, which is shared by the individuals or groups standing in solidarity relations with each other. These networks therefore are not simply ones of mutual aid or care. They unite around such a shared commitment to justice, particularly understood as the elimination of oppression, and they facilitate concrete collective action to this end (or at least reflect a readiness to undertake it). As I have argued elsewhere, important to this sort is solidarity is *deference* to the needs and interests of those people seek to support.[34] In this way, solidarity in this meaning eschews neocolonial impositions of values on others, by force or other means. Yet given the shared commitment to justice, we can suppose that the growth of such networked solidarities in increasingly global communicative interactions can help in the wider fulfillment of human rights.

CIVILIZATIONAL CLASHES OVER GENDER?

We can return in conclusion to briefly reconsider the putative diremption between civilizations, asserted by Inglehart and Norris, with which we began this essay. Their view is that the fundamental clash is not about democracy any longer (if it once was) but about gender equality. Yet, in view of the recognition of the multifarious and dynamic nature of cultures, it is clear that we need to be wary of such generalizations. The context in which the survey questions they relied on were asked and the answers obtained undoubtedly played a role, and not a neutral one, in the survey's results.

But to the degree that the study these authors summarize does reflect genuinely discrepant views among cultures in regard to women's equality, we can observe that any imposition of values and norms will not be helpful. Indeed, it seems likely that gender identities of male dominance may become hardened by such impositions, particularly where the interventions are by force, as they have been recently. We can suggest that coercive impositions have a tendency to produce humiliation, which in turn exacerbates existing tendencies on the part of some men to control women, while also contributing to extremism of other sorts. Positively, by contrast, it seems likely that a commitment to human rights, taken as emerging in their specificity from across different cultures, is important in remedying these problems and producing less conflicting forms of interaction and understanding. I have argued that women's human rights play a central role in such an alternative approach, and I have also pointed to the idea of rights to care. It is legitimate too, I have proposed, to support others in their own efforts to eliminate oppression and meet human needs. Such a feminist conception of transnational solidarity, one that avoids imposition but also offers support, can be seen to be an important supplement to the establishment of human rights more globally.

Chapter 3

WHO PAYS FOR GENDER DE-INSTITUTIONALIZATION?

Shelley Wilcox

In debates about gender identities within national contexts, some feminists implicitly refer to globalization as a positive catalyst for change, while employing a one-dimensional analytical lens that obviates the diverse effects of globalization on women's lives. For instance, in feminist discussions in the United States, it is sometimes suggested that women have overcome many of the constraints once imposed upon them by traditional gender roles and expectations. Paradigmatic examples of this "de-institutionalization" of gender involve women's increased participation in the public sphere, a process facilitated by the expansion of capitalist markets. Yet, while more married, middle-class American women are employed than ever before, and women have made notable advances in professions once closed to them, an intersectional and transnational feminist analysis reveals that gender de-institutionalization under globalization is highly uneven, both within and across national boundaries. In the United States, expanding opportunities in the public sphere have enabled many white, middle-class women to develop new gender identities. However, these liberatory identities are increasingly predicated upon a "re-institutionalization" of traditional gender identities for the migrant workers who replace them in the domestic sphere.

This paper explores this paradox of paid domestic work within the global context of the feminization of labor migration, global economic restructuring, and an increasingly "international division of domestic labor."[1] It proceeds as follows. Section I describes the cultural, social, and economic contexts of paid domestic work in the United States. Sections II and III develop my normative evaluation of the practice. I begin by discussing several feminist criticisms of commodified domestic work, and then I argue that the practice contributes to the exploitation of individual domestic workers by employers, migrants by citizens, and ultimately, the global South by the global North. In Section IV, I recommend several policy reforms to remedy these injustices. Finally, Section V highlights some general conclusions concerning the themes of this collection that follow from my arguments.

DOMESTIC WORK IN THE UNITED STATES

The demand for domestic services has been rising steadily in the United States. Upper-class women have always employed domestic workers to clean their homes and provide personal care for themselves and their children. Recently, however, middle-class women also have begun to hire domestic workers as a strategy for managing the demands of the double workday. As we know, more middle-class women participate in the US labor force now than ever before, and many have advanced in professional occupations in the technology, legal, pharmaceutical, and business and financial sectors, which have flourished under global restructuring.[2] However, stubborn patriarchal attitudes continue to shape women's choices in both the public and private spheres. Women with professional careers must conform to a masculine career model emphasizing professionalism, competition, individualism, and commitment, measured in terms of progressively longer hours on the job. Yet despite women's participation in male-modeled professions, a sexual division of labor based on traditional gender roles stubbornly persists in heterosexual households. Although most men do more childcare and housework than their fathers, the burden for these duties stills rest primarily upon women, even in dual career households.[3]

Ironically, standards for home cleanliness have increased as more middle-class women have begun to participate in the labor force.[4] Standards for proper childrearing have also changed dramatically, as middle-class professionals have become increasingly influenced by "the ideology of intensive and competitive mothering."[5] According to this model of parenting, the standards for successful mothering are measured in terms of the ability to raise children who will have a competitive advantage in a capitalist society. As Tronto explains:

> Mothers are urged to provide their children with the right music, to have them participate in the best activities, attend the right schools, and so forth, to improve their chances later on in life. . . . While mothers may unselfishly love their children and try to do the best for them, in a

competitive society they must also try to gain and keep
competitive advantage over other people's children.[6]

Intensive and competitive mothering is costly, in terms of
both the money it requires and the tremendous demands it
places on mothers' physical, mental, and emotional energies.

To meet the gendered requirements of the public and
private spheres, many middle-class women find it necessary
to delegate some of their household and caring responsibilities to other women. Historically, female family members
have been available to care for the children of their working
relatives. Today, however, many extended families are too
geographically dispersed to share day-to-day domestic
responsibilities, and many of the sisters, aunts, and grandmothers who once might have helped out are themselves
working outside the home. In absence of adequate public
funding for social services, such as childcare, working women
increasingly turn to the market for needed domestic goods
and services, including prepared meals, housecleaning services, day care, and a variety of lessons and activities for their
children. However, there is a relative scarcity of affordable,
convenient, high-quality childcare centers and preschools,
especially those that will accept infants and toddlers. Even
when such facilities are available, many parents fear that
these settings do not provide a sufficiently enriching environment for their children. For many working parents, hiring
a private domestic worker is an attractive alternative.
Domestic workers provide convenience and flexibility not
available in day care programs, and many parents believe private childcare workers offer more consistent, personal, and
intensive care for their children.[7] Ironically, private domestic

workers also may be less expensive than formal service providers, especially if employers avoid paying wage and social security taxes. These savings are multiplied if a single domestic worker serves as both nanny and housekeeper.

Domestic workers perform the domestic duties assigned to women under the sexual division of labor, including cleaning, laundry, mending, gardening, cooking, and the care of children and other family members. Sociologist Pierrette Hondagneu-Sotelo distinguishes three common types of domestic jobs.[8] Live-in nanny/housekeepers live and work full-time for one family, usually doing both housework and childcare. Live-out nanny/housekeepers also work full-time for one family, doing both housework and childcare, but live in their own homes. Housecleaners clean houses, working for several employers on a contractual basis, and usually do not do childcare. My analysis will focus on live-in and live-out nanny/housekeepers.[9]

Owing to its historical legacy in slavery, native-born African-American women predominated in these domestic positions until well into the twentieth century, when the 1964 Civil Rights Act made it possible for many black women to enter occupations previously formally closed to them. In different historical periods, different groups of migrant women also have been overrepresented as domestic workers. Until the beginning of World War II, domestic work was the most common source of employment for European migrant women, most of whom initially migrated as wives or daughters of labor migrants and then were forced into wage work to supplement the low incomes of their husbands and fathers. Today, the US demand for private domestic workers is filled by growing numbers of women from Mexico, Latin

America, and the Caribbean who themselves migrate to find work, often without their families. Neo-liberal globalization has contributed to this feminization of labor migration. Trade liberalization and the associated deregulation of labor markets have increased economic inequalities between countries in the global North and those in the global South. As a result, middle-class women in developing countries often can earn higher incomes as domestic workers in the United States than as teachers, nurses, or administrative or clerical workers in their home countries. Structural adjustment policies, imposed by the IMF and WTO, have led to significant cutbacks in social services in many developing countries. These neo-liberal cutbacks have exacerbated economic insecurity, thereby impelling more women to consider labor migration as a means to support their families. Indeed, remittances sent by female labor migrants play an increasingly important role in helping national economies service their foreign debt.

EVALUATING THE PRACTICE OF PRIVATE, PAID DOMESTIC WORK

In the previous section, I described domestic work and situated it the context of the sexual division of domestic labor, ideological models of parenting, global economic restructuring, and the feminization of labor migration. While I have implied that these phenomena are morally dubious, I have not argued that practice of paid domestic work itself is unjust. In this section, I will discuss four feminist objections to domestic work, paying particular attention to the ways in which immigration and citizenship status intersects with the axes of gender, race/ethnicity, and class to increase domestic workers' vulnerability to disrespect, mistreatment, and abuse.[10]

POOR WAGES AND LACK OF EMPLOYMENT BENEFITS

Private, paid domestic work is distinctive in being regarded as something other than real employment.[11] Cultural notions of domestic work contribute to this understanding. Domestic work takes place in the home, which is considered to be a place for kinship and leisure, and thus by nature antithetical to work. Moreover, domestic tasks are associated with women's so-called natural expression of love for their families and thus not considered "real work" at all. These cultural understandings of domestic work contribute to its low social status and market value. Hours are long for domestic workers and wages are extremely low, particularly for live-in workers.[12] Domestic workers usually do not receive health insurance, retirement benefits, worker's compensation, or paid sick leave or vacation.[13] The ambiguous, quasi-familial position of domestic workers within the household also increases their vulnerability to economic abuse.[14] Employers who view domestic workers as "just like part of the family" are less likely to think of themselves as employers, with a responsibility to pay taxes and provide employment benefits. Though rarely genuinely treated as such, domestic workers who believe they are considered to be part of the family may feel too guilty to ask for a day off, request a raise, or demand overtime pay.

Migrant domestic workers almost universally earn lower wages than native-born workers.[15] The idea that domestic work is a "bridging occupation" is thought by some to justify this wage disparity.[16] The occupation is often described as entry-level position for migrant women, offering social mobility and the ability to move on to higher-status and better-paying jobs. Some theorists go so far as to praise domestic work for "furnishing rural, traditional immigrant women with exposure to the modern world in a protected and supervised environment" thus giving them opportunities to learn middle-class values and preparing them to enter the formal labor market.[17] The patronizing, sexist, and ethnocentric notion that "traditional" migrant women benefit from modernization belies the fact that many of the migrant women working as private domestic workers in the United States are college-educated and held relatively high status jobs in their home countries. Moreover, although domestic work was a transitional occupation for some earlier European immigrants, the class- and race-stratified US labor market ensures that most migrant women today experience domestic work not as an intermediary occupation, but rather as an occupational ghetto that neither pays the bills nor provides access to better-paying jobs.

DIFFICULT WORKING CONDITIONS, DISRESPECTFUL TREATMENT, AND ABUSE

Working conditions for private domestic workers can be as bad as the wages. Since domestic workers work in the private space of their employers, they have little power or authority within their workplace.[18] Their lack of autonomy is complicated by the asymmetrical yet personal nature of the employer-domestic worker relationship and the inequalities based on class, race/ethnicity, and citizenship/immigration status that inevitably shape it. Domestic workers are immersed in the details of the lives of their employers, yet structural inequalities often prevent employers and workers from forming relationships of genuine mutuality and respect. Employers exercise a great deal of power over domestic workers and may change the terms of employment, act erratically, or insult or degrade workers.[19] Since there are no universally accepted standards for what counts as good housework or childcare, employers may hold workers to unreasonable standards. If the employer-worker relationship is especially personal and emotionally charged, employers may become critical of workers for reasons that have nothing to do with their job performance. Employers may even fire domestic workers whom they perceive as rivals for the affection of their children. Domestic workers are vulnerable to sexual harassment or abuse by household members.

Working conditions are especially difficult for live-in workers, who have precious little time or space to call their own.[20] Since they live with their employers, these workers are essentially on call both day and night. Some are required to share a child's bedroom, and even those who have their own private rooms report that they feel uncomfortable using other rooms of the house, including the kitchen. Ironically, although live-in domestic workers are usually surrounded by other people, many suffer from intense loneliness and social isolation. Undocumented migrants are more likely to seek live-in domestic employment than other domestic workers. Although many newly arrived immigrants choose live-in work in order to minimize their expenses and secure urgently needed housing, undocumented immigrants, many of whom are terrified of deportation, seek live-in positions as protection against exposure to immigration officials and the police. However, the costs of live-in work may outweigh the benefits, since live-in domestic workers are especially likely to experience overwork, lack of privacy, disrespectful treatment, sexual harassment, and isolation.[21]

OPPORTUNITIES FOR RECOURSE

In most jobs, workers have several options for resisting disrespectful treatment and employer abuses. Workers can form unions, engage in collective bargaining, and ultimately go on strike. In absence of collective action, individual workers can refuse to perform the most oppressive of their assigned duties and report severe abuses to regulatory authorities. However, the private and relational nature of domestic work complicates each of these options for domestic workers. Domestic workers have few opportunities for collective action because they work in separate households. Since care is inherently relational, domestic workers cannot shirk their caring responsibilities without imposing tremendous harm on their charges.[22] Most domestic workers are reluctant to put the children they care for at risk, and especially so once they have developed ongoing caring relationships with them.

Furthermore, because domestic work takes place in the private sphere of the home, few legal protections pertain to domestic workers. Indeed, domestic workers are explicitly excluded from coverage under three of the four most important federal employment laws in the United States: the

National Labor Relations Act, which guarantees workers the right to organize and engage in collective bargaining; the Occupational Safety and Health Act, which protects workers against occupational hazards; and Title VII of the Civil Rights Act of 1964, which prohibits workplace discrimination. The Fair Labor Standards Act, which guarantees the right to receive minimum wages and overtime pay, was amended in 1974 to include most private domestic workers.[23] However, it still exempts personal attendants, including nannies, from minimum wage and overtime protections, and live-in employees from overtime coverage.[24] Some state employment statutes provide partial remedies to these exclusions. New York, for instance, requires employers to pay overtime to live-in workers who work more than forty hours per week.[25] However, most state laws reinforce federal exclusions, exempting employers of domestic workers from worker's compensation requirements, state anti-discrimination protections, and state occupational safety regulations.[26]

Recent nativist immigration legislation creates additional obstacles for migrant domestic workers who wish to leave oppressive jobs. Ironically, while migrant women are increasingly chosen to reproduce traditional American families, immigrants are popularly represented as a threat to the American way of life. Critics contend that immigrants, and especially undocumented immigrants, cause severe social problems in the United States, including overburdened public schools and social welfare programs.[27] Underlying this charge is the assumption that migrant women enter the United States to obtain social services and ultimately citizenship for their children. This sexist, racist, and xenophobic rhetoric, which scapegoats migrant women for domestic social ills, has initiated a series of legislation that bars nearly all non-citizens, both documented and undocumented, from access to most publicly funded social services. While there is no evidence that such restrictive legislation reduces the alleged social costs of immigration, these laws intensify the vulnerability of migrant domestic workers by constraining their options should they wish to leave oppressive or abusive jobs.

TRANSNATIONAL MOTHERHOOD

Like most working mothers, domestic workers often must struggle to find good childcare for their children while they are at work. This task can be especially difficult for migrant domestic workers, since migrant women, particularly those without papers, often must leave their families behind in their home countries when they travel to the United States in search of work. Most migrant domestic workers leave their children in the care of grandmothers, other female relatives, or husbands; some hire nannies either as sole care providers or as aids to family caregivers. Feminists have demonstrated that isolationist, privatized mothering is a culturally specific model; however, this model informs many migrant women's ideals about parenting.[28] Thus, as Parreñas points out, domestic work is both a "labor of love" and a "labor of sorrow" for many migrant women.[29] Migrant domestic workers are able to send needed remittances home to their families, yet they must transgress deeply ingrained ideals about good mothering in order to do so. Migrant women sometimes are criticized for "aban-

doning" their families, and many report that feelings of anxiety, helplessness, loss, guilt, and loneliness are associated
with their separation.[30] The emotional strains of transnational parenting can be further intensified by the caring
tasks of domestic work.[31] Although children in transnational families appreciate the material gains provided by
their migrant mothers, they also experience intense feelings
of loneliness, insecurity, and vulnerability.[32]

PRIVATE, PAID DOMESTIC WORK AS EXPLOITATION

In the previous section, I discussed four feminist criticisms
of paid domestic work. Some feminists conclude from these
criticisms that hiring domestic workers is intrinsically unjust
because it harms domestic workers and their children.[33]
While I do not wish to deny that such harms occur, I believe
that attempts to capture the injustices involved in paid
domestic work solely in terms of individual morality are
misguided, for three reasons. First, the claim that hiring
domestic workers is *intrinsically* unjust falsely implies that
employers necessarily harm the domestic workers they
employ. While the practice of paid domestic work certainly
involves significant moral hazards as it is currently structured, at least some employers are aware of these hazards and
treat the domestic workers they employ with the appropriate
professional respect.

Second, the claim that hiring domestic workers is intrinsically unjust would seem to blame individual working
women for the childcare decisions of their families without
acknowledging the broader, patriarchal context in which

these decisions are made. I have argued that several factors influence the decision to hire a private, domestic worker, including the masculine professional career model, the sexual division of labor, the lack of affordable, high-quality public childcare, and increased standards for home cleanliness and proper childrearing. While the ideologies underlying the latter standards arguably should be discounted or ignored, the former three factors place real structural constraints on working women with children. Failing to acknowledge the ways in which these patriarchal constraints shape childcare decisions leaves these constraints unproblematized and may play into the hands of cultural conservatives who wish to see middle-class women return to the home.

Finally, evaluating the practice of paid domestic work solely in terms of individual morality provides too narrow an account of the injustices associated with it. Since individual morality focuses on the relationship between individual employers and domestic workers, it tends to ignore the broader political and economic forces in which the practice is embedded. These realities not only constrain childcare decisions as I have mentioned, but also shape the practice itself in ways that contribute to its injustice. To evaluate paid domestic work within this broader context, it is necessary to analyze the practice in terms of its potential for exploitation. Theorizing paid domestic work as an exploitative practice is particularly conductive to the global context because it enables us to articulate its associated injustices as injustices between groups.

According to a general normative account of exploitation, such as that developed by Iris Marion Young, exploitation "occurs through a steady process of the transfer of the results of the labor of one social group to benefit another" in absence of adequate recognition or fair remuneration.[34] Furthermore, the social rules that govern the labor—the rules that determine the meaning of the work and the conditions under which it is carried out—enact relations of power and inequality between the groups. These relations of inequality are reproduced, in Young's words, "through a systematic process in which the energies of the have-nots are continuously expended to maintain and augment the power, status, and wealth of the haves."[35] Importantly, while the exploiting group is enhanced in this process, the exploited group is diminished by even "more than the amount of the transfer, because [members of the group] suffer from material deprivation and a loss of control, and hence are deprived of important elements of self-respect."[36]

According to this account of exploitation, employers tend to exploit domestic workers in much the same way that housewives are exploited within the patriarchal family.[37] Like patriarchal husbands, female employers clearly benefit from the labor of domestic workers. Hiring a domestic worker frees female employers from the day-to-day execution of their culturally assigned domestic duties, thereby enabling them to participate in the public sphere as equals to men. In this way, domestic workers allow their employers to develop non-traditional gender identities outside their roles as mothers. Yet, since the "products" of commodified domestic work—clean homes and well-tended children—tend to be attributed to employers, women who hire domestic workers may also satisfy cultural expectations for good mothering. In this way, domestic workers enable employers to enjoy the advantages of gender de-institutionalization without sacrificing the more traditional aspects of their gender identities. However, since domestic work is socially devalued as "women's work" and largely invisible, even to those who benefit the most from it, domestic workers rarely receive the compensation and recognition they deserve.

Like patriarchal husbands and housewives, employers and domestic workers enter into the employment relationship from very different social positions. Although employers and domestic workers are typically both women, they are almost invariably differentiated by class, race/ethnicity, and citizenship/immigration status. Domestic work reproduces these structural inequalities. By performing work that employers cannot or wish not to do, domestic workers enhance the labor market position and social status of their employers, yet because domestic work is socially devalued and underpaid, domestic workers receive no comparative socio-economic gain. Moreover, given the asymmetrical power relations between employers and domestic workers, their daily interactions often enact systems of domination and inequality similar to those played out in patriarchal households. Like traditional housewives, domestic workers often suffer from the dependency, social isolation, and loss of self-respect that accompanies working alone in the home.

This suggests that the practice of paid domestic work is conducive to the exploitation of domestic workers. However, the exploitation associated with domestic work is not confined to individual employers and domestic workers. Since most domestic workers are migrants and most employers are citizens, the practice also contributes to the broader exploitation of migrant workers by US citizens. Like domestic workers, other labor migrants perform socially necessary labor; in addition to domestic work, migrants are overrepresented in the agriculture, construction, and garment industries. Yet while migrant workers perform some of the most arduous, dangerous, and degraded jobs in the country—work that citizens themselves refuse to do—they typically receive poverty-level wages and are denied health insurance, retirement benefits, and paid sick leave, while being vilified in the media for "stealing" Americans' jobs. Moreover, the rules that govern migrant labor, as codified in US employment law and immigration policy, formalize stark inequalities between migrant workers and citizens. Employment laws tend to exclude occupations in which migrants predominate, thereby providing migrant workers with fewer legal protections than citizen workers. Migrant workers are also systematically excluded from most of the civil, social, and political rights granted to citizens. This two-tiered system of rights, together with other policies designed to prevent the long-term settlement of migrant workers, enable US citizens to exploit the disempowerment and disenfranchisement of migrant workers. Undocumented migrant workers are especially vulnerable to such exploitation because the fear of discovery and deportation usually prevents them from exercising the few legal rights they possess.

The practice of paid domestic work also contributes to an international division of labor in which migrant women from the global South increasingly reproduce the families of citizens in the global North. This international division of labor is exploitative insofar as it enables citizens in the United States to benefit from the labor of migrant domestic workers while externalizing its social costs to their home countries. Legal restrictions on the social rights of migrant workers and policies preventing family members from accompanying them facilitate this transfer. Immigration admissions policies also play an important role. Current admissions policies strongly privilege "skilled" workers, such as engineers, physicians, and academics, over "unskilled" workers, such as nannies and housekeepers. By arbitrarily limiting the number of domestic workers legally admitted, despite the increasing domestic demand for their labor, these policies leave domestic workers no choice but to migrate through irregular channels. Since undocumented immigrants have even fewer social rights than documented immigrants, virtually the entire social cost of their labor is externalized to their countries of origin.

REMEDYING EXPLOITATION

I have argued that although hiring domestic workers is not intrinsically unjust, the practice of paid domestic work is conducive to various forms of exploitation and may involve harms to individual domestic workers. In this section, I will discuss several reforms required to remedy these injustices. First, regulations must be implemented to improve the occupation for domestic workers in the United States. Formalizing and regulating domestic jobs is a necessary first step. Existing federal and state employment regulations, including minimum wage, overtime, social security, employee safety, and anti-discrimination laws, should be strengthened to provide full protection to all domestic workers, including live-in workers and personal attendants, without regard to immigration status. Domestic workers and their employers should be informed of their legal rights and obligations under these regulations and the laws should be enforced consistently. Formalizing employment through written contracts would allow domestic workers to negotiate the terms of their employment. Moreover, by depersonalizing the employer-domestic worker relationship, formal employment contracts may also encourage employers to see themselves as employers and to treat workers more consistently and with greater respect.[38] Formalization may also enhance opportunities for labor organization and collective action in pursuit of improved wages and working conditions.

However, formalizing and regulating paid domestic work will not suffice to remedy the problems of structural injustice that leave domestic workers vulnerable to exploitation. Racial, ethnic, gender, and class stratification in the labor market disadvantage domestic workers, as does discrimination on the basis of immigration status. Acknowledging the real social and economic value of domestic work may help to ease these contributing factors. Formalization is a first step toward improving wages, working conditions, and benefits for domestic workers. Yet as many feminists have argued, domestic work will not be properly valued as long as the sexual division of domestic labor remains firmly in place. Of course, men must do their fair share of housework and childcare in order to eliminate this division of labor. Policies to help equalize the care burden along gender lines, such as more generous parental leave allowances, and increased state funding for the provision of childcare may also play an important role in increasing the perceived social and economic value of domestic work.

Since current US immigration policy increases the vulnerability of migrant workers to exploitation, preventing the exploitation of domestic workers will also require progressive immigration reform along the following four lines. First, access to publicly funded social services should be restored to all long-term immigrants and their dependents, regardless of their immigration status. Such access would remove one important obstacle to leaving exploitative jobs. However, merely extending social rights to migrant domestic workers will not sufficiently diminish the existing inequalities between migrant workers and citizen employers. As long as civil and political rights are linked to citizenship, migrant workers will be vulnerable to exploitation unless they have access to naturalized citizenship. Thus, second, a short path to citizenship should be established for all long-term immigrants, including undocumented immigrants and immigrants who originally entered on temporary worker visas. This policy should include full "amnesty" for undocumented workers already living in the United States. Third, immigrant admissions policies should index employment visas to the national demand for domestic labor. This would increase the number of visas available to domestic workers, thereby ensuring that workers who migrate to the United States to meet domestic labor demands are able to do so through regular channels. Fourth, family reunification policies should be expanded to allow migrant parents to bring their children with them to the United States.

Finally, a comprehensive remedy to the injustices involved in domestic work must acknowledge that global economic restructuring, and particularly neo-liberal structural adjustment policies, play a large role in stimulating labor migration. The decision to migrate for work should reflect a voluntary choice, not a desperate response to avoidable local poverty. Thus, global economic policies should be revaluated from the standpoint of the global poor and reformed to meet their needs.

CONCLUSIONS

I have argued that in absence of broad reforms, the practice of paid domestic work is unjust. I would like to conclude this essay by relating my arguments more explicitly to the topic of gender identity and globalization. As I have argued, the practice of paid domestic work, which is necessitated by the lack of publicly funded childcare and facilitated by the feminization of labor migration, enables some class-privileged American women to meet the gendered demands of the public and private spheres. Hiring a domestic worker allows female employers to participate in the public sphere as equals to men while ensuring that their culturally imposed domestic duties are fulfilled. Employers of domestic workers are thus able to develop new, more liberatory gender identities while retaining some of the positive aspects of traditional gender identities, specifically, the identification as good mothers. However, since the sexual division of labor remains firmly in place, the oppressive aspects of traditional gender identities have not been abolished, but rather transferred to the migrant women who replace these privileged women in the private sphere. Paradoxically, the positive aspects of traditional gender identities may be unavailable to domestic workers since the job often entails long separations from their own families.

Two general conclusions can be drawn from my analysis, each of which is itself an invitation to further discussion. First, I have shown that gendered ideologies, social structures, and juridical systems continue to shape the identities of women. Since gender is mediated by other systems of inequality, including class, race/ethnicity, and importantly, citizenship/immigration status, it follows that gender de-institutionalization is an uneven process. Second, my analysis suggests that gender identities are no longer formed solely within distinct nation-states, but rather in relation to global politics and economic restructuring. Within this context, women's gender identities are developed not only in relation to men and masculinity, but also in relation to other women, and increasingly to women of different nationalities. Thus, under globalization, the gender identities that some women experience as liberatory may depend upon the imposition of oppressive gender identities upon other women. While gender de-institutionalization is certainly a worthwhile feminist goal, we ought not fully embrace its instantiations without first subjecting them to an intersectional and transnational feminist analysis.

Chapter 4

PERSONAL IDENTITY AND GENDER
A Revised Aristotelian Approach

Melissa Moschella

To what extent are gender differences the result of social or personal construction? This question has been a source of debate not only between feminists and non-feminists, but also among feminists themselves. The androgynous ideal championed by Simone de Beauvoir and the eradication of even the most basic biological differences between men and women as advocated by radical feminists such as Shulamith Firestone now, at least among some feminists, seems to have largely given way to an emphasis on revaluing the unique qualities and experiences of women, even though most feminists consider these qualities and experiences to be uniquely female only because of the social and cultural formation of gender distinctions. In recent years it has become increasingly clear that what most women want above all—especially if we include the preferences of non-Western women—is not liberation from maternity and its responsibilities, but rather recognition of its social importance, and policies that make it possible for them to carry out these responsibilities, without necessarily having to forfeit professional goals as a consequence.[1] Even some landmark feminist thinkers such as Betty Friedan, Germaine Greer, and Naomi Wolf have modified their initial views after coming to recognize the importance of motherhood in their own lives and in the lives of other women. Such recognition in no way implies the need for a return to institutionalized gender differences, but rather is important, among other things, for fostering economic and social policies that can make career and family more easily compatible, for removing the current cultural stigma against women who choose to dedicate themselves full-time to the care of their family and household, and for overcoming the undervaluation of caring professions typically carried out by women.

Iris Marion Young describes this shift in feminist theory during the late 1970s and early 1980s as a rejection of the ideal of androgyny and a turn "to accounts of the social and psychological specificities of femininely gendered identity and social perspective derived from gender roles. While not at all explained by biological distinctions between men and women, nevertheless there are deep social divisions of masculine and feminine gendered dispositions and experience which have implications for the psychic lives of men and women, their interactions with one another, their dispositions to care for children or exercise authority."[2] Although this approach soon came under attack as "essentialist," some elements of it still survive in a more nuanced form. One example of attention to the unique experiences of women particularly in moral philosophy is the ethics of care. This view has recently been presented as an all-embracing feminist account of morality by Virginia Held in her book, *The Ethics of Care.*

At the heart of Held's ethical theory we find a conception of the person as relational and interdependent, in contrast to the emphasis on individual autonomy in Kantian and utilitarian approaches.[3] Although Held does not want to embrace an extreme constructivist view and defends a modified understanding of autonomy for relational persons, she never explains what constitutes the nucleus of personal identity that is not constructed by society, or—if she in fact does not accept the existence of such a nucleus—on what basis it is possible for moral agents to transcend social and cultural limitations in order to act with genuine freedom.[4] I find it difficult to reconcile Held's conception of the person "as an embodied nexus of relations" with her statement that "we are not prisoners of our upbringings and circumstances."[5]

Relationships and social context certainly shape identity profoundly, and it is important to draw attention to these aspects of selfhood and to their ethical implications. Yet while I share Held's critique of the atomistic self at the center of dominant moral theories, it seems to me that Held's relational self cannot account for the moral capacity to formulate a radical critique of one's socio-cultural environment and to forge a personal identity that severs one's constitutive network of relations when such relations prove oppressive. Indeed, if the self is actually constituted by relations, from where does one derive the agential powers that would make possible a radical critique or severing of those very relations that constitute us? If we are really the product of our social relations, how can a woman raised in a patriarchal environment transcend that environment in order to criticize it and to form an identity in opposition to it?

Diana T. Meyers is likewise concerned with these weaknesses in care-based visions of moral agency that see the self as relational. She argues that "women typically confront countless situations in which care-based agency seems mal-adapted if not doomed," referring to problems such as employer discrimination, sexual harassment, and anorexic ideals of female beauty.[6] In such contexts, what Meyer terms "oppositional moral agency" is called for. Feminist theorization of oppositional moral agency tends to rest either on a materialist (Marxist) or discursive (postmodern) conception of the self.[7] However, Meyers warns that "the socially constructed self has a sinister side. It is disquieting that influential thinkers are trumpeting the dissolution of the self and agency just when women are claiming agentic powers and gaining recognition as moral agents."[8]

Similarly, Ann Ferguson criticizes poststructuralist theories because they ignore the fundamental question "of whether there is a subject that has the agency to resist bodily disciplines and gender discourses."[9] Even the solution that some have proposed with the notion of a "subject-in-process" does not seem satisfying, because "there must be some relatively stable elements in such a self-process in order for it even to take on the goal of changing itself."[10] Although I agree with Ferguson's critique of poststructuralist gender theory, I am not convinced that her account of subjectivity, which attempts to combine Marxist materialist and psychoanalytic approaches, succeeds in providing a vision of the subject that is sufficiently unified and independent of social construction to act as a free and responsible moral agent.

Therefore, without undermining Held and other care theorists' basic point regarding the importance of relations for personal identity and the fact of human interdependence, I believe that a more robust notion of individual identity is necessary to defend the dignity and rights of women and of human beings in general.[11] Without such a defense, the ethics of care is incomplete, because it fails to explain why, to what extent and in what circumstances we have an obligation to care for others, and they for us. These questions become particularly pressing when considering the problem of care for the disabled, which is the focus of Eva Feder Kittay's discussion in *Love's Labor*. Richard Gottlieb, for example, poses the difficult issue of how parents can balance other ethical obligations—to their spouse and other children, at work, in the community—with the demands of raising a seriously disabled child.[12] Also commenting on Kittay's work, Martha Nussbaum argues that a care ethic is insufficient for improving the situation of the disabled, because we also need to consider the demands of justice, the legal rights of the disabled, the obligations that society as a whole has to establish the conditions in which the disabled can participate with a certain independence in the civic and economic life of the community.[13] Nussbaum suggests that to determine and defend the rights of the disabled and the corresponding obligations of caregivers and society as a whole, what we need is an Aristotelian concept of the person "that emphasizes the thorough oneness of human rationality and human animality."[14]

Keeping in mind the complex constellation of issues that surround feminist approaches to selfhood and gender identity, in this paper I would like to offer a revised Aristotelian notion of the person,[15] drawing on the work of Margaret Archer and Alasdair MacIntyre. I believe that the insights offered in these accounts enable us to locate a core of human identity sufficient to establish the existence of a stable, unified subject that is the bearer of rights and capable of free and responsible moral agency. At the same time, unlike Kantian notions of personhood that focus exclusively on autonomy and individuality, the modified Aristotelian conception that I will defend also accounts for human interdependence, the importance of embodiment, the influence of relationships on the formation of personal identity, and the impact of social structures on the exercise of human agency. By using Archer's and MacIntyre's theories to distinguish the various elements that constitute personal identity, I hope to offer a framework that, when applied to the question of gender, can avoid the pitfalls of both extreme constructivism and biologically deterministic essentialism.

THE ARISTOTELIAN NOTION OF *PRAXIS*

Aristotle's conception of personal identity is closely connected to his notion of *praxis*. When speaking of human actions, Aristotle distinguishes among *poiesis, praxis* and *theoresis*.[16] *Theoresis* refers to acts of speculative reason whose objects are eternal and immutable, while *praxis* and *poiesis* refer to acts of practical reason concerned with changing and contingent realities. The difference between the two is that *praxis* contains its end in itself, as opposed to *poiesis*, whose end is found not in the action itself but in the object.[17] Although *praxis* is most frequently used to refer to moral actions, Aristotle also applies this term analogically to vital operations.[18] For example, the act of seeing is inseparable from its end, which is precisely to see. And it is the agent, not the object seen, that is perfected in the act of seeing. This is interesting insofar as it manifests Aristotle's insight, in opposition to Platonic dualism, that human identity is not that of a pure spirit for whom the body has no real importance. The soul, or *psyche*, for Aristotle is not a prisoner of the body as Plato would have it, or a ghost in the machine in the Cartesian expression. Instead, the soul is the first act of a living being, the act of living itself, which includes all of that being's potencies. In the case of human beings, the soul as an active potency includes all vital operations, as well the affective and intellectual faculties, in an ordered unity ordained to the perfection of the whole.

This framework has its limitations due largely to the overly rigid distinction among *poiesis*, *praxis* and *theoresis*, that makes it difficult to explain, for example, the moral value of manual work (unless you realize that every *poiesis* is embedded in a *praxis*). Nonetheless, in trying to understand personal identity, the Aristotelian notion of *praxis* offers helpful insights, precisely because it includes both the vital operations of the individual and moral actions which necessarily imply social relations. It can therefore perhaps be useful in working toward a notion of personal identity that avoids the extremes of constructivism and essentialism. As we have seen, to overcome a constructivist notion of identity that would reduce the person to a mere pawn of social forces incapable of making any genuinely free contribution to the shaping of his or her own identity, or to a mere existentialist "empty point" lacking the basic tendencies and inclinations that make agency possible, it is necessary to locate the existence of a nucleus of identity that has a certain independence from social relations and individual choice.

Perhaps the locus of this core identity can be found at the level of vital *praxis*. It is true that the type of identity that corresponds to this level of bodily operation is best described as animal identity rather than fully human identity. Yet for human beings it is impossible to establish a sharp separation between those elements of our nature that are properly human and those that we share with other animals without falling into dualism. Therefore I believe that it is worthwhile to pause and reflect further on the extent to which we can establish the existence of a core identity at this level, always keeping in mind that the distinction between vital *praxis* and moral *praxis*—between the animal and the properly human elements—is analytical, as in reality the two are always intertwined. The explanation of human identity formation via "embodied practice" that Margaret Archer offers in *Being Human* offers valuable insights in this regard.

MARGARET ARCHER'S CONCEPTION OF HUMAN IDENTITY

Drawing on the phenomenological analysis of Merleau-Ponty, neuroscientific research on memory, and studies regarding early childhood development of reasoning capacities carried out principally by Jean Piaget, Archer attempts to demonstrate that the person's primordial sense of self derives not primarily from social interaction, but from embodied relations with the natural world—that is, Aristotle's vital *praxis*. At the outset of her analysis, Archer makes a crucial distinction between what she terms the "*sense* of self" and the "*concept* of self."[19] While the concept of self is socially formed and evolves over time, the sense of self provides a stable core of identity because it is "naturally grounded."[20]

Archer's analysis begins with a phenomenological explanation of how in the earliest stages of development infants
come to acquire this sense of self. They recognize themselves
initially as individual objects distinct from the other objects
that surround them, then as self-conscious subjects in a
world of objects, and finally as self-conscious subjects surrounded not only by objects but by other subjects as well.
First, Archer explains how Merleau-Ponty's account implies
the importance of the body and its sense capacities in perceiving reality, the intentional nature of our perception and
the distinction between the perceiver and the object perceived. Both perceiver and perceived have certain characteristics that determine the outcome of the act of perception, as
the perceiver always perceives based on the body's particular
perspective and sense capacities, and the perceived object has
certain characteristics that do not permit just any interpretation. As Archer points out, "we cannot take the gaps between
the trees as figures and the trees themselves as background."[21]

Important for Archer's argument is that bodily perception of the world in the earliest stages of human development is completely independent of the linguistically determined social and cultural context: "To Merleau-Ponty, our
natural relations have priority over our social relations, both
in the sense that they are prior to human development, but
also in the sense that the former continuously grounds the
latter and indeed obtrudes at every phase of our life
course."[22] Phenomenological analysis of perception has
demonstrated how the body acts as an "archimedian point,"
as that in comparison with which we measure nature as tall
or short, big or small, close or distant, etc. The body's func-

tion as "a scale against which to calibrate nature" presupposes a distinction between the perceiving body and the object perceived.[23] At this stage perceiver and perceived are related as object and object, because establishing subjectivity on the part of the perceiver requires a demonstration of the perceiver's self-consciousness.

Phenomenology helps us to understand the emergence of subjectivity via the body's capacity to distinguish between sensing itself and sensing another object, thus progressing from object/object relations to subject/object relations.[24] Our consciousness at this stage is not linguistic, but practical, based on the bodily memory of past actions, what Archer speaks of as the "habitual body."[25] This "'habitual body' of familiar actions" acts as "the sedimented memory through which the body declares various manipulative possibilities to the consciousness."[26]

Subject/subject relations arises in two stages according to Merleau-Ponty's account. First, one recognizes the difference between human bodies and other objects of perception via libidinal promptings that react to human bodies as sexually significant.[27] Secondly, one comes to see the other not only as a human body but as a subject by discovering the similarities between one's own bodily reactions to the world and those of others, thus implying that they are also self-conscious subjects.[28]

Finally, language arises as an outgrowth of embodied practice shared in common with other human beings. Like other forms of practice, language is acquired through habit, and makes intentional reference to reality.[29] The development of the object/object, subject/object, and subject/subject distinctions constitute a prerequisite for the acquisition of

language, based on "public and collective references to natural reality and to (the new) social reality."[30]

The importance of Merleau-Ponty's account for Archer's
argument is that language and therefore dialogical social
relations arise only at the end of the process, after the formation of self-consciousness. Phenomenological analysis—
even that of an author like Merleau-Ponty who does not
share Archer's commitment to realism—thus supports
Archer's claim that the sense of self at the core of our identity emerges independently of discursive social relations.
This claim does not imply that infants can develop without
human care and affection. People are necessarily included
among the objects with which infants interact and play a
crucial role in their growth. The very distinction among
inanimate beings, animals and human beings, however, must
itself be learned through practical interaction with the
world. Archer's point is not that babies grow and develop in
isolation from society, but rather that their relationships
with people remain at the practical, non-discursive level.[31]

To establish the continuity of this sense of self that arises
through embodied relations with the natural world, Archer
turns to neuroscientific studies on visual and procedural
memory, as opposed to declarative, linguistic memory which
is socially dependent. On this basis, Archer attempts to
develop a notion of identity following the neo-Lockean tradition, which relies both on bodily identity and continuity of
consciousness.[32] Studies have found that up until puberty
children tend toward visual or eidetic memory, which is
non-verbal, while in adults memory tends to be a practice of
active recall, depending on our interests.[33] The development
of visual capacities is itself dependent upon environmental

exposure, as the visual system tends to develop in response to external stimuli. Archer refers to experiments carried out with kittens, demonstrating, for example, that kittens reared in environments that had only vertical stripes did not respond to horizontal cues later on.[34] These findings seem to corroborate our earlier conclusions about the formation of a sense of self based primarily on natural relations with the world. Furthermore, the existence of non-verbal memories that in themselves provide a certain degree of continuity of consciousness helps to support the claim that there is a core of human identity that does not depend on discursive social relations.

Also particularly interesting for our current purposes are scientific studies regarding the relative independence of procedural and declarative memory. Procedural memory can be retained even when declarative memory has been lost. Archer cites, among other examples, the case of subjects suffering from brain damage who cannot remember the word "bike," but still remember how to ride one.[35] Memory of such embodied practical skills remains with the subject throughout life. Only the highest level of memory, the declarative, is linguistic in nature and is therefore inextricably tied to the social and cultural realm.[36]

Even the logical principles at the basis of language and therefore of dialogical social relations have their origin in practical interaction with the world. As we saw earlier in relation to the phenomenological analysis regarding the emergence of the distinction between perceiving subject and object, interaction with the natural world leads children to recognize that objects have distinct causal properties and powers independent of their own. This recognition, argues

Archer, is tantamount to recognition of the logical principle of identity.[37] Experiments carried out by Jean Piaget on chil dren under five years of age support this insight. Piaget attempted to determine how children come to understand the physical principle of conservation, which is inherently related both to the principle of identity and to the principle of non-contradiction.

In one of the experiments, children had to transfer equal amounts of liquid from two identical glasses to two glasses of different diameters, after having assented to the equality of the liquids in the first stage. After transferring the liquids, there appeared to be more in the tall thin glass than in the short wide one. Many children recognized that, despite appearances, there still must be an equal amount of liquid in each glass, and those who were fooled by the appearance realized that they needed to justify the difference, explaining, for example, that some of the liquid must have spilled when transferring the water. Piaget's experiments demonstrated that children were more likely to recognize conservation when they were practically involved in the setting up and carrying out of the experiment, thus indicating the impor- tance of practical interaction with objects for the develop- ment of the principles of identity and non-contradiction.[38] From these and similar studies, Archer draws the conclusion that embodied practice is pivotal to knowledge, a conclusion reminiscent of Aristotle's principle that all knowledge comes to us via the senses. Such a conclusion is incompatible with seeing identity as a mere social construction, because it implies that language is likewise grounded in embodied practice.

Archer's analysis helps to demonstrate not only that

identity is not the outcome of *social* construction, but also that it is not entirely the outcome of construction at all, either social or individual. In other words, the subject himself seems to face certain limits in the determination of his or her identity. Embodied knowledge, which, as we have seen, is crucial for the establishment of stable individual identity, is subject to certain conditions, for it depends upon the properties and powers of the body, and those of objects in the world. As Archer explains, "in the natural order . . . nature encodes information about possible practice, given the way it is and the way we are, which is disclosed in our relations."[39] It is for this reason that embodied knowledge can be classified as "right" or "wrong." The correctness of embodied knowledge differs from that of theoretical knowledge, because—although an error could also be explained theoretically—mistakes are demonstrated to us by the body itself. One example which we have all certainly experienced is the disequilibrium that results from mistakenly taking an "extra step" at the top or bottom of a staircase.[40]

The point may seem almost too trite to state explicitly, but it is clear that our personal and social identity—which do indeed develop via the interplay of free human decisions and unchosen social and cultural circumstances—are also influenced by our core human identity based on embodied practice in the world. As Archer argues:

> Our human relations with things . . . helps to make us what we are as persons. Not only do these supply that part of us which is not a gift of society, but also predispose us towards those *social* practices which we will seek and shun. They are influential structurally in conditioning the

roles, careers, sports, or relationships in which people engage voluntarily, and equally so culturally, since practical knowledge serves to sieve the propositional knowledge which we willingly acquire or dismiss.[41]

Few would contest the fact that people tend to engage in and to enjoy the activities that they perform well, and that skill depends not only on education but also on natural talent. While it may sometimes be the case that circumstances do not allow individuals to assume the social and professional role for which they are best suited, their natural inclinations still remain, and undoubtedly influence the way that they carry out that role. A dedicated father may, for example, decide to set aside his talent and passion for playing the violin when he sees that a career in business will enable him to earn a more stable income to support his family. Yet his mode of carrying out his work will almost certainly be quite different—perhaps more creative and original—than that of his colleague with a passion for numbers and a degree in accounting. As Archer explains, "We do not make our personal identities under the circumstances of our choosing, since our embeddedness in nature, practice and society is part of what being human means."[42]

This example also highlights the interplay among what Archer distinguishes as three orders of identity: human, personal, and social. I have focused above all on the human or natural order, because it is at this level that we can establish the existence of "a human being with a continuous sense of self, which anchors human identity through eidetic memory and procedural knowledge."[43] However, it is important to note that Archer's isolation of these three orders is primarily analytical, for the purposes of avoiding reductionisms and better understanding the mechanisms that come into play in the formation of identity.

In fact, *personal* identity, which corresponds to what most people think of when they speak of identity in ordinary conversation, is formed in relation to the natural, practical, and social orders. Each level has its corresponding concerns—physical well-being at the natural level, performative achievement at the practical level, and self-worth at the social level.[44] In real life, one lives in these three orders simultaneously. Personal identity is forged precisely by establishing a harmony among them, ordering them in relation to one's "ultimate concerns," established through a reflective process of discernment, deliberation and decision-making that Archer calls the "internal conversation."[45] As personal identity is neither reducible to identity in the biologically determined natural order, nor to identity in the discursively defined social order, it acts as the key for avoiding the extremes of essentialism and constructivism.

I characterize Archer's separation of the natural, personal and social orders as *primarily* but not entirely analytical, because she does in fact accord temporal priority to the development of a sense of self via embodied practice in the world. This position has led Diana Tietjens Meyers to criticize Archer's theory as "a systematic defense of materialism and individualism," as painting a completely solitary portrait of identity formation, and failing to give due importance to the role of parents and caretakers in infant and early childhood development. In addition, while Meyers finds Archer's emphasis on the importance of embodiment to be refreshing, she is disappointed that Archer's theory, as she

understands it, downplays the influence of embodiment in
the formation of personal identity.[46]

I am sympathetic to both aspects of Meyers' criticism,
but I believe that at least the essential elements of Archer's
theory survive the critique. Like Meyers, I also find that
Being Human lacks a recognition of the importance of
human attention and affection in infant development. However, it seems that such a recognition is not inherently
incompatible with Archer's theory, but only that Archer
wanted to abstract from these aspects of personal development in order to emphasize her point regarding the non-discursive foundation of identity, similar to that achieved by
other higher animals. Furthermore, regarding the influence
of embodiment in personal identity formation, I also miss a
fuller discussion of this point, but I believe that it is implicit
in Archer's theory.

PERSONAL IDENTITY IN ALASDAIR MACINTYRE'S *DEPENDENT RATIONAL ANIMALS*

Considering these criticisms, it seems to me that we can find
an excellent counterpart to Archer's work in Alasdair MacIntyre's theory of identity in *Dependent Rational Animals*.
MacIntyre emphasizes that we need to understand human
identity as primarily bodily, animal identity.[47] This position
seems to be a philosophical complement to Archer's sociological account of human identity formation. Archer's pre-
discursive sense of self formed via embodied interaction
with the world—what Archer terms "human identity"—
seems to correspond to what MacIntyre calls "animal iden-

tity." Indeed, at this level of identity there is no actual distinction between human beings and other animals. MacIntyre also refers in passing to the importance of Merleau-Ponty's phenomenological analysis of identity as bodily, but does not elaborate on this point as Archer does, nor complement it with other data regarding memory and early childhood development. With regard to the formation of our bodily, animal identity, therefore, Archer's theory provides support for claims that MacIntyre basically takes for granted.

On the other hand, with regard to the passage from initial animal identity to distinctively human personal identity, MacIntyre's theory offers us several insights, particularly with regard to the role of parents and caregivers. To see the connection, it is necessary to overcome differences in terminology and focus in the two authors' approaches. MacIntyre, as a moral philosopher, uses terminology that emphasizes his focus on ethics, while Archer's approach is that of a sociologist who wants to "save humanity" from theories that would reduce the person to a mere social construction. MacIntyre does not explicitly distinguish, therefore, between three levels of identity—human, personal, and social—as Archer does. However, what Archer speaks of as achieving personal identity by ordering our desires in accordance with our ultimate concerns, seems to correspond to what MacIntyre describes as the process of becoming an independent practical reasoner.

The insight that MacIntyre offers to moral philosophy is precisely that we never lose our animal nature and identity, and that this fact is of crucial importance for ethics, because properly human reasons for acting presuppose our animal nature, because our very exercise of rationality is that proper

to "one species of animal," and because our animality implies
that dependence and vulnerability are central features of the
human condition.[48] The first two points correspond clearly
to Archer's insistence on the natural order as an ineluctable
source of concern that needs to be given its proper place as
we harmonize our concerns in the formation of personal
identity. However, the third point—that animality involves
dependence, both physical and rational—implies the importance of other human beings in developing and maintaining
our personal identity. It is here that MacIntyre's analysis can
serve to fill in an important gap in Archer's theory. MacIntyre's insights do not contradict Archer's view, but simply
highlight elements that Archer leaves in the background.

Regarding the very earliest stages of development, Mac-
Intyre emphasizes a point that Archer only alludes to in
passing:[49] that our most basic level of identity is not distinctively human, but is comparable to that of other higher animals such as dolphins and chimpanzees. MacIntyre uses dolphins as a point of comparison throughout the book,
drawing on studies of dolphin behavior to establish the similarities and differences between dolphins and human
beings. MacIntyre argues that "we owe to parents [and other
caregivers] that care from conception through birth and
infancy to childhood that dolphins also owe to elders who
provide maternal and other care."[50] However, although at the
most basic level there are commonalities, the care that
human beings need from other human beings involves much
more than the care that dolphins need from other dolphins.
To develop into independent practical reasoners (or, using
Archer's terms, to develop personal identity), we need relationships that foster "the ability to evaluate, modify, or reject

our practical judgments," as well as "the ability to imagine realistically alternative possible futures," and "the ability to stand back from our desires."[51] These abilities coincide with those necessary, on Archer's account, for successfully ordering the competing concerns of the natural, practical and social orders via the internal conversation.

Drawing on studies carried out by D.W. Winnicott, MacIntyre demonstrates that the first condition necessary for the child to develop these capacities is a sense of security and unqualified trust in the caregiver (earned by the caregiver's loving recognition of the child and responsiveness to its needs).[52] A secure environment enables the infant to relax, opening the conditions for creative experimentation with the environment, or play. Interestingly, play, on MacIntyre's account, seems to correspond to what Archer speaks of as embodied practice in the natural world. As MacIntyre explains, "Play is important because it is exploratory, because it extends both the range of activities found worth pursuing for their own sake and the range of pleasures that can be taken in such activities, and because in moving from the kind of playfulness exhibited both by humans and dolphins to more sophisticated forms of play we move from animal intelligence to specifically human reasoning."[53] The sense of self acquired through playful interaction with their surroundings is a necessary basis for acquiring practical reasoning capacities, because without such a sense of self one would lack the necessary independence for making ethical decisions.

With regard to the continuity of personal identity, MacIntyre does not rely only upon the biological continuity of our animal, bodily identity over time, but also recognizes the social aspect of identity confirmation. MacIntyre mentions this double aspect of identity in a discussion about the importance of self-knowledge for successful practical reasoning. Self-knowledge grows through experience, through the memory of past actions and their outcomes, which presumes continuity of identity over time. When I remember my past actions as successes or failures, I assume that I am the same person who committed those actions, "and it makes no sense to ask me *how* I know that I am the same human being who did or failed to do so and so."[54] However, when others judge me to be the same human being, they *do* rely on certain criteria. Confirmation of our presumed continuity of identity by the objective, criteria-based judgments of others, is key for our confidence in the reliability of our self-ascriptions. This is true to the extent that "I can be said truly to know who and what I am, only because there are others who can be said truly to know who and what I am."[55]

INTERPERSONAL RELATIONSHIPS AND THE "INTERNAL CONVERSATION"

Does this assertion contradict Archer's account of personal identity formation? In my opinion, it does not. It only completes it. The necessity of adequate self-knowledge for the development of personal identity is likewise implied in Archer's theory, as is the role of social relations. As Archer's aim is to defend the existence of a *private* inner life, in *Being Human* she rarely draws explicit attention to the need for sympathetic external interlocutors to confirm our self-conception, as well as the need for trusting relationships, especially during infancy and childhood but also throughout life, to provide the security necessary for healthy personality development. Important insights on this point arise, however, in Archer's most recent work, *Structure, Agency and the Internal Conversation*, in which she develops more fully her theory of personal identity formation and analyzes what she calls the "internal conversations" of twenty interviewees.

Archer considers reflexivity to be "the process that mediates the effects of structure upon agency," or how agents respond to the constraints and enablements offered by social structures in the formation of their personal and social identity.[56] The successful exercise of reflexivity—one in which the internal conversation has practically efficacious results—"depends upon agents exerting their personal powers to formulate projects and to monitor both self and society in the pursuit of their designs."[57] From her interviews, Archer found that there are variations in the way that people exercise reflexivity, and divided them into three categories: "communicative reflexives," "autonomous reflexives," and "meta-reflexives." Communicative reflexives mistrusted their own internal conversations and constantly sought advice and confirmation from trusted friends and family members.[58] The opposite was the case for the autonomous reflexives, who mistrusted and avoided the "intrusions" of others into their internal conversation; but even so, the influence of others was still inevitably present.[59] Finally, meta-reflexives—who are distinguished by their commitment to an ideal and their constant self-monitoring regarding the coherence of their lives with that ideal—actively seek the support of "at least a small group of colleagues or friends who are on the same 'wavelength.'"[60] Archer's observations thus confirm MacIntyre's assertion regarding our reliance upon others for the formation and confirmation of our personal identity.

Particularly interesting is Archer's discussion of "fractured reflexivity," generally involving tensions and lack of trust in interpersonal relationships. Archer qualified as "fractured reflexives" those whose internal conversations failed to mediate efficaciously between social structure and personal agency, because they lacked clear priorities with which to harmonize their concerns and take control of their actions and of the situations in which they found themselves. The result was passivity in the face of social and cultural circumstances.[61] The most extreme case is that of Jason, who exhibits only minimal reflexivity. A seventeen-year-old with a rough family background, who took to the streets at the age of thirteen and at various points in time was kicked out of the house by both his father and his mother (his parents are divorced), Jason focused much of his internal conversation on discerning the trustworthiness of others. When asked about instances in which he engages in internal conversation, Jason gave the following example: "Well, like people talking to me and I just think more about what they're saying and just try to see if they're lying or telling the truth, I suppose. Because I've got a problem with trust. That's about the only thing I ever think about—whether I can trust them or not."[62] As a result, Jason (along with the other fractured reflexives, although his case was the most extreme) lacked a capacity for active agency, and tended to be thrown about passively by circumstances. Jason clearly lacks the sense of security about himself, derived from trusting relationships, that constitutes a prerequisite for developing a personal identity, or, in MacIntyre's terminology, for becoming an independent practical reasoner.

PERSONAL IDENTITY AND GENDER

Although neither Archer nor MacIntyre offers an explicit analysis of the relationship between gender identity and personal identity, their theories provide useful insights regarding possible approaches to this topic that avoid the extremes of essentialism and constructivism. As we have seen, grounding human identity in a basic sense of self—what MacIntyre speaks of as our initial animal identity, which is independent of discursive social relations—serves to avoid extreme versions of constructivism. Since some irreducible element of our identity is grounded in our animal nature, we cannot be entirely products of social forces, nor even of our own self-creation. At the same time, the accounts of personal identity formation offered by Archer and MacIntyre also avoid biological essentialism. Using Archer's distinction among human, personal, and social identity, we can understand gender as an element of personal identity, grounded on biological sex differences, but influenced in its personal expression by both social structures and personal choice.

This distinction also offers important insights regarding the relationship between agency and personal identity, which, as we saw earlier, presents difficulties for many feminist theories. Both Archer's and MacIntyre's accounts help to clarify that the human capacity for active agency has both metaphysical and ethical aspects. We can consider the metaphysical aspect as the indispensable core identity that gives the self unity over time as well as a nucleus of biologically-rooted capacities, inclinations and tendencies (Aristotle's vital *praxis*) that serve as the minimal prerequisite for self-directed action. Here we are at the level of animal identity (in MacIntyre's terms) or human but not yet personal identity (in Archer's terms). Arrriving to the level of personal identity, however, is an ethical task that involves both personal choice and adequate education.

Indeed, forming and maintaining a "strict personal identity," or becoming and sustaining oneself as a successful independent practical reasoner, is a lifelong process always capable of further progression. Here we are at the level of Aristotle's ethical *praxis*. Archer's analysis of her interviewees' internal conversations has shown us that to the extent that one falls short of attaining a strict personal identity—which implies establishing a coherent equilibrium among one's concerns, arising both as a result of our physical inclinations and of our social and cultural situation—one becomes a merely passive agent, with only a minimal capacity to formulate and execute goals. This failure could be due primarily to factors external to the person's control—such as a traumatic childhood, as in the case of Jason—or to poor personal choices, or (as is the case in all but the most extreme situations) to a mix of less-than-ideal social circumstances and less-than-ideal responses to those circumstances on the part of the individual.

Even in highly unfavorable external circumstances, human beings almost always retain some capacity to determine their response,[63] and the free choices that this involves are decisive for personal identity. The only cases in which one might argue that free choice is completely or largely absent are those in which a person has failed to form even the most basic sense of self as a result of extreme neglect and abuse in infancy and early childhood. Arguably, examples of such extreme situations could include that of the Wild Boy of Aveyron and of children raised in Romanian orphanages during the Ceausescu regime, who exhibited a range of emotional, cognitive, and motor impairment as a result of the atrocious conditions in which they were raised. Some improved after being incorporated into a loving family, but the difficulties were less remediable for those who had spent more time in the orphanage. The Wild Boy of Aveyron—who was almost murdered and then abandoned at the age of six and survived on his own for three to five years in the forest before reentering society—never learned how to speak, read, or write. Meyers refers to these examples in order to demonstrate the importance of loving care and attention for the formation of identity.[64]

Considering the great influence of the way a child is treated in infancy and early childhood, Meyers extends her argument to make the claim that subtle differences in the way parents and caregivers treat boys and girls are decisive for the formation of gender identity, to the extent of minimizing and perhaps even overriding the influence of biological differences.[65] This position, at least in its extreme form, seems to run the risk of conflating the distinction between vital praxis and ethical praxis, thus calling into question the existence of a core identity that is prior to discursive social relations. As we have seen, denying this core identity makes it difficult to defend the capacity for self-directed action, and particularly the capacity to exercise what Meyers herself calls oppositional moral agency. Thus the determination to downplay the biological aspect of identity in order to avoid biological determinism in the conception of gender differences tends to undermine the non-discursive core human identity without which it is impossible to criticize and challenge the dominant social structures that often place women at a disadvantage.

How can we overcome this paradox? Perhaps a bit of reflection on some of the biological studies of sex differences can help us to clarify what is at stake. While culture certainly plays a large role in shaping gender identity, a number of recent studies suggest that some aspects of gender difference may find their roots at least partially in biology. As an exhaustive analysis of the research on this topic is well beyond the scope of this paper, here I will briefly mention only a few of the most representative and noteworthy findings over the past few decades.

Perhaps the most provocative case—which I detail here as representative of the outcome of numerous similar cases—is that of "John," a male child whose penis was extensively damaged during a medical intervention. Taking the advice of Dr. John Money of Johns Hopkins University, the parents decided it would be best to raise him as a girl. Accordingly, surgery was performed to give "Joan" the appearance of female genitalia. Joan's parents did everything possible to socialize her as a girl, but she constantly resisted these attempts. Diamond summarizes Joan's childhood experiences as follows: "Girl's toys, clothes and activities were repeatedly proffered to Joan and most often rejected. Throughout childhood Joan preferred boy's activities and games to those of girl's; she had little interest in dolls, sewing or girl's activities. Ignoring the toys she was given, she would play with her brother's toys. She preferred to tinker with gadgets and tools and dress up in men's clothing; take things apart to see what makes them tick. She was regarded as a tomboy with an interest in playing soldier. Joan did not shun rough and tumble sports nor avoid fights."[66] Fed up, at the age of fourteen Joan declared herself to be a boy, and is now married to a woman, with adopted children.

The case may seem merely anecdotal, and it would be if it were simply an isolated incident. However, over twenty similar cases have likewise been documented, and an extensive literature review reveals that "there is no known case where a 46 chromosome, XY male, unequivocally so at birth, has ever easily and fully accepted an imposed life as an androphilic female regardless of the physical and medical intervention." Diamond draws the following conclusion: "This last decade has offered much support for a biological substrate for sexual behavior. In addition to the genetic research mentioned above there are many neurological and other reports which point in this direction. The evidence seems overwhelming that normal humans are not psychosexually neutral at birth but are, in keeping with their mammalian heritage, predisposed and biased to interact with the environment, familial and social forces, in a male or female mode."[67]

A number of other studies likewise suggest that perhaps some aspects of gender difference have a biological basis. Particularly interesting is the work of Simon Baron-Cohen, a self-proclaimed feminist who wanted to show that sex and gender differences are largely the result of social construction, but whose research yielded the opposite conclusion. After studies on twelve-month old infants suggested that females are more people-centered and males are more object-centered, Baron-Cohen and his team at Cambridge University's Department of Experimental Psychology and

Psychiatry decided to conduct a similar experiment with newborns in order to determine whether those differences are due to biological factors or to socialization.[68] They tested 102 one-day-old babies, comparing the amount of time that boys and girls spent looking at a face or a mobile of similar shape and color, controlling to make sure that those who measured the times did not know the infants' sex. The research demonstrated that boys showed a statistically significant preference for the mobile (a mechanical object), and girls for the face (a social object).[69–70]

Researchers postulate that these differences can be explained at least in part by males' greater exposure to testosterone in the womb. An inverse correlation has been found between prenatal testosterone levels and amount of eye contact shown by twelve-month old infants.[71] Further, "many studies show that testosterone affects development and behaviour, not only in humans, but also in other mammals. Testosterone sponsors development of the male phenotype, and can influence behaviour even of animals of the same sex. For example, giving older men testosterone specifically improves their ability with those spatial tests on which males normally score higher than females."[72]

Neurobiological studies have also demonstrated significant differences in the male and female brain, particularly in areas of the hypothalamus related to maternal behavior and sex behavior in general,[73] and in the hippocampus, which responds differently to stress in men and women, and which is important for spatial mapping.[74] Jill M. Goldstein of Harvard Medical School and her colleagues have also found that, in proportion to overall brain size, "parts of the frontal cortex, the seat of many higher cognitive functions, are bulkier in women than in men, as are parts of the limbic cortex, which is involved in emotional responses. In men, on the other hand, parts of the parietal cortex, which is involved in space perception, are bigger than in women, as is the amygdala, an almond-shaped structure that responds to emotionally arousing information."[75] Of course, as these findings are based on studies of the adult brain, they may to some extent be explainable by differences in the way that boys and girls are treated during childhood.

What conclusions, if any, can we draw from these studies? Determining if and to what extent gender differences find their roots in biology presents many difficulties, and certainly requires further research. However, if Diamond's critique of Dr. Money's psycho-sexual neutrality theory is correct, it seems that the most basic anatomical differences between men and women, differences directly related to the complementary roles of males and females in human reproduction, are not irrelevant to identity. In itself, this represents a difference in core identity at the level of vital praxis. The question becomes more complex if we try to relate this basic anatomical difference to the existence of certain tendencies that stereotypically characterize gender difference, such as people-centeredness versus object-centeredness, the tendency that Simon Baron-Cohen and his team attempted to verify experimentally. Once we begin to speak about tendencies and inclinations, it is extremely difficult to separate biology from cultural influence. Furthermore, even if it were clear that there is a direct link between biological sex differences and the tendencies and characteristics typically considered to be masculine or feminine, determining whether or not those tendencies should be followed is a task for ethical reflection, not biological experimentation. To consider something good simply because it is the result of natural[76] tendencies is to fall into the naturalistic fallacy. For human beings biology is not destiny, and both personal choices and social forces shape our tendencies and determine the way that we direct them.[77]

Considering how other aspects of our embodiment affect the personal and social identity that we form, it seems reasonable to admit that embodied sex differences, formed pre-discursively as part of our embodied sense of self, also have an influence on personal identity, an influence mediated by culture and personal choice. Just as recognizing, for example, that a certain individual or race tends to have a body shape particularly propitious for running does not imply that all such individuals ought to take up a career as Olympic runners, women's biological capacity to bear and nurse children does not imply that all women must make marriage and childrearing their first priority, or even a priority at all. Such decisions require personal ethical reflection—as Archer would explain it, it is necessary to prioritize among often-conflicting desires in order to become an active agent. Here, however, it is also important to remember MacIntyre's point about the need for accurate self-knowledge in order to become an independent practical reasoner. Awareness and acceptance of one's biological capacities, tendencies, and limitations constitute an important element of that self-knowledge. Among these we could include, for example, women's generally stronger inclination to have and nurture children, certainly influenced by culture, but also explainable in biological terms by the greater prominence in women of hormones such as estrogen, progesterone, peptide oxytocin and prolactin, the last two of which are secreted in especially high levels during pregnancy and breastfeeding, and foster nurturing emotions.[78] Of course, some women may experience these tendencies with greater force than others, just as some men may also have a strong desire to be fathers and to nurture their children. In addition, since dovetailing one's concerns requires freely deciding which to prioritize, in some cases women and men attracted to parenthood may nonetheless forego this option or place it low on their list of priorities in order to dedicate themselves more fully to a career or to an important cause for which they have a great passion.

An interesting case in point is that of feminist Susan Brison, who relates how she had initially rejected physical maternity as incompatible with her feminist ideals and academic career. However, after reading Ruddick's *Maternal Thinking* and, around the same time, learning from her gynecologist that she may have difficulty conceiving a child, her "philosophical bias against maternity . . . suddenly gave way to the startling realization that I might *want* to experience the particular kind of embodiment and connection that pregnancy and motherhood provide."[79] The interplay between the biological and the ethical here is fascinating. First, Brison initially rejected any possible maternal tendencies because of her ethical commitment to feminist ideals. However, when she realized both that becoming a mother does not necessarily imply disloyalty to the feminist cause (from Ruddick's book) and that she would need to begin attempting to get pregnant soon or foreclose the possibility forever, she decided to include motherhood among her priorities. Awareness and acceptance of her own desire for

maternity proved to be an important element of self-knowledge that enabled Brison to avoid making a choice against
motherhood that she may have later regretted, as did many
of the women whom Sarah Hewlett interviewed for her
recent book, *Creating a Life: Professional Women and the
Quest for Children.*[80]

On the public policy level such knowledge is empowering for women as well, because it provides a basis on which
to demand, for example, sufficient maternity leave, the
option of a career-and-family track in businesses, and perhaps even something like a government-provided child care
voucher that parents could either use to pay for day care or
keep as compensation for their own childcare work within
the home. As feminist Tina Chanter argues, "Feminists
working in the area of legal studies and social and political
philosophy have recognized the need to acknowledge that
there are important respects in which women's needs are different from men's, and that women consequently require different treatment."[81] Although such benefits should be open
to both women and men, it should not shock us if more
women prefer to take advantage of them, as has been the case
with parental leave policies in Sweden. On the contrary, not
recognizing biological sex differences could lead—or, as
Brison's and Hewlett's accounts suggest, already has led—to
a sort of reverse oppression of women by fostering policies
and cultural expectations that push women *not* to make
motherhood a priority even if they are personally inclined to
do so.

While a full analysis of this complex question goes well
beyond the scope of this paper, here my aim has only been to
offer a brief sketch suggesting that an open-minded

approach to the study of possible biological bases for gender differences does not require falling into a deterministic form of essentialism or advocating a re-institutionalization of gender roles. It does, however, help to overcome the danger of constructivism and the problems that this entails for feminist theory's account of agency. Above all, an account of gender identity that takes into account both vital and ethical praxis—biology, culture and personal choice—will most effectively be able to recognize, respect and forward the wide range of women's interests in today's global society.

Chapter 5

BODIES BETWEEN GENDERS
In Search of New Forms of Identity

Lucia Ruggerone

When introduced in the 1970s, the notion of the sex-gender system and, by implication, the definite distinction between sex (biological) and gender (cultural), seemed a great step forward toward conceptual clarity and men-women equality. Thirty years later, we must acknowledge that, although in everyday life the situation of some women has improved, at the theoretical level, the introduction of that notion marks the start of a long lasting debate, still unsolved to date.

It is perhaps fair to say that for a long time after the distinction was introduced, feminist theory has tended to concentrate on the gender side of the dichotomy;[1] especially it tried to explore and understand the various social and cultural processes through which gender is constructed and subordination against women realized.

Some authors, especially in the field of psychology and psychoanalysis, have tended to disregard the distinction and defined femininity and masculinity as sets of properties rooted in such deep psychological make-up that they come to sound virtually "natural." In particular Nancy Chodorow[2] and Carol Gilligan[3] argue that gender differences can be traced back to the very early phases of identity formation (in the pre-oedipal phase of an individual's life): due to the nearly ubiquitous social arrangement whereby the infant's (female or male) first relationship is to a woman, Chodorow and Gilligan argue that boys and girls construct their identities in two distinct ways leading to the development of two different moral universes.[4] In their work the sexed body remains a fixed biological background to the processes of personality formation, while the construction of gender identity, though depending on a social arrangement, emerges as virtually immutable. This explains why Chodorow and Gilligan have often been labeled as "essentialists" by members of other schools of feminist theory.

At the same time, outside the field of psychology, most second wave feminists, (including scholars and active members of the feminist movement of the 1960s and 1970s) acknowledge the distinction of sex and gender, but tend to ignore the issue of the possible variability of sex. For the authors the focus of attention is constituted by gender whose social construction needs to be analyzed and possibly modified in order to eliminate its discriminatory effects. It is perhaps worth noting that during these same years the issue of the cultural construction of gender was being addressed by sociologists outside the domain of feminist theory and again not necessarily aware of the distinction between sex and gender as posed by Rubin. One of the best known examples of this kind of work is Goffman's *Gender Advertisements* and

The Arrangements Between the Sexes[5], where he shows that the institutionalization of gender difference can be traced back to the micro-level of interaction rituals which are constantly crystallized in the collective representations provided by commercial images.

Prior to Goffman, the socially constructed character of gender (and the medical construction of sex) is described in Garfinkel's study of Agnes,[6] where the author narrates the story of an hermaphrodite with a penis who successfully passed for a woman for many years before undergoing a sex change operation. Incidentally, it should be noted that the story could also be read as reflecting the position transsexuals seem to embrace and somehow embody: that biological sex is changeable, but not psychological sex, i.e., what we may call, gender.

The idea that sex should not be considered a biological given, but itself a social construction or discursive effect has enjoyed growing popularity in the theoretical debate especially in the last ten to fifteen years as a consequence of two main factors. Firstly the work of some authors has proved crucial, first of all Judith Butler,[7] who, by questioning normative heterosexuality, ultimately criticizes our binary system of perceiving the world as divided between males and females.

Secondly (and partly as a consequence of Butler's work) the emergence and growing popularity of queer theory and queer studies have extensively opposed the idea that sex is a natural immutable category, arguing that it is rather an expression of our traditional knowledge frames.

The idea that sex too is the result of cultural conditions and particularly that the binary division of sexes is culturally enforced has been supported also by feminist scientists like Anne Fausto-Sterling[8] whose work describes how the assignment at birth to one or the other sex category is indeed the result of human decisions and often of active medical intervention.[9]

GENDER IDENTITY UNDER ATTACK

Against this background, my concern here points to the role that changing notions of sex and gender play in the processes of the construction and consolidation of women's identities.

Identity is, of course, a pivotal concept in sociological and cultural studies and millions of pages have been written on it. Although I am not going to address the width of that debate, I shall nevertheless clarify my stance as a starting point: unlike a vast part of classic and, to some extent, contemporary sociological production, I do not consider the body a marginal, unimportant element of identity. On the contrary I position myself within the phenomenological tradition which sees the body, or more precisely our corporeal experience, as our way of being in the world. Within this perspective the site of subjectivity is very much located in the body (if I had a different body I would be and feel as a different person, I would have constructed, in collaboration with others, a different kind of identity), where the body is no pure materiality, rather it is, at the same time, subject and object of my consciousness. The grade of availability or remoteness of the various techniques through which I can perform my agency (i.e., through which I can act in the world) depend on the kind of body I have/am.[10] Like Goffman, I do not see the body as a mask behind which lies a purely spiritual identity, but as an integral part of my, albeit provisional, situational, contingent identity. In this perspective, acting on the body is a process of identity management, a technology of the self[11]; manipulating one's body means to change (albeit temporarily) one's identity, to adorn the body reflects on identity, as fashion studies and work on bodily modifications show us. Following Foucault,[12] I see the body as the crucial site of the exercise of power in modern societies; power is performed through control of the bodies framing and forging identities that people later perceive as of their own make.

For a long time in western societies, the ideologies of femininity and masculinity based on the sexed bodies have functioned as powerful determinants in the formation of identity: alongside race and social class, the sex one was born with had a strong impact on the destiny he/she would have and on his/her everyday participation to the social world. Being male or female meant possessing a set of precise and different physical and psychological characteristics. Processes of socialization were strongly informed by beliefs about what boys and girls were "naturally" gifted for and ideas (very often later proved wrong) about the different things a male or female body could do or not do. Up to a certain point in western history various elements of culture unanimously concurred in reinforcing these ideas: language, clothes, rules of interaction, but also art, law, medicine, politics. Sexual difference was, in other words, more or less consciously, culturalized, institutionalized and thereby turned into sexual inequality. Sexual inequality is inscribed in the western social order and it is fundamental to the persistence of the social system as we have known it so far.[13]

Rubin's sex-gender system[14] has provided the theoretical basis for feminists to start fighting sexual inequality by deconstructing ideologies of femininity which had lost their secure foundation in "natural, sexual difference." Some of these feminist scholars started their work in the 1970s and many of them found inspiration in Foucault's notion of power and docile bodies. Focusing his analysis on modernity, Foucault argues that power circulates through society and that rather than possessed, it is exercised through control and management of the bodies and the identities of subjects who then become themselves creators of the structure controlling them. Although Foucault makes very few references to women and gender, his attention to the exercise of power outside the political arena and inside people's everyday lives inspired feminists' attempts to uncover the mechanisms of patriarchal power even in the most private domains, such as marriages, maternity, personal relationships, and finally in the rituals governing the relationships between women and their own bodies. Foucault's idea that the body is targeted by power mechanisms and thereby rendered docile has been taken up by feminist theorists to analyze contemporary forms of subordination obtained through the control of women's bodies.

FEMINIST CRITIQUES OF STEREOTYPICAL FEMININITY

Foucault's work has admittedly functioned as a point of reference for two radical second wave feminists who have focused their attention on the body: Sandra Bartky[15] and Susan Bordo.[16] Both these scholars have extensively empha-

sized the importance of the relationship between women
and their bodies and have identified in the so called "beauty
practices" a crucial site where to explore and uncover the
mechanisms through which women's subordination is
achieved. Bartky, for instance, supplies a detailed exploration
of some of the physical manifestations of gender. She argues
that recognizably male and female bodies are constructed
through three types of practices, "those that aim to produce
a body of a certain size and general configuration, those that
bring forth from this body a specific repertoire of gestures,
postures, and movements, and those that are directed toward
the display of this body as an ornamented surface."[17] Bartky
specifically discusses also the social creation of physical
gender differences in walking, eye contact, smiling, touching,
stance, skin, and hair, among other things, by referring to the
sum total of these physical social practices as "the social construction of the feminine body."[18]

Bordo emphasizes the power of images, especially commercial ones, in setting beauty standards that women then
struggle to achieve by continuously manipulating their
bodies. She also remarks that women spend an enormous
amount of time and resources in "doing looks" and that,
after a relative break in 1970s, in the 1980s and 1990s women
have returned to all forms of "doing looks" with renovated
enthusiasm and energies[19]; a confirmation of this trend
would be the growing popularity of plastic surgery among
women. In other words, in contemporary western society,
women's bodies are perceived and represented as "never
good enough"; they need to be constantly controlled in their
natural manifestations and continuously reformed, embel-
lished, adorned, and so on. And what is worse most women

take this for granted as their destiny, or one of their "duties," as part of their normal routine, a set of activities assigned to them or imposed on them almost by nature.

In the United States at the beginning of the 1990s Naomi Wolf suggested, in her bestseller, *The Beauty Myth*, that by obsessively following superimposed and often unrealistic standards of beauty women end up subtracting large amounts of energies and effort from active and successful participation in public life and from effective competition with men for positions of power. So, although the majority of women are no longer wearing corsets and crinolines to impede their movements, nevertheless the unavoidable imperative of pursuing beauty in order to achieve a socially acceptable appearance and a respectable social identity, pushes women into a position of subordination in at least two ways: it takes away energies that could be more effectively employed to challenge power structures and, more importantly, it encourages women to perceive their own body as an object, ultimately objectifying their being in the world.

Through beauty practices, women are turned into sexual objects for the pleasure of men and paradoxically feel like that too. On this point French feminist Monique Wittig says:

> The category of sex is the product of heterosexual society that turns half of the population into sexual beings. Wherever they are, whatever they do (including working in the public sector) they are seen (and made) sexually available to men. . . . They must wear their yellow star, their constant smile, day and night.[20]

Despite differences among them, the approaches mentioned above seem to all come to the conclusion that, all through modernity, the ideology of femininity, i.e. the standard for socially accepted female gender identity, has been aimed at controlling women's bodies, trying to keep them docile and ultimately to confine them in their subordinate place in society by employing historically different strategies.

On this subject, fashion history provides us with some interesting and significant examples. In the 19th century, unhealthy and constrictive fashion items, of which the corset is the most eloquent example, physically reduced women's ability to move, act and work; in contemporary times it is the beauty myth dictating the rules of feminine attributes and behavior. In fact even nowadays it is hard to deny that the obsessions about one's body—still much more common among women than men—reveal a tendency to confirm the traditional social organization and to oppose attempts to change current power relations in as much as it objectifies women and leave men to play the role of the only subjects in society.

However, in the last ten years this negative view of beauty practices and fashion has been opposed by members of the sometimes called "third wave feminism." These authors take a critical stance against some of the analyses and ideas circulated among the previous, "radical" generation of scholars. Animated mainly by the cultural studies notion of the "active consumer" third-wave postmodern feminists refuse to depict women as "cultural dopes," as semi-conscious or unconscious collaborators in bringing about their own subordination. On the contrary, they emphasize the pleasure women experience when engaging in fashion and beauty practices. Talking about women and fashion, Elizabeth Wilson[21] and others underline the playfulness involved in choosing what to wear and argue that fashion can be made transgressive when used in contrast to mainstream stereotypes of class and gender. As much as clothes and make up can help us create our femininity, in the same way they could be used to fake it; our body can be presented and shown as a sign of opposition to moral norms and standards. The excitement people experience with fashion and makeup is often described as a result of using beauty practices to play with identities, to construct, like a theatre play, as many different identities as we like, thereby uncovering the cultural origin of masculinity and femininity.[22]

As fascinating as these views might be, I think they still elude the basic issue. Given that we can deconstruct the ideology of femininity by uncovering the performative elements of which it is constituted, and if, as feminists, we refuse to "buy into" traditional patriarchical notions of femininity, what alternative and new discourses can we find or create to refer to women's subjectivities? In other words, Butler's position and its derivates are very powerful deconstructive tools, but they leave us at loose ends when it comes to propose a viable alternative to dominant culture.[23]

EMBODIED SUBJECTIVITIES

While drag queens and habitual cross-dressers can entertain themselves with continuously changing identities, I think that the vast majority of people are faced with the problem of constructing an identity, or better of defining a (perhaps varying) notion of their own subjectivity. Compared to centuries past our freedom in doing so has probably increased:

nowadays we can say that in most cases class is not a destiny, nor is race. But can we say so about gender, or sex? Radical feminist theory shows us that we should not fall prey of the beauty myth proposed by the flood of mediated and commercial images we are constantly exposed to; not only do they make us unhappy with ourselves, but also help keeping us in a subordinate position.

Third wave feminists, on the other hand, tell us to relax and enjoy popular, commercial culture instead of demonizing it: we are after all expert consumers and critical beings, able to use commodities to join the postmodern bandwagon of "fun at all costs." Anyway we don't have a unique identity and so we might as well enjoy ourselves creating as many as we can manage. With Butler's theory we are told that culture and discourse does it all for us: because of the circulating narratives, we'll have some views about masculine and feminine which will only allow us to see two sexes and there's not much we can do about it all. Of course we have a body, but whether it is a man, a woman or a Martian only culture can tell.

So the question of what it means to be a woman or a man in a given society (here, our western late capitalist society) is virtually left unanswered in the sex-gender debate I have tried to present here. How can we possibly tackle that? Is there anything in the literature or in the world that could give us hints about how femininity can, may be performed and/or alternatively represented nowadays?

As I said before, I think a discussion on identity must involve a discussion of the body. But to think and talk about woman's body means stepping on dangerous, unfirm ground, if, as I have tried to show, the dominant discourse on the body (both male and female) has been created in a male dominated culture. Even in the conceptualization/culturalization of their own bodies women seem to have had no voice. So the first step should perhaps consist of finding ways to de-construct the dominant discourses on female bodies which are man-made artifacts.

On this issue, important and interesting work has already been done especially, I think, in psychoanalytically based literature on women's health and in women's art. Many authors have recently focused on those typically feminine health problems, such as eating disorders and the depression occurring at particular times of life, such as pregnancy and after a child's birth. At the same time in the field of art, various women artists have placed the female body at the centre of their inspiration and have come out with some very interesting pieces of work that boldly exposes the monstrous, uncontrollable flesh that western culture traditionally attributes to women's bodies in contrast to the rational, "under control" body usually attached to manliness.

In a recent and fascinating volume about women's bodies and representations of femininity, Jane Ussher[24] identifies some crucial points in women's life in which their bodies are positioned as monstrous, dangerous, and disgusting. Starting from the taken for granted, namely that in western culture woman's reproductive body "is deemed dangerous and defiled, the myth of the monstrous feminine made flesh,"[25] Ussher goes on to explore the common cultural practices routinely employed to hide and control women's bodies through narratives and discourses that become accepted in society as "regimes of truth." The operations of these regimes can be detected with the highest evi-

dence around the bodily manifestations of women's fecun-
dity (incidentally, those properties of the body that men
lack): the menarch, pregnancy, giving birth, breast-feeding,
and menopause. Each of these events is subjected to a whole
set of socio-cultural protocols, of regimes of control that,
previously nested mainly within religion and magic, are
nowadays often created and enacted within the field of medicine and health care. Although Ussher's analysis is rich and
detailed, her argument can perhaps be summarized by
saying that these narratives are aimed at either silencing or
hiding these manifestations away from the social arena (as in
the case of the disgusting menstrual blood), or at patholo-
gizing, medicalizing them, as it happens with pregnancy,
child birth, and menopause. The enactment of these
"regimes of truth" turns the woman's body into the object of
expert monitoring and surveillance, while very little or no
space is left to the woman's first hand experience of these
events, in other words to the woman's subjectivity.[26]

The lack of an authentic, independent subjectivity, as
well as the cultural perception of women's bodies as monstrous, dangerous, and imperfect is also central in the work
of some women artists. One of the best known examples is
provided by Cindy Sherman, an American photographer
that has worked extensively on these themes during her
career. In the 1970s she did a series of black and white photographs where she depicts herself in various disguises,
scenes, poses and dresses, reminiscent of American movies of
the 1950s. These pictures aim to represent the emptiness of
femininity; "the observer goes from one image to another,
each endlessly displacing and deferring a 'real core' or sub-
stance."[27] In this series femininity emerges as a "masquerade

hiding nothing,"[28] perhaps suggesting, along with radical second wave feminists, that femininity is nothing but a man-made stereotype powerfully imposed by popular culture. As Betterton notes, there has been an important evolution in Sherman's work on femininity: in more recent work the plastic fetishized image of femininity, the socially present-able one, has opened up "to reveal its disturbing interior."[29] In a more recent series of large color photographs, *Untitled*, Sherman "reconstructs her own body in a monstrous anatomy made up of prosthetic parts or else fragments it in a waste of bodily fluids, decaying food, etc. . . ."[30] So, in other words, Sherman's more recent work tackles the problem of the monstrosity associated with female bodies in a male dominated culture and forcefully exposes scenes and elements that are normally and normatively hidden. Whether or not this kind of exposure of the "shameful" parts of women's bodily functions is useful to transform normative discourses about women's sex as monstrous and unclean, is still a debated issue in feminist art criticism. Surely, I think, the work of women artists on the body constitutes an effective way to denounce and reveal to the public the misogyny engrained in the culture and its deep hostility to (and fear of) the female potentially reproductive body.

By being denied the "authorship" of discourses about their own bodies through beauty practices, on the one hand, religious and later medical discourses, on the other, women have then become deprived of the primary material for the construction of their own subjectivity: in modern western thought, the apparently neutral subject is actually a man; white, middle class, heterosexual, and capable of objective, disembodied thought and knowledge. So the question for women becomes: how are we to re-appropriate our bodies and how are we to create new narratives about them so that we can replace the definition of "the Other" with forms of independent subjectivity?

THE SITUATIONAL BODY

Thinking about this problem and searching for possible paths toward a solution, I find myself brought back into phenomenological fields. In particular the phenomenological notion, firstly proposed by Merleau Ponty and later taken up by de Beauvoir, of the "body as situation." As Toril Moi has eloquently shown in her famous essay *What is A Woman?* approaching the problem from this perspective re-frames the debate and evaporates some of the *empasses* it seems to have run into.

In particular, as I see it, from the broad debate emerging from the intersection of the various positions within feminist studies one general conclusion might be drawn: that it is very difficult and perhaps not even coherent to propose a universal and absolute concept about women's subjectivity and women's body to replace the objectified stereotype that patriarchal society has left us with. In other, perhaps more illustrative, terms I do not think that a shabby appearance and lack of shaving is needed to free oneself from the beauty myth, nor that lesbianism is the answer to normative heterosexuality, nor giving birth at home the antidote to the medicalization of maternity. To do all this probably makes a statement but I don't think it empowers women as independent subjectivities, in as much as it doesn't get them out of the position of "the other," which many authors like Irigaray[31] and, before her, de Beauvoir,[32] have used to define womanhood. To adopt counter-attitudes to the stereotype just ends up promoting other stereotypes that ultimately universalize the notion of "woman," once again disregarding or plainly ignoring the simple fact that women, like men, are not all the same and do not all feel the same.

To treat the body as a situation, I think, re-locates the issue at a different level: the level of naturally occurring episodes of social life in which non-predefined individuals continuously create subjectivities using their bodily being in the world both as a set of resources and a set of constraints for their agency, i.e. their specific project at hand. When defining the term "situation," Sartre[33] said that a situation is a structural relationship between our projects (our freedom) and the world (which includes our bodies). So the body is at the same time something that discloses for us a limited set of possibilities to carry out whatever plan we might have, and something upon which depends the meaning we give to the world: depending on my body (and my project) the world appears to me in one way or another, as one set of resources and constraints and not another.

The idea of the body as a situation is central in de Beauvoir's feminist thought, which has often been accused of essentialism by poststructuralist feminists in as much as de Beauvoir fundamentally accepts the binary division of sexes and defines woman as somebody bearing female sexual characteristics. Although in many passages of her work she, implicitly or explicitly, reveals her mixed feelings and ambivalence towards motherhood (sometimes even implying that women's reproductive function is the reason for their subordinate place in society), on the other hand, the ways in which she uses the notion of the "body as a situation" in the context of her discussion of women's position seem to open up very promising scenarios. Moi[34] reminds us that in one passage of *The Second Sex*, de Beauvoir says that the problem for women is not their biological/sexual make up; the problem is that women somehow are *imprisoned* in their sex, their sexual nature socially becomes a cage from where it is very difficult to get out and where traditional and popular representations do their best to confine us. To continue the metaphor, I could add that the iron bars of this cage are ideological discourses about women's bodies that are continuously reconfirmed and consolidated in commonly shared rules of interaction.[35]

But if we break free of the patriarchical discourses about our bodies which stop us from entering the domain of thought,[36] if we start considering our bodies as the source of our experience of the world and therefore of our knowledge, the prison could suddenly be turned into the runway towards our freedom as subjects.

In this phenomenological perspective, the making of subjectivity is a life-long process, a series of encounters between my embodied being and the world, whereby women are "always in the process of making themselves what they are. We give meanings to our lives by our actions"[37] and, I would add, in all the different situations of interaction in which we engage and by which we are modified. This is probably not such a different stance than the one taken by Goffman[38] when he says that one enters an interaction projecting a "face," "a proposed *self*" for a course of action; this face is usually a combination of situational constraints and one's project at hand. The face chosen is a key to apprehend the world around as an ensemble of more or less relevant elements on and through which to display one's body techniques. The body is obviously at the centre of this scene, it is a fundamental element of the face, "a historical sedimentation of our way of living in the world, and of the world's way of living with us."[39]

So being a woman, i.e. bearing female sexual characteristics, is certainly a fundamental starting point to construct my lived experience in the world, but it is not enough to predict what will happen next and therefore what it will mean *for me* to be a woman. In this perspective there is obviously no straightforward answer to the question "what is a woman?" because each woman's experience of her body is bound up with her projects in the world and depends on the ways in which she encounters gender norms, stereotypes and patriarchal ideology.[40]

The problem women have with so-called gender identity derives, I suspect, from an universalistic (and therefore masculine) approach to the notion of womanhood as an essence located in one particular body form: confronting themselves with the stereotypical woman, some women make it the project of their life to meet that standard. This may be true in various degrees, but, I think, affects nearly all women: for some, in some phases of life, it is a priority; others might have other plans but at the same time try, while attending these other plans, to fit gender norms as much as possible. The struggle to look beautiful and thin is ever lingering upon western women in everyday life; even for those who are very conscious of the background issues and problems. And when we don't succeed in this we might feel not fully satisfied, not entirely fulfilled, simply not good enough. Patriarchal society's attempt to locate the essence of womanhood in the body (the normalized, docile body of fashion and cosmetic adverts) might be then read as an attempt to prevent women from seeing all the potential they have *besides* the cultivation of their bodies to meet a man-made standard; the common tendency to propose a ready made ideal of woman can be seen as a sneaky way to stop real women from elaborating new, alternative, unpredictable versions of living their embodied (and dangerous for man) existence and ultimately to emerge as independent subjects of knowledge and thought.[41]

If we let our body be disciplined without listening to it, if we collaborate in putting our body under rules we did not author, we become the first to treat our body as an object, we'll be the first to silence the body as if it was just pure flesh and not the history of our being in the world. If we silence the body, we won't be able to tell the stories about how it feels to be pregnant and have a baby, or how it feels to be looked through at a business meeting or to be subjects of hints and harassment on the workplace. Seeing the body as a situation perhaps gives us back a sense of freedom without which it is impossible to author the scripts of our lives instead of having them dictated.

MASCULINITIES IN A
GLOBALIZED WORLD

Chapter 6

TRANSFORMING MASCULINITIES
Globalization, Dislocations, and Insecurities; Masculinities/Modernities

Victor J. Seidler

If we can think of an Enlightenment vision of modernity as the project of a dominant white European masculinity we can begin to think in different terms about gender identities within a globalized world. We begin to acknowledge that globalization has taken different forms and that projects of empire and colonial domination were themselves global projects that were to bring the benefits of modernity such as reason, knowledge, and science to colonized others who had in the eyes of a dominant colonial imaginary been deprived of them. Supposedly it was only through accepting gratefully subordination to their European colonial masters that the uncivilized "others" were to be able to make a transition from nature to culture, from tradition to modernity. Ever since 1492 and possibly before, European powers imagined their futures in globalized terms. Often these imaginations were framed through notions of heroic masculinities of "discovery" and "exploration."[1]

If European powers sought to remake the world in their own image, it was often within the image of a dominant masculinity. At some level, this was also to be reflected in the assumption of a rationalist modernity that reason itself was to be cast, through its radical separation from nature, within masculinist terms. This has left traces within the relationship between philosophy and social theory and particularly within a Kantian inheritance, that as I argued in *Kant, Respect, and Injustice: The Limits of Liberal Moral Theory*, was framed through its radical distinction between reason and nature. This reflected a Cartesian assumption that has been reflected universally but was largely framed within masculinist terms whereby consciousness was identified with reason and mind and so with a disembodied conception of knowledge. Through a dualism of mind and body, the body was framed as part of a disenchanted conception of nature.[2]

As I showed in *Unreasonable Men: Masculinity and Social Theory* this meant that a dominant masculinity could alone take its reason for granted and it assumed a power to treat emotions, feelings and desires—gathered together by Kant as "inclinations"—as if they could only lead people astray from the path of pure reason. This is specifically *not* to argue in essentialist terms that reason is somehow "masculine" and emotions "feminine" but it is to sensitize us to the power that a dominant masculinity had to trivialize and delegitimize women's speech as "emotional" and thereby as "irrational."[3] Of course it is difficult to think in such general terms but it can help to frame the ways that feminism has presented a significant critique to modernity in its refusal to accept the prevailing distinction between reason and emotion. Not only have they helped to validate emotions and feelings as sources of knowledge, but feminist theories have also illuminated complex relations between knowledge and power and the ways men have been able to use their power to silence and to invalidate different ways of knowing.

I recall these concerns because they help us grasp a relationship between a dominant masculinity and language and a tendency for men to be able to legislate for others because they alone have, as Kant assumed, an inner relationship with reason. They can reinforce their power through a claim to be "impartial" and "objective" in their judgments and they can insist that they do *not* really need to listen to what others have to say. Traditionally, within patriarchal families, fathers were able to legislate that it was "good" for their sons to follow in their footsteps and attend a similar boarding school. Since the family was making a financial sacrifice, this is something a child should be grateful for. This is a decision that could traditionally be made without having to *listen* to what a boy has to say, for reason allowed the father to legislate impersonally. There was no need for dialogue or narrative with his son, so that if the son says he does not want to leave home, he only shows his ingratitude and his "failure to understand" the benefits he is being offered. It might be said that this is understandable because the point of going is to be separated from his mother so that he can become independent and autonomous.

But this also silences mothers who traditionally would have been expected not to question their husbands, at least in public. They would have been treated as irrational if they seemed to stand in the way of providing a good education for their sons. Sometimes sons can feel isolated and betrayed if their mothers refuse to speak up for them, though they might also recognize the reality of patriarchal power and the authority that fathers can assume within the family which they "head" as the representative of divine authority. Their word is supposed to be *law* so that if you dare to question, this is a sign of disobedience that shows you are deserving of punishment. Again it was crucial for Second wave feminisms in the West to reveal the dynamics of silencing and ways that patriarchal relations of power worked to undermine a woman's sense of self-worth and could make it difficult for them to value their different voices.[4]

Often men learn to use language not as a means of expression but as a mode of self-defense and as a means of affirming their right to legislate for others. This means that they can often speak in general terms about what is good for others, *before* really being able to speak more personally for themselves. Their voice, as Gilligan suggested, is often an impersonal voice that wants to be able to discern what is "right" through an impartial reason, framing moral issues as if they can always be solved, as if they were mathematical puzzles.[5] Though Gilligan has been accused of essentialism, the insight that has often been lost is how gender relations of power work to silence certain forms of moral thinking. The guiding insight was how a Kantian tradition had fostered a notion within Kohlberg's work that there was a scale of moral thinking in which their capacity to think in terms of universal moral principles was validated as the highest value. What Gilligan realized was that there was some kind of relationship between a Kantian ethical tradition of universal moral principles and the silencing of a different voice, often a woman's voice that was concerned with an ethic of care.

Of course there is a place for universal moral principles, but we have to be careful about the ways they are generated and the kind of dialogues between different cultures and civilizations that they allow. But as we think about the shift of gender relations within a globalized world we need to think more carefully about the power that a dominant Western masculinity has had in establishing the *terms* of discussion and debate. Not only do we need to be able to listen to different voices but there is a particular task for men to be able to recover their own personal voices so that they can enter dialogue on different terms. There is a danger, as Wittgenstein was aware of, of language becoming disconnected and abstracted so that people needed to be reminded of the meanings of terms they are using. As Stanley Cavell reminds us in his early paper, "Must We Mean What We Say?" "When the philosopher who proceeds from ordinary language tell us, 'You can't say such-and-such,' what he means is that you cannot say that *here* and communicate *this* situation to others, or understand it for yourself. This is sometimes what he means by calling certain expressions 'misuses' of language, and also makes clear the consequences of such expressions: they break our understanding."[6]

In his seminal essay on Wittgenstein in the same collection, "The Availability of Wittgenstein's Later Philosophy," Cavell recalls Wittgenstein in the *Philosophical Investigations* writing:

One human being can be a complete enigma to another. We learn this when we come into a strange country with entirely strange traditions; and, what is more, even given a mastery of the country's language. We do not *understand* the people. (And not because of not knowing what they are saying to themselves.) We cannot find our feet with them.

Cavell recognizes "In German the last sentence employs an idiom which literally says: 'We cannot find ourselves in them.' We, who can speak for one another, find that we cannot speak for them. In part, of course, we find this out in finding out that we cannot speak *to* them. If speaking *for* someone else seems to be a mysterious process, that may be because speaking *to* someone does not seem mysterious enough."[7]

This insight can also be useful for understanding difficulties that men and women can have speaking with each other. This was a realization that informed Gilligan's work but she, along with Cavell, possibly does not identify issues of power that are also involved. As fathers traditionally assumed within patriarchal families that they could speak *for* their wives as well as for their children, so traditionally colonial relationships of power were framed through a discourse of fathers and children with indigenous peoples being figured "as" children. But within a dominant European discourse of modernity, the colonized were often assumed to be uncivilized so that they could not be reasoned with. The "strangeness" of the encounter was hidden as the indigenous were defined as *lacking* a culture and few recognized, in Wittgenstein's terms, that they had "come into a strange country with entirely strange traditions" and that "We do not *understand* the people." As Simone Weil appreciated, the colonial encounter assumed that the ignorant sailor who had hardly been schooled had everything to teach and nothing to learn because he had "modernity" while they were still to be regarded as "primitive."[8]

Cavell does not think easily within gendered terms but he does recognize the significance of the fact "that so astonishingly little exploring of the nature of self-knowledge has been attempted in philosophical writing since Bacon and Locke and Descartes prepared the habitation of the new science. Classical epistemology has concentrated on the knowledge of objects (and, of course, of mathematics), not on the knowledge of persons. That is, surely, one of the striking facts of modern philosophy as a whole, and its history will no be understood until some accounting of that fact is rendered." For me this striking fact has to do with masculinities and the ways in which philosophy and social theory have been shaped through a radical distinction between reason and nature.

At the same time Cavell acknowledges "philosophers from Socrates onwards have (sometimes) also tried to understand themselves, and found in that both the method and goal of philosophizing. It is a little absurd to go on insisting that physics provides us with knowledge of the world which is of the highest excellence. . . . Our intellectual problems (to say no more) are set by the very success of those deeds, by the plain fact that the measures which soak up knowledge of the world leave us dryly ignorant of ourselves." He also recognizes that "Wittgenstein has not first 'accepted' and 'adopted' a method and then accepted its results, for the nature of self-knowledge—and therewith the nature of the self—is one of the great subjects of the *Investigations* as a whole."

But it might be, as I discovered, that it was not through philosophy alone that we can explore these issues. For me there was a resonance between the promise of Wittgenstein's later work and the kind of explorations of the personal as political that were being encouraged through feminism and sexual politics. It helped to remedy what Cavell through Bernard Williams recognized that English and American academic traditions in philosophy "unconcern with the knowledge of persons and particular with self-knowledge" has to do with "its neglect of history as a form of human knowledge."[9] It was through the recovery of Hegel and Marx that some of these connections were being made, though it was likely to be in social theory, rather than in philosophy, that you would discover hospitality for these ideas.

But these issues again would be quickly silenced through a poststructuralist tradition that sought a particular reading that could create its own silence through too quickly identifying explorations of self with an "essentialism" or a "humanism" that has to be firmly rejected. Of course these concerns returned later through an attention to issues of subjectivity and an awareness of the fluidity and fragmentation of self. Enriched through an engagement with poststructuralism issues of memory, trauma, and history are being explored across the humanities and social sciences and even finding echoes in some philosophy departments.

Cavell's concerns expressed over forty years ago still find a resonance when he says, "Because Wittgenstein does fuller justice to the role of feeling in speech and conduct than any other philosopher within the Anglo-American academic tradition, it is disheartening to find his thought out of reach. Pole extends the line of those who, shocked at the way aca-

demic reasoning is embarrassed by the presence of feeling—
its wish to remove feeling as the 'emotive' accompaniments
of discourse, out of the realm of intellectual assessment—
counter by taking feelings too much at face value and so
suffer the traditional penalty of the sentimentalist, that one
stops his feelings seriously." Again the references are to a
male gender but at least it opens up a space that has been
explored through feminisms, queer theory, and critical
studies in relation to men and masculinities. It helps to
unsettle a dominant rationalist tradition that is still so powerful in shaping the concerns of academic philosophy.[10]

But if we are to find an appropriate language that can
move across different registers of the personal and the
impersonal and does not set them in opposition to each
other then we have to be wary of uneasy generalizations.
Often it is through narrative and ethnographic methods that
we can appreciate the significance of "thick descriptions" as
Geertz has framed it and so find ourselves working with concerns about the difficulties of understanding and communi-
cating across cultures within a globalized world that
Wittgenstein also helped to identify.[11] This is to open up a
form of analysis that is not simply concerned with catego-
rizing into pre-given classifications but can recognize the
need for dialogue around the transformation of masculinities across different cultures, histories, and traditions. I want
to explore how globalization has worked to shape gender
identities in the North as well as in the South, in similar and
also in different ways.

An awareness of the historical framing of a rationalist
universalism within modernity should hopefully also make
us aware of a need to rethink traditions of hegemonic mas-

culinity that too easily reinstate Anglo-American assumptions. We need to be wary of analyzing masculinities as relationships of power in ways that echo, rather than subvert, traditional splits between reason and nature. Given the existence of patriarchal relations of power across diverse cultures, there is bound to be a resonance with examples drawn from the Anglophone North, particularly say over men's control over women's bodies and sexualities. But even here we need to recognize how women are being undermined and silenced also through the invalidation of their experience. There is little doubt that globalization is working to frame particular cosmopolitan masculinities at the same time as it creates pressures upon women to conform to these new techniques of appraisal and regulation especially within corporate sectors. But if there is to be resistance and men and women learn to negotiate for a different kind of balance between work, family, and intimate relations, then we need to shape different relationships to language so that people can also be more in touch with themselves and their own values as they negotiate for more equal gender relations within a globalized world.[12]

BOUNDARIES

Young men who have grown up with new technologies and the Internet within a globalized world have learned to draw upon a variety of sources of information. They are often very quick in their responses and have grown up with visual and aural cultures to deal with a complexity of sensory activities. It is as if they are constantly alert to where the next piece of information is coming from and the immediate response that it might require. This is part of an adrenalized culture in which young men are often responding to a variety of stimuli at the same time. They can expect themselves to be able to process information very quickly from a number of diverse sources. This forms the gendered experience of young men and women who can expect immediate access to information and feel frustrated if they do not have it. This can make it so difficult when a hard drive goes and a computer crashes because people can feel suddenly powerless and unable to communicate. For men it can feel almost catastrophic as if they cease to exist for themselves if they cannot communicate with others.

Sometimes young men will feel that if they do not get an immediate response then they will give up and move on to something else. They might feel that they have said what they wanted to say and if they felt that it was not understood immediately, there is no point keeping on about it. They might hope that things change and that it never happens but they will often "hold" their emotions within themselves. They might have little experience of staying with issues, especially emotional ones, and have inherited a sense that they should be able to deal with whatever emotional problems they have on their own. Within new capitalism what is important is the capacity to get on with people quickly and then to be able to disengage with them when a task is over. This was a quality that Richard Sennett recognized in *The Corrosion of Character*, but he does not explore whether and how it might be gendered. For it might be easier for young men to sustain an instrumental relationship with self and so get on with people even if they do not like them. They might not get caught up in the relationships as young women can be more inclined to do.[13]

It might be helpful to explore an example that shows how a global corporate masculinity is being framed and how it also works to pressure women to become a particular identity within regimes of a supposed gender equality. In the BBC show *The Apprentice* in which young people are competing to be the assistant of Alan Sugar, it was often the women who would get tangled up in relationships with each other while it was the men who often seemed able to put personal conflicts aside to get on with the job at hand. But the men were often less able to listen to others in their teams and would simply expect that if an instruction had been given, it would be obeyed without question. But this meant if others had a different idea of how a task might be done or wanted to approach people in a different way, some men could be slower to respond and feel more threatened in their authority. As the leaders of a particular task they were often more tied up with their own authority and could feel threatened when others made what could be useful suggestions. They could also be less flexible in their thinking once a certain direction had been set.[14]

If men can be clearly focused upon a task at hand they can be less aware and sensitive of what is going on around them. They can find it harder to "tune in" to what is happening for others and so respond to anxieties that often remain unspoken. This is not to frame gender difference/s but it is to acknowledge how growing up within particular gendered cultures can shape expectations and qualities that young men and women can have of themselves. Of course when we are reflecting upon *The Apprentice* we are focusing upon high achieving women and men who are ambitious for themselves in business and have proven track records that have allowed them to be chosen to take part. They want to win and are highly competitive. They often say that want to win "more than anything else" and they are prepared to do "whatever it takes." This shows the "qualities" that are necessary to succeed within the competitive world of neo-liberal new capitalisms. People bring different qualities with them and it is often not the people you might expect that prove themselves most able in the different tasks they are assigned. But it is clear that personal skills and the capacity to communicate with others that have traditionally been associated with women have become important within the new managerialism.

Young men are often brought up within competitive cultures so they learn to police their experience so as to eradicate the slightest signs of weakness. In this way they create "tight boundaries" around themselves. Of course some men are more porous and they absorb the feelings of others around them even if they are unaware of their meso-morphic bodily type. Men grow up with different body types that can encourage them also to respond to experi-ences differently. But if they grow up within cultures that teach them to disavow their emotions as sources of weak-ness, so they will also learn to attack their awareness in dif-ferent ways. They might be so focused upon the demands of work that they can be less sensitive to what is going on in their intimate relationships.[15]

In the West young men can grow up to be more emo-tionally literate than their parents' generation and more attuned to what is going on emotionally. But they are also more likely, with their relationship to new technologies, to find it harder to stay with their experience to take in what is going on for them. They might think that because they have said something about a troubling emotional situation, that this is enough to make sure that it is registered by others. For them it can be akin to sending an email where once the message is sent you expect that others will read it and respond appropriately. But with person-to-person relationships things do not work that way and often you have to make sure that what you have expressed has been registered appropriately. You can need to check *how* you have been heard and how it has been interpreted.

Younger generations of men in their early twenties and thirties can be more likely to expect that what they have said will receive immediate attention and so get a quick response. As it is with emails so often people can expect with life. Traditionally with heterosexual relationships women were expected to be supportive of their husbands and so ready to listen to what happened for them during the day. There was a clear gender division of labor in which women were expected to organize their time so they could do the emotional labor that so often sustained the relationship. Often this was a dependency that men took for granted without appreciating the effort and energies that went into it. Since men are often identified with an image of themselves as independent, it makes it difficult to appreciate the support they receive. Often they can also assume that with the establishment of the relationship it can provide a supportive background to their work lives. Traditionally this meant that women often felt taken for granted and undermined in their sense of self-worth as they became invisible within the relationship. Women were not expected to respect their own time and space, but rather were supposed to sacrifice themselves when their husbands were around. They were to find happiness indirectly through making their partners and children happy.

Second wave feminism had a global impact through its demand that women should be able to exist in their own right and that their time was of equal value and that they needed a space of their own. It was the recognition that women ceased to exist for themselves that was so threatening to Western philosophical traditions that assumed with Descartes that if women were conscious they thereby existed. Liberal feminism had historically affirmed the rationality of women, challenging a Kantian ethical tradition that argued that women could only secure a strong enough inner relationship with reason if they were ready to subordinate themselves to men. As I argued in *Kant, Respect and Injustice*, it was Kant's insights into the workings of power and dependency that threatened his vision of the autonomy of morality. Because of this I argued morality could not be separated from politics and knowledge from power.

Traditionally work was imagined as part of the public sphere and so as a realm of reason and power. The domestic realm was the space for women and it was the sphere of emotion. It was the space in which children were to be brought up until they were ready to enter the world of work as rational selves. It was men who supposedly moved between different worlds, between a public realm that was supposedly a sphere of reason and so shaped as a masculine space in which men could be relied upon to make decisions based on reason alone and a private realm in which they often seemed to be visitors or guests. Through a Kantian modernity reason was deemed to be radically separated from nature, so that bodies were not recognized as sources of knowledge. Rather men were encouraged into an instrumental relationship with their bodies that they owned as property at their disposal. At some level, it was the mind—reason alone that was "human" and, given that a dominant masculinity could alone take its reason for granted, it was bodies that remained "animal." This frames masculinity as a relationship of self-control where it is reason that is to be in control of bodies that are the sphere of emotional life. In some sense bodies "belong" at home in the domestic space though it is significant that men's bodies do not supposedly have any emotional needs.[16]

The traditional split between work and family was gendered because for a long period it was men who were supposed to work outside of the home while it was women who were supposedly confined to the home. This still holds true in many traditional cultures. This means that women do not belong outside of the home. If they move out of the domestic space they are supposedly entering foreign territory. They are entering men's spaces and they should be fearful and on their guard. In these spaces they need to be protected by other men such as their fathers, brothers, or cousins. This also means that men do not "really" belong at home and that there refuge there is temporary. They are spending time in women's spaces where they can be looked after and nourished before returning to work where their male identities are shaped and they can really "belong."

Dis/locations

Where do men belong? This is a useful question to bring out how different cultures frame the spaces of men. It also gives us a sense of how quickly things have changed in post-traditional societies in which gender divisions of labor have been challenged. Within Scandinavian countries, where there is the strongest identification with notions of gender equality, there is a vision that men and women belong equally at work as they do at home with shared responsibilities for childcare and domestic work. These activities are not gendered as they were traditionally imagined but are often deemed to be neutral activities that have to be more or less equally distributed according to the particular demands of the moment. In the 1970s and 1980s women learned to give the same priority to work than men did and the State often took over responsibilities for childcare from an early age. There was high quality provision in countries like Denmark where children were looked after in small groups that allowed them to be socialized with other children.[17]

But though women and men were often happy with these arrangements, it was striking that some women, especially with their second child, wanted to make different choices. They expressed a desire to stay at home with their young children, often organizing a break with work where this was possible. Some women felt they had "missed out" with their first children and wanted to have a closer, more intimate engagement with their second child. They felt this was not an experience they wanted to miss. It was something they wanted for themselves. This meant that childcare was not being imagined as labor that could be shared out but as an experience, often frustrating and difficult but also full of joy they wanted to have for themselves as mothers.

I'm not sure whether many men made similar decisions about fathering but some certainly did chose to become house husbands with their partners going out to work and there assuming major responsibilities for childcare and home. This could work but sometimes men felt isolated and undermined in very similar ways than reported by women. If they were accustomed to the respect of a high profile job they often found it harder. They could also miss contact with other adults that could be harder to organize for men. Though many were supposedly welcomed into childcare facilities, there were often fewer other men around they could relate too.

In the West there have been important experiments in alternative forms of living, especially in the 1970s and 1980s. There were experiments in communal living and childcare that need to be carefully evaluated. Interviews conducted by Lucy Rhoades with women in their late twenties who grew up in intentional communities in Britain show a diversity of experiences with some women feeling it was a difficult time, especially if they wanted to be more "feminine." They could feel pressure to behave more like tomboys. But they could still treasure the spaces they had in rural communes and the time for relationships with other children. Reflecting back at a moment in their lives when they were thinking about what kinds of families they wanted for themselves, they often valued being able to relate to other adults and also to a group of children but, as with the experience in Kibbutzim in Israel, they also wanted to have closer relationships with their children than they felt they sometimes had with their parents. They found divorce and separation difficult to deal with, especially when they had to deal with the sexual relations of their parents with the idea that because sex was "natural" it should not be hidden away from them. They appreciated the honest conversations about sex but often did not want to "take on" their parents' new partners.[18]

The emotional literacy and ideas of gender equality that were shaped in the communities became mainstream within Western urban cultures in the 1980s and 1990s. Often children had responsibilities and were encouraged to take initiatives in organizing events for themselves that helped shape ideas of choice and responsibility that were taken up by libertarian thinking on the right within neo-liberal economies. Sometimes these notions were taken out of context and the interrelation between creative individuality and communal recognition and support was lost. But within a globalized economy young people are expected to take more responsibility in organizing their own lives. They are encouraged to be entrepreneurial in the ways they face opportunities and to shape themselves according to the demands of the market.

With Thatcherism in Britain, it was the dominance of the market and the realization that a younger generation would have to continually upgrade their skills if they were to be able to compete in a global market that became significant. Living in an uncertain world often means that young men feel a need for maps that allow them to feel more confident and give them a sense of control over their futures. They can feel a need for a sense of direction and a vision of the different steps they need to take to achieve. This is allowed for in the career gradings in multinational corporations and organizations that give young people a sense of future direction within a precarious world. It shows stages on life's way.[19]

But with young women being encouraged to think of themselves as "career women" they can find themselves facing similar predicaments. They might be more conscious of a feeling of lack in their lives if they are without a relationship, but secure in their own living situations they might also enjoy the freedom that comes with singleton life. They might not want commitment and they might be happy with serial monogamy or with diverse relationships at the same time as long as they feel a sense of control over their lives. In this way "control" can become as important for women as it traditionally has been for men. But men might "hold on" to emotional issues much longer without expressing what is going on for them. They might have said something but then, when there was no immediate response, reckoned that "there was no point" so switched to something else. It is this capacity to move on to different territory and so distract yourself emotionally that can connect men from different generations.

A young man might be upset because he has broken up with his girlfriend. They might have been together for a while but he made a decision to move to a different city because of his career. She might have been disappointed possibly because she would have wanted him to stay and possibly because of what it might have said to her—but not to him—about the future of their relationship. They might have continued with the relationship for a while finding ways to deal with the distances involved and where he thought they were doing well, she might have been thinking about ending the relationship. She might have felt she was giving out all kinds of signals but he had not registered them. This is partly because men can be more literal, though they can also be concerned emotionally at another level about what is going on in the relationship but not really know *how* to put this into words. But what might be striking is the sadness he feels at the breakdown of the relationship and the ease with which he can talk to his mother and friends about it. This might be quite new for him, but it might also be the first time that he has been "dumped," so that it is a new situation for him.[20]

The ways men can learn to tune in and tune out of situations is a skill that can be fostered through a new media culture. Of course this is something women also learn to do but men can often more easily be distracted when a situation begins to get emotional. Being able to switch attention and "turn off" can also mean that men can find it harder to allow themselves to be touched and affected. It can be hard for them to recognize that people can be interested in their stories of their lives because it is only through "doing things" and achieving or excelling in some way that they think you can become interesting to others. It is what you do rather than who you are that can be interesting to others. But this can reflect a lack of depth and a fear of a deeper contact with self that men often carry. They can be dismissive of their own experience and unable to appreciate what they have been given by life. This can make it harder to *connect* with what is going on in the present because they can be so identified with plans they have for the future.[21]

Feelings can be difficult because they can disturb the narratives that people have prepared for themselves. Men can find it threatening when they feel insecure or unsure how they want to respond. Often they can switch into doing and feeling what is expected of them because in this way they can affirm a threatened masculinity and so show themselves to be "in control" of what is going on. So often it is easier for men to disavow their feelings and behave as if they do not exist at all. If they are in managerial positions within firms or organizations they can seek protection through adopting the organizational rhetorics as their own. They learn to do what is expected of them. But this can also mean they learn to feel only what they can rationally defend in advance. They can seek refuge in predictability and can fear being taken by surprise in life. Rather, life is to be controlled and for men it has traditionally been easy to identify life with work. Sometimes they feel frustrated and affirm "there has to be more to life than work" but they can soon settle back into their routines and habitual behaviors. It is partly because of the fear of spontaneity, of being taken by surprise that they need to affirm control.

Often this means that within contemporary Western cultures men feel a need to be in control of relationships. Often they can use language without really connecting to what they have to say. Rather, language is often performative as a way of creating a favorable impression or else getting their way in situations. Young men can be adept at saying what others want to hear and being aware that they are doing this while they are doing it. They know that they are being instrumental but if they think that it what is required, even expected by others if they are to win promotion or find themselves noticed by those in authority, they will be prepared to do it. This is the way they find themselves organizing their relationship to future time. It also makes a difference to the ways they inhabit their bodies and shape their experience.[22]

Finding security in having a clear goal of promotion into a higher grade, young men and women can do whatever is required because they have accepted that the means justify the ends, though they might never affirm this openly. They often fail to recognize how they might be attacking their own awareness and undermining their relationship with their inner selves. They might talk about integrity but so often this becomes empty language. It is the ways that language can so easily become emptied of meaning that is a theme in Wittgenstein's later philosophy, though he does not identify it as a particular feature of performative masculinities in late capitalism.

PRECARIOUS LIVES

People can live precarious lives in different ways. For some it is a question of insecure employment and the scarcity of jobs. They might not know what the following day will bring. Will they have enough food for their families? Sometimes what was a secure form of income as a fisherman is no more because the stocks of fish are no longer available and waters could have been polluted. Through no fault of their own, there means of livelihood have become precarious. But there can also be invisible viruses that can also make life precarious, as with HIV/AIDS. Since 2001, MMAAK—the Movement of Men Against Aids in Kenya has concentrated on preparing men to play a more prominent role in Africa's response to HIV prevention. One of their main partnerships has been with the fisherfolk living along the shores of Lake Victoria.

On the toilet of a small hotel close to the Dunga Beach resort on Lake Victoria is a poster showing a well-built man, smiling and showing off his magnificent biceps. Above the man's head are the words: "I wanted to . . . she didn't." Beneath the torso is the caption: "And so . . . we didn't." The location of the picture is significant because the hotel is frequented from time to time by local fishermen and their jaboya—a Luo word for a customer who is also a lover. Women fishmongers regularly buy fish from specific fishermen and in return give sexual favors to guarantee a regular supply of fish. Henry Osalu and around twenty other fishermen meet regularly with MMAAK in a small shack close to Dunga Beach's bustling fish processing market. He has been a fisherman since the late 1960s, when the supply of Nile perch and tilapia was plentiful. As he explains, "The practice of jaboya started when the lake fell into poor health. Now when fishermen come to shore, you can see the women fighting over the catch. If a woman's children are going hungry, and having sex with these men is the only way of giving her an income, it's unlikely she will say no."[23]

Michael Onyanga, MMAAK's national director, says many fishermen have the virus but believe they should suffer in silence to protect their masculinity. They also do not want to bring shame to their families and think that others will reject them and they will lose standing in the community. As he remarks, "In Kenya, traditionally, men are not empowered or given skills to deal with sex and sexuality. Yet they make most of the decisions at home, in the workplace, in parliament and in religious institutions." It can be shameful to talk about sex and sexuality and people can feel embarrassed to approach the subject. But men often conceal their own ignorance and do not want to acknowledge their own lack of knowledge for this can also threaten their male identities and image of themselves within the community.

Onyanga feels the fishing community has been overlooked. "Men are not hard to reach. Many assume they are not affected. Few belong to organized groups. So the workplace becomes one obvious alternative." But as Charles Juma another fisherman recognizes it takes time and determination to change behaviors. There are also cultural traditions like wife inheritance within Luo culture that calls for men to have non-protected sex with the wives of their deceased brothers. This was a cultural practice that traditionally sought to give economic security to widows but it no longer works in this way. It is not permitted to use condoms for this would mean that the ritual was not effective and bad things could happen to the family.

But as long as there is denial about the virus and as long as women are not economically empowered with sources of income on their own that could allow them to negotiate on slightly better terms, it is important to reach men where they can be talked to in ways that do not threaten their male identities. Services need to be culturally aware and also framed at appropriate times. As Juma says, "Free testing, counseling, and distribution of anti-retroviral treatment won't do much good if they're scheduled when men are out fishing or have moved on. The nomadic lifestyle of men here has to be considered if the project is going to make an impact."

Nick Were from MMAAK recognizes that fishermen

learn that the more sexual partners they have, the *more* masculine he will be. Sex becomes a way of affirming your masculinity and also strengthening it through the number of sexual contact you have. Fishermen often spend months away from their wives and children and so seek out sexual relationships. But as Were recognized, "Positive men can feel emasculated. They do not want to disclose to their wives. They fear discrimination and stigma at work." This can partly explain a resistance to the tests since they can prefer not to know their status. But this makes issues of denial complex and means they cannot be understood in rationalist terms alone, as a matter of the distribution of health messages encouraging men to take HIV tests and to use condoms. Rather, cultural beliefs about condoms also need to be engaged with so that we grasp their relationship to ideas of virility and male potency. Possibly as people see the devastation wrought by the virus and the children who are left fatherless, men can be reached through appealing to their responsibilities as fathers to protect their children. The poster is also an attempt to show that a man can still exercise his masculinity and sexual prowess by showing restrain and being gentle.[24]

But these affirmations of masculinities involve questioning some of the Anglophone models that have been developed in the West and have tended to think of masculinities as relationships of power. They have been helpful in appreciating the centrality of empowering women through giving them sources of income. But they can too easily assume that men will be obliged to change through these economic negotiations. We also need to engage with cultural masculinities and silences around sex and sexualities. As

Nick Were realizes, "By building partnerships, by rejecting the idea that all men are intrinsically bad, oppressive and promiscuous, we find we are able to involve more people in the fight against HIV/Aids."

Within Second wave feminist discourses in the West there has been a tendency, especially in some radical feminist discussions around violence against women, to regard men "all men (as) intrinsically bad." This has tended to frame women as innocent victims of male power. This is significant in grasping the patriarchal control that men so often assume within specific cultures over women's bodies and sexualities. Traditionally within Luo culture it has been men who have decided that the couple is ready for sex. But at the same time we need to be aware of issues of cultural translation and a tendency for Western discourses, including feminisms, to be framed in universal terms so obscuring the ways they express particular historical and cultural conditions within the global North. We need to be wary of tendencies to universalize or to assume that theoretical developments that have their origin in the North can simply be "modified" in relation to local cultural conditions.

For international organizations like UNICEF and other UN organizations it can be important to recognize how gender equality is not simply an organizational issue of gender parity at different levels but informs the projects that people are engaged with around the world. But this can be difficult to appreciate if gender still remains seen as an issue about the empowerment of women that does *not* really engage with issues of men and masculinities. Often men are resistant when it comes to exploring the making of their own masculinities. This calls for a process of reflection that men can experience as a loss of power and so as a threat to their male identities. It can be scary to make themselves vulnerable in front of others, especially other male colleagues because this can be experienced as "feminine" and so as undermining of their male identities. So men can feel in a double-bind of wanting to change but not really wanting to engage in a process of change that involves them engaging more personally with how cultural masculinities have been shaped and how they continue to limit them in the present.

INSECURITIES

Often it is a fear of "losing face" in front other men that can bind men to their inherited masculinities. They fear showing more of themselves partly because often they do not know these aspects of self well enough and have never really grown a connection with their emotional lives. It can feel too risky to share yourself emotionally when you suspect that whatever you say will be used by those you work with against you within a competitive relationship. Even when men want to reach out towards others they often find they can only do this with their childhood friends, where there is enough trust established. Relationships at work remain too provisional and uncertain and within a globalized neo-liberal economy people are constantly being moved on in their jobs.

Men often have many acquaintances but hardly any friends. They have learned to get on with people well enough but they are constantly disciplining themselves so they hide any sign of weakness or uncertainty. They will conceal their doubts and feel they have to deal with issues on their own.

They can be so used to betraying their inner knowledge of themselves in order to behave in ways expected by the organization, that they hardly recognize they are doing this. Rather, these behaviors are somehow expected of them and they are ready to do whatever is required to "get on." If other colleagues seem to reveal more of themselves, this is often taken as a sign of weakness that reflects a lack of self-control.

Children grow into adults but men rarely have a sense of how they might grow from being alpha males to developing a deeper masculine in their late 50s and 60s. We tend to have an appreciation of physical growth and possibly intellectual growth but little cultural grasp in the West of emotional and spiritual growth. Often within secularized Protestant modernities men can be haunted by a sense that they are *not* loveable or really deserving of love. If people say they love them this shows they do not really understand who they are. Rather, for men love is something that has to be earned through individual success and achievement and even then men can feel insecure about it. Often they need to hear their partners share their love for them, but this is a need that often goes unrecognized. It is women who will often more easily ask for reassurance that they are loved, but young career women within "post-feminist" corporate cultures can fear intimacy as much as men. Rather than interpret this is as a move "beyond gender" we need to explore generational differences and *listen* for the different terms in which a younger generation articulates their own experiences.

Vulnerability can bring feelings of insecurity. Often men will do their best to project a "front" and will tend to blame others for their own feelings. Since emotions were traditionally expelled from the office and men were expected to show self-discipline and self-control through keeping their emotions in check, it could be difficult for men to read the emotions which had *leaked* everywhere into the workplace. Since they were often living in denial of their own emotions, they would do their best to conceal their own responses that might be visible to others, often to women in the office.

Traditionally men had learned that if they had not expressed their emotions, say about who they fancy in the office, then there was no way for others to realize what was going on. Insensitive to atmospheres and ways they are created in their intensities through suppression and denial, men would often be blind to what was going on around them. They are often quite surprised to learn about office affairs and who has been seeing whom. A younger generation has learned to be more emotionally attuned but also often more adept at projecting their emotions onto others. Within postmodern consumer cultures they are more aware of their *look* and how they present with others. But often they can be caught by the surface appearance of what is going on, since for them it is often image and presentation that matter most.[25]

Of course there is a much darker side to office and work relations, especially if people are emotionally involved with each other out of work. Sometimes people are having affairs with people at work that their families do not know about. They cannot always expect their workmates to keep a secret so they have to hide what is going on. Others might know but not feel free to talk about it, at least not to relevant parties. Gossip is often the energy that keeps a workplace going with different circulations of information. Sometimes men can feel insecure because they know others are talking about them, but they do not know how much they know and about what.

Since men often want to feel "in control" of their lives, they can feel insecure about what is going on around them. Often gossip can be confined to particular layers in the organization and people in management positions might be quite unaware of what is going on. Women are often more attuned to what is going on at different levels so can often foretell a crisis before it has broken into the open. They are often aware that "their reality" is in tension with the male norms of the organization and so can be more accustomed than men to recognizing different levels of experience. They can often more easily switch between different realities and they are less likely to think that there reality is necessarily shared by others. Often men can be too focused on the task at hand to realize what is happening around them.

Often people can feel insecure because they sense that other people are talking about them and often they expect the worst. This is a form of self-protection that men can assume, feeling that the worst is likely to happen. This is what can make it difficult for them to take pleasure in what is going on in the present because their attention can be focused upon what might go wrong in the future. They can be haunted by a catastrophic consciousness that always expects something terrible to happen. They can feel that if they allow themselves to take pleasure in what is going on in the present, it will be more likely to happen. This can mean that men can feel as if they are living other people's scripts and often not taking the risk to find happiness for them-selves. Sometimes this means they will stay in a marriage that is not working and where there is little love, because they feel a sense of duty and obligation. They do not want to hurt others, nor do they want to acknowledge *how* love has drained out of their marriage. Often expecting very little for themselves men can feel fearful about "rocking the boat" and as long as things seem to be working reasonably well, they can often prefer to put up with things.

Again these generalizations can only be helpful if they encourage men in diverse cultures to reflect upon their own situations in order to define what they identify with and what is different for them. Often it will be easier for men to conclude that the narratives I am sharing do not fit for them and so can be disproved. This means they do not have to listen further and they can be excused from thinking that if these narratives do not fit with their particular class, racial, or cultural experience, what does. For men have often learned that attack is the best form of defense so that, rather than make themselves vulnerable, they sustain a distance that allows them to question the validity of what is being offered. As soon as it has been proved to be false, they need give it no further attention. So, for instance, young men might insist that they were *not* brought up to treat emotions as "feminine," so the proposition is disproved for them at the same moment as it speaks in a helpful way to older men brought up in diverse cultures. This can help them to name a feeling of insecurity in relation to their own emotions that would otherwise remain unspoken.

Though we need to be careful to talk about men and masculinities in ways that are historically and culturally specific, we also need to speak in ways that can encourage forms of recognition on the part of men themselves. This is not a matter of presenting them with abstract theories in relation to masculinities, but giving them openings that allow them to recognize tensions they might experience themselves between their experience as men and prevailing cultural masculinities. This is a tension men can often be blind to within rationalist modernities in which they can be encouraged to identify themselves with the prevailing cultural ideals of masculinity. Often men learn to conceal their inner feelings especially when they are in tension with cultural ideals because they do not want to "lose face" in front of other men. Rather, they can be hard on themselves as they blame themselves for letting themselves down. This can leave them feeling personally inadequate and insecure. They can conceal the tension especially when they have become so identified as men with the ways they perform their masculinities.

Sometimes men can be spiteful about men they are working with behind their backs. This is partly because masculinities are set within competitive terms and often men can only feel good about themselves at the expense of others. They put others down so they can feel good about themselves. Sometimes in working class occupations there are solidarities developed between men as forms of resistance to capitalist power. They do not want to be "pushed around" and they want to feel that their mates will stand up for them if they are being victimized by their supervisors or bosses. Traditions of working-class solidarity have been built up over generations, but they have been undermined and attacked within neo-liberal economies.

Young people often do not carry the trade union traditions of their parents and are less likely than earlier generations to sustain their male identities through their trade-union affiliations. There has been a displacement of historical awareness and young people are more likely to feel that they live in a radically different world from their trade-union parents. They live within a more individualized culture in which they feel they have to make it on their own as individuals. Unsure of future employment possibilities, they learn they can only rely upon their own skills and abilities on the labor market.

In some organizations it is through being noticed by those with leadership positions in the hierarchy that assures you of promotion. This means that what matters is not only what people do but also the success they have in promoting what they have done to others. Skills of self-presentation and the manufacture of appearances become important within a global culture where people are constantly moving between different teams and gaining promotions through moving firms. Often they do not stay around to see their plans come to fruition before they are planning to move on the basis of what they helped put in place and the initiative they can show they have taken. This means that young people learn to adopt an entrepreneurial relationship towards themselves that often involves an externalized view.

Within multicultural organizations that gather people from very different class, racial, and ethnic backgrounds, you have to learn to get on with people with very different histories, cultures, and traditions. Racial difference, like gender and sexual differences are framed as concerns of equal access but are supposed to become invisible within the organization where promotions are organized on the basis of individual skill, talent, and performance. Within a post-feminist culture both men and women can be encouraged to draw a sharp boundary between personal lives at home and public lives at work. At work, people can be concerned with their self-presentations and their identities remain performative.

What matters is what you present to others, though it is recognized that this can be radically in tension with inner feelings and anxieties. There might be a few people at work you can share more of yourself with and these might be friends who also know you out of work. But often there is a disciplined split that is carefully monitored and regulated.

Such splits, when they are tightly maintained, can create their own insecurities, for you rarely get honest feedback about how others see you at work. This can leave you feeling relatively isolated and alone and it can create insecurities around what others really feel about you. For as you are aware of how false you are with others, so you are often suspicious about how they are with you. There might be an official discourse to do with respecting differences and living with integrity but so often these become empty institutional rhetorics. But this does not stop people hiding behind them and often voicing them as their own. For people can seek a sense of security through closely identifying with their organizations. Sometimes men come together through trivializing emotional life and quietly ridiculing others who might take it more seriously. This can make it difficult for men to engage in a process of personal change because in their turn they can feel vulnerable to the ridicule of others. Often there will be resistance unless concerns with gender equality and organizational cultures are adopted by men in leadership positions at the highest levels of an organization. Often they can help to legitimate these concerns for others.

Chapter 7

RE-THINKING HEGEMONIC MASCULINITY IN A GLOBALIZING WORLD[1]

Chris Beasley

INTRODUCTION

Masculinity Studies writers can be credited with bringing to attention not just how gender is part and parcel of social life and social organization, but in addition how masculinity in particular is implicated in all aspects of sociality.[2] As Michael Kimmel points out, masculinity is almost invariably invisible in shaping social relations, its ever-present specificity and significance shrouded in its constitution as the universal, the axiomatic, the neutral. Masculinity, he notes, assumes the banality of the unstated norm—not requiring comment, let alone explanation. Its invisibility bespeaks its privilege.[3] "One of the principal ingredients of men's power and privilege" then becomes men's indiscernible status *as men*:[4]

> [t]he very processes that confer privilege to one group
> and not to another are often invisible to those upon
> whom that privilege is conferred...men have come to
> think of themselves as genderless, in part because they can
> afford the luxury of ignoring the centrality of gender . . .
> And the invisibility of gender to those privileged by it
> reproduces the inequalities that are circumscribed by
> gender.[5]

Thus rendering gender and masculinity visible offers a challenge to existing power relations and their continuing reiteration.

In similar fashion, Masculinity Studies writers—like Kimmel and R. W. Connell amongst others—have drawn attention to how globalization and global politics are not gender-free and largely privilege forms of masculinity in an emerging world gender order. While "most theories of globalization have little or nothing to say about gender,"[6] Masculinity Studies writers make visible the gendered character, for example, of the rhetorically gender-neutral neo-liberal market agenda in global politics, diplomacy, institutions, and economics.[7] However, as Connell points out, existing analyses of masculinities in many regions and countries cannot be simply be added together to produce a "global understanding of masculinities." In an ever more globalised world, local analyses are no longer sufficient. Rather, a grasp of large-scale social processes and global relationships is necessary to understand "masculinities on a world scale."[8]

Masculinity Studies writings on global matters are as yet in their infancy.[9] Despite the critical importance of this work, according to Connell "there are still only a handful of studies of masculinity formation in transnational arenas."[10] Similarly, in the "Introduction" to the *Handbook of Studies on Men & Masculinities,* Kimmel et al. state that research in this field on a world scale is very uneven and "still mainly a First World enterprise."[11] All the same, precisely because the investigation of gender and masculinities in global politics is indeed of great significance, I suggest that perhaps this is the moment to pause and look sympathetically but somewhat more closely at the theoretical and terminological tools developed by Masculinity Studies writers. I am encouraged in this endeavor by Connell's own view that it is timely to reassess these tools.[12] In particular I suggest that by focusing upon the term hegemonic masculinity—which is almost ubiquitously used in analyses of masculinity about local and global arenas—I can offer some useful directions for situating the as yet relatively undeveloped analysis of gender and masculinities in a globalizing world.

In concert with William Connolly, I consider that analysis of conceptual tools is a means to clarifying the political implications of different perspectives. Connolly goes so far as to say in *The Terms of Political Discourse* that, "[c]onceptual disputes…are surface manifestations of basic theoretical differences that reach to the core."[13] I do not presume that my discussion of the term hegemonic masculinity reveals incommensurable divisions between perspectives, but Connolly's point does signal that examination of this conceptual term is no mere abstract exercise. As Lakoff and Johnson put it,

> [t]he concepts that govern our thought are not just matters of the intellect. They also govern our everyday func-

tioning, down to the most mundane details. Our concepts
structure what we perceive, how we get around in the
world, and how we relate to other people.[14]

In other words, this paper presumes a role for theory in
political praxis and regards concepts as political interventions.[15] In keeping with this view, close examination of the
term hegemonic masculinity provides a contribution to both
theoretical and political dialogue.

EXISTING PROBLEMS IN THE TERM "HEGEMONIC MASCULINITY"

Jeff Hearn has drawn attention to Connell's early development and ongoing usage of the term "hegemonic masculinity"—a term which is now virtually omnipresent in
Masculinity Studies literature,[16] as well as being very widely
employed in Feminist, Sexuality and International Studies
writings. Because this terminology has unparalleled usage
and occupies a uniquely privileged positioning in the study
of men and masculinities within local gender orders, it is
clearly a crucial term for situating masculinities per se. In
addition, it is viewed by Connell and the vast majority of
Masculinity Studies writers as framing analysis of masculinities in a global context.

The term "hegemonic masculinity" is most importantly a
means to recognizing that "all masculinities are not created
equal"[17] and invokes a framing that draws attention to the
diversity within masculinities, to multiple masculinities. Masculinity in this reading is not all of a piece, nor simply about

power externalized. It is not only about men's power in relation to women. Rather masculinity is de-massified as masculinities and these are not equal. Hegemonic masculinity
holds an authoritative positioning over other masculinities
and will "dominate other types in any particular historical
and social context."[18] However, at this point, as a number of
writers within Masculinity Studies have indicated, the term
becomes more slippery. Michael Flood has noted, for
example, that Connell's own usage of the term slides between
several meanings.[19] In short, I suggest that these may be summarized as a slippage between its meaning as a *political mechanism* tied to the word "hegemony"—referring to cul-
tural/moral leadership to ensure popular or mass consent to
particular forms of rule—to its meaning as a descriptive word
referring to *dominant (most powerful and/or most widespread)*
versions of manhood,[20] and finally to its meaning as an
empirical reference specifically to *actual groups of men.*[21]

This slippage produces certain problems. Firstly, as
Flood notes, it is politically deterministic and defeatist to
assume that the most dominant (in the sense either of most
powerful or most widespread) ideals/forms of masculinity
are necessarily the same as those which work to guarantee
men's authority over women.[22] Dominant forms of masculinity, for example, may not always, at all times, legitimate
men's power and those that do legitimate it may not always
be socially celebrated or common. Connell himself has
acknowledged this slide in his writings between the meaning
of hegemonic masculinity as legitimating strategy and as
merely dominant.[23] Relatedly, he cautions that hegemonic
masculinity may in fact describe the position of a minority
of men or may only loosely correspond to the lives of actual

men,[24] and has recently re-emphasized that he does intend the term to be defined by its political strategic function in legitimating patriarchy.[25] Nevertheless, the problem of a slide towards a usage that refers to socially dominant types of men reoccurs in his work.[26] In his most recent clarification of the concept of hegemonic masculinity published in December 2005, Connell—in concert with his co-author Messerschmidt—uses the term "socially dominant masculinities" as an equivalent, and later refers to economically "privileged" men as "bearers" of hegemonic masculinity. The inclination towards the merely dominant is evidently deeply implicated in the term, since Connell and Messerschmidt state that "certain masculinities are more socially central, or more associated with authority and social power than others."[27] The slide also reappears in his work on the global context, as I will discuss shortly.

This raises a second issue. The understanding of hegemonic as simply socially dominant opens up a further slippage in which hegemonic is often understood even more fixedly as *actual* particular groups of men. As Flood points out, actual men may or may not conform to cultural ideals concerning masculinity, even when these are associated with power or are pervasive.[28]

Such a focus on actually existing groups of men generates a third related problem concerning the association of hegemonic masculinity with *types* of men in the sense of actual men exhibiting a list of specific *characteristics*. The social malleability of hegemonic practice is lost in equating gendered power with assumed fixed personality types, as Connell is well aware. Yet this is a common inclination in many Masculinity Studies writings.[29] As Kenneth Clatterbaugh argues, such models prohibit asking which traits might be crucial to masculinity (and hence to hegemonic masculinity) and which are incidental.[30]

Usage of the term to refer to dominant actual men and their characteristics is certainly understandable pedagogically and in the context of political activism, in that it gives gendered power a human face, a visceral reality, and makes the term more accessible and less abstract. Moreover, the cascading slide from hegemonic masculinity as the mechanism of patriarchal legitimization towards socially dominant (powerful and/or widespread) types of men, towards actual men, and finally towards a cluster list of generalized personality traits, is not a question merely of sloppy usage, theoretical confusion, or theoretical underdevelopment. In all fairness, it must be said that these are *not* entirely discrete definitional entities.

All the same, the slide to dominant types of men/actual men—even if understandable and related to an attempt to give embodied materiality to the political mechanism of a legitimating cultural ideal—has problematic consequences. For example, to put Connell's conception of hegemonic masculinity as political mechanism to work, it is important to be able to disentangle hegemonic from merely dominant types/dominant actual men and their associated personality traits. It is important to be able to perceive that a senior manager in the major accounting firm KPMG Australia[31] and his mates may represent a dominant masculinity in that he wields a widely accepted institutional power and may even perhaps have particular personality traits associated with that dominance, but may not necessarily be the politically legitimating cultural ideal invoked by the term hegemonic masculinity. Accountants—even those with consider-able authority—are scarcely deemed the mobilizing model of manliness to which all men should aspire. They may exercise power, but are not able to legitimate it. As Connell himself notes, many men who hold significant social power do not embody hegemonic masculinity.[32]

By the same token, but in reverse, while actual working class men may not wield institutional power, muscular working class manhood *is* commonly employed as a highly significant mobilizing cultural ideal intended to invoke cross-class recognition and solidarity regarding what counts as a man. Witness, for example, a current advertising campaign for Holden cars in Australia. Holden, as the only originally Australian-owned car manufacturer, has an iconic association with Australian national identity. Holden's advertising is precisely pitched at and reliant on evoking a widely shared sense of quintessential Australian-ism, and specifically Australian manhood.

The current Holden Rodeo car advertising campaign begins with a presumably married couple sitting up in bed. The wife turns to her husband and asks, "what's your *ultimate* fantasy?" We are then shown him secretly fantasizing about vigorously driving a big muscular (and expensive) four-wheel-drive utility—a workingman's vehicle, "a ute with grunt" in Australian parlance—over rough country.[33] A buxom long haired blonde (not his wife) in a flannelette shirt and tiny shorts appears by his side.[34] The sexy blonde, specifically demarcated by her clothing as a workingman's sort of woman, is also recognizable to Australian audiences as a former "handyperson" host on a TV program called *Changing Rooms*, and is particularly known for her capabilities with power-tools.[35] She is then depicted leaning over the stationary car and polishing its chassis. The final caption reads, "it's what every bloke wants." While public debate about this campaign has focused on the question of its treatment of women,[36] there has been no comment on its far more explicit engagement with a notion of the *ultimate* "everybloke." Evidently stereotypes of femininity are demeaning to women, but stereotypic masculinity could not possibly demean men. The advertisement was received as if it were a bit embarrassing because it was amusingly revealing, amusingly "true." It seemed that Australians widely accepted that, yes, every man does *really* deep down want a big macho car and a fantasy handmaiden. This idealized working class-inflected blokehood is at a considerable distance from actual men, yet it can only work as a generalizable representation of proper, honored manliness—that is, as a form of hegemonic masculinity (a point to which I shall return).

The significance of such a form of masculinity in Australia is reflected in the mobilization by the two major political parties of a language of "mateship" as the core of national identity, a language which historically draws upon working men as its exemplars—that is, manual workers, bushmen and ordinary soldiers.[37] For instance, the previous leader of the social democratic Labor Party, Mark Latham, recently equated what is specific to Australian culture with mateship and hence to a particular form of Australian muscular "blokey" manhood that is decidedly not white collar middle-class. He described what he saw as this essentially Australian manhood in terms of "mates and good blokes," who were to be distinguished from much despised "nerds," "nervous wrecks," and "metrosexual knobs."[38] In similar fashion Bethan Benwell has noted in relation to British 'new lad' magazines that mobilizing models of desirable masculinity can involve drawing upon notions of working class manhood, notions intended to justify "sexism, exclusive male friendship and homophobia" as fundamental to "real" as against wussy metrosexual manliness.[39] Working class blokes may not actually wield power, but they can provide the means to legitimate it.

Both the example of the actual KPMG accountant and the ideal of the working class "every-bloke" indicate that it is a matter of some importance to be able to distinguish hegemonic from merely dominant men, from actual men, or from their specific personality traits.

PROBLEMS AS THE TERM GOES GLOBAL

The problems that seem to haunt the term hegemonic masculinity in local western settings are not surprisingly magnified on the larger stage of the global. Connell, Hearn, and Kimmel assert in concert that "the most obviously important" issue in the future of the field researching masculinity in the setting of globalization "is the relation of masculinities to those emerging dominant powers in the global capitalist economy, the transnational corporations."[40] Connell's particular contribution to this field, which appears largely accepted by Masculinity Studies writers,[41] is that globalization in creating a world gender order involves the re-articulation of national hegemonic masculinities into the global arena. Specifically he refers here to "transnational business masculinity," which he describes as definitively taking the leading role as the emergent gendered world order, an order associated with the dominant institutions of the world economy and the globalization of the neo-liberal market agenda. In this account transnational business masculinity is asserted to have "achieved a position of hegemony," to occupy the position of a hegemonic masculinity on a world scale—that is to say, a dominant form of masculinity that embodies, organizes, and legitimates men's domination in the world gender order as a whole.[42]

As is the case with the account of local western hegemonic forms, the political legitimating meaning of hegemonic masculinity in the global arena quickly slides in Connell's analysis towards its meaning as the "dominant" masculinity and how an actual group of businessmen "embodies" this dominant positioning, including how this group exhibits particular personality traits. Connell asserts that "world politics is now more and more organized around the needs of the transnational capital," placing "strategic power in the hands of particular groups of men—managers and entrepreneurs"—who self-consciously manage their bodies and emotions as well as money, and are increasingly detached from older loyalties to nation, business organization, family and marital partners.[43] These men are, in his account, dispositionally highly atomistic—that is, competitive and largely distanced from social or personal commitments. They embody a neo-liberal version of an emphasized traditional masculinity, without any requirement to direct bodily strength.[44]

Connell's account of the hegemonic status of "transnational business masculinity" reveals further issues in the term. It is in the first instance not clear why Connell is so adamant that business masculinity occupies world hege-

monic status, and why he regards other potential contenders—he draws attention to military and political masculinities—as of less significance in this legitimating and
mobilizing role. There seems at minimum here a limited
engagement with the burgeoning and highly fractious literature on globalization.[45] For instance, Connell does not
engage with those writers who question the very notion of
economic globalization. Nor does he contend with those
writers who might dispute this focus and by contrast propose multiple, uneven, and contradictory globalizations.
Mann provides an example of the latter view, suggesting that
unprecedented hegemony is more characteristic of contemporary military power than economic relations.[46]

Whatever the force of different perspectives on globalization, the point is that it is no simple matter to claim that
transnational business masculinity, a masculinity organized
in relation to economics, is *the* hegemonic form on a world
scale, legitimating men's dominance in the global gender
order as a whole. Given this, why does Connell make the
claim? Connell, in his global and macro historical moments,
is inclined to presume that masculinity (a gender category)
is to be understood by its constitution through class relations.[47] Though Kate Hughes' summary of Connell's perspective is not intended to make this point, it supports this
interpretation. She says Connell

> provides an interesting analysis of the ways in which glob-
> alization has exported a version of patriarchy . . . to cul-
> tures whose economies have come to be vulnerable to such
> [transnational executives] and to such corporations.[48]

While gender in this approach certainly gives particular characteristics to globalizing capitalism, it seems to be carried along by and within host class relations—a comparatively passive and responsive sub-structure. Gender here tends to subsumed within class, as it was in traditional Marxian analyses, and in the same vein class becomes shorthand for relations between men, while women's contributions to the shaping of global history seem to disappear.[49] Such a perspective seems curiously at odds with Connell's overriding conception of gender as a shaping force in local and global social relations. It also sits uneasily alongside Connell's assertion that hegemonic masculinity is a relational concept and his recognition—following Brod—that looking only at men and proceeding without including women in the analysis of gender relations is highly problematic.[50] This is precisely a point on which feminist analyses of global politics have proved more robust.[51]

Connell's framework—with its tension between gender as riding on the coat-tails of class and gender as actively socially constituting—is frequently replicated in Masculinity Studies writings, even in the work of those who are far less wedded to an economic focus in research on the politics of masculinity on a world scale.[52] Yet the crucial feature of the term hegemonic masculinity is precisely that it enables the Gramscian conception of power as more multi-faceted than mere coercion, including economic coercion, and that it is not supposedly to be equated with economic or military dominance. Connell's term has the great advantage that encourages a creative and subtle understanding of power as constitutive, as always associated with the mobilization of consent and complicit embodied identities. However, Connell, along with many other Masculinity Studies writers, tends to fall back into more limited, even economistic readings of hegemony when dealing with the global.

I am not suggesting that the leading contender for the position of hegemonic masculinity on a world scale is not transnational business masculinity, nor am I necessarily disputing that the other contenders are military and political. The point here is simply to stress that the term does not actually enable these judgments at present and Connell's approach is insufficiently tied to demonstrating how transnational business masculinities have achieved a hegemonic role specifically *in relation to the gender order*, rather than merely as an auxiliary handmaiden to the "current stage of capitalism"[53] and as a dimension of globalizing western institutions.

Indeed, broadly speaking, it is not clear how one would assess whether any particular version of masculinity has an over-arching legitimating function. There is very little information in Connell's work on the crucial matter of how the *legitimation* of gendered power occurs and thus how to assess which masculinity is the hegemonic one.[54] It is not self-evident overall how to judge which masculinity (or masculinities) might be deemed hegemonic over all others.

WHAT TO DO?

This discussion of the term hegemonic masculinity suggests that situating masculinities in global politics is no simple matter, and that usage of the term may require further analysis. In particular, I am arguing on the one hand for a narrower clarification of meaning[55] and, on the other, under this narrowed rubric, for a taxonomical expansion of particular instances. What is the aim of this re-thinking of the term? Why might it be worth undertaking?

I have already noted the slippage in Connell's work and in that of other Masculinity Studies writers in the concept of hegemonic masculinity from its political function—as a political mechanism producing solidarity between different masculinities in a hierarchical order—towards an emphasis on socially dominant men at the moment and their particular characteristics. I also pointed out that this slide has several problematic implications, including raising concerns about political defeatism, claiming the monolithic, global *hegemonic* status of a specific group of actual businessmen, and relatedly offering an account of the gendered character of globalization—largely without reference to women—as a primarily economic, uniform and indeed top-down phenomenon. In re-thinking the concept of hegemonic masculinity, I intend firstly to focus the term hegemonic masculinity on its *political* function—to *narrow* the characterization of the term—and, secondly, to undertake a taxonomic *expansion* of its forms, in order to resist this slippage in its meaning and thus avoid the associated problematic implications of this slippage.

It is after all politically important not to simply equate dominant masculinities as a matter of course with hegemonic masculinity—that is, with the legitimization of men's authority over women—since it is hopefully imaginable that dominant (socially powerful or prevalent) masculinities might not be constituted by gender hierarchy. Moreover, it is politically useful in terms of policy development, including educational policy development, and political strategies to *recognize* that challenging hegemonic legitim*iz*ation with regard to gender may not coincide with challenging a specific group of actual men who hold significant institutional power. It may also not coincide with attending only to men. Yet Connell's account of global hegemonic masculinity in practice assumes that challenging hegemonic masculinity does coincide with concentrating upon dominant, economically powerful businessmen and their particular characteristics. What if, however, these socially dominant men do not occupy the pinnacle hegemonic position in the global hierarchy of masculinities, legitimating and bonding together men in the world gender order as a whole, as Connell asserts? And, what if gendered *globalization* is less singular, less one-way, more complex and nuanced than Connell's account proposes? In my view, our understanding of gender and masculinity in this *globalizing* world shapes the political directions we might undertake to advance gender equality. For this reason, to the degree that the concept of hegemonic masculinity may be both insufficiently *focused* and overly monolithic, I would suggest that a re-thinking of the concept is not merely of abstract theoretical interest, but a crucial element in assessing contemporary social trends and our responses to them.

NARROWING THE MEANING OF THE TERM

I will now turn to my first argument. I have asserted that a more focused conceptualization of "hegemonic masculinity" is required. In short, I am arguing for the term to be conceived more narrowly.[56] With regard to this clarified meaning, I suggest in particular a more focused characterization of hegemonic masculinity as concerned with a *political ideal* or model, as an enabling mode of representation, which mobilizes institutions and practices. Contra Connell's approach and in keeping with that of Mike Donaldson, the concept of hegemonic masculinity is likely to retain what I have described as its centrally important concern with political legitimization and promoting solidarity between men by explicitly differentiating it from the study of masculinities associated with actual socially dominant men.[57] Characterizing hegemonic masculinity in relation to a narrowed meaning as a political ideal prevents a slide towards depictions of men with institutional power and instead concentrates the term upon its legitimating function, which may or may not refer to men with actual power. Such a clarification enables us to acknowledge the hegemonic significance, for example, of working class-inflected models (along the lines I noted earlier) in sites like Australia. Indeed, it seems to me that attention to such models is crucial to analysis of Australian masculine identities and gender relations.[58]

This suggested re-thinking of the concept of hegemonic masculinity—towards a focus upon a mobilizing political ideal—may however not be acceptable to Connell or other Masculinity Studies writers like Jeff Hearn or Kenneth Clatterbaugh, who tend to display antagonism to any focus on "the symbolic," "representation," or "discourses." They adopt a form of macro sociological social constructionism, which involves dividing off "discursive" from "material" processes, structures, interests and practices. The division between discursive and material is depicted rather along the lines of the materialist base/superstructure metaphor—a metaphor which assumes the ultimate critical status of activities deemed material and particularly the economic infrastructure.[59]

In this context, it is worth pointing out that Connell appears to oscillate on this question. On the one hand, Connell and Messerschmidt, when discussing who represents hegemonic masculinity, argue that "an *ideal* masculinity" is frequently not associated with "men who hold great social power." Hegemonic masculinity is at this point equated with an ideal. Similarly, they employ words like "models," "ideals, fantasies and desires," "collective images," "common cultural templates," and "exemplary."[60] Yet on the other hand, they insist that while hegemonic masculinity

> involves the formulation of cultural ideals, it should not be regarded *only* as a cultural norm. Gender relations also are constituted through *non-discursive practices*, including wage labor, violence, sexuality, domestic labor, and child-care.[61]

This seems initially to be an inclusive approach, a "not only but also" framework, in which hegemonic masculinity is identified with a discursive cultural norm but additionally with "non-discursive" elements. However, what is important here is an ongoing inclination in Connell's approach to maintain a distinction between discursive and non-discursive—described in terms of an opposition between non-material and material—alongside a prioritization of the latter.

This separation between discursive and material and prioritization of the latter is evident in his rather dismissive view of postmodern perspectives, of "discursive approaches" as about culture, representations, and personal voluntary tactical choices—as against material practices, interests, and inequality which are lined up with employment, violence and childcare. Not surprisingly Connell argues in the "Introduction to the Second Edition" of *Masculinities* (2005), just as he did in earlier work,[62] that "discursive approaches have significant limits. They give no grip on issues about economic inequality and the state."[63] No wonder, given the materialist base/superstructure presumptions evident in his depiction of "discursive approaches," that Connell understands hegemonic masculinity in "the world gender order as a whole" as transnational *business* masculinity and globalization itself in primarily economic terms. No wonder, when dealing with macro and global, his analysis tends to subsume gender within class, with class primarily depicted as relations between men.

Connell's presumption that discursive approaches are at odds with "material" concerns may lead him to dispute my suggestion that we should re-think hegemonic masculinity as a political ideal, as a discourse. However, it is worth considering whether such a re-thinking also enables us to re-think Connell's assumptions regarding what counts. Precisely because he is committed to the separate and determining authority of what he deems "material," he tends to slide away from the political legitimating meaning of hegemonic masculinity towards equating hegemony with "dominant" masculinity, since this masculinity is associated with "material" authority and institutional social power.[64] In short, Connell's investment in "the material" may well go some way to explaining the problematic slippage in his usage of the term hegemonic masculinity. By extension, questioning Connell's conception of what counts may not only enable us to reconsider his terminology but also his analysis of globalization and conclusions regarding the global masculine hegemon. If his base/superstructure account of the separation between discursive and material and the priority accorded the latter is questionable, then not only may hegemonic masculinity be understood differently but there is no reason to presume that the global gender order is *necessarily* and monolithically *legitimated* by elite transnational businessmen in a top-down fashion. This is no trivial matter.[65]

Debating Connell's antagonism to "discursive approaches," and his associated commitment to "the material," might also lead us down another tack. His usage of hegemonic masculinity—along with that of other Masculinity Studies writers—has become unnecessarily, and perhaps inadvertently, positioned in the first wave of globalization scholarship and at a distance from recent developments in understanding globalization and international political economy. First wave globalization scholarship assumes that globalization is simply a fact out there, an unproblematic given, and is straightforwardly an economic phenomenon, demanding an emphasis on the multinational firm. Similar assumptions arise in Connell's focus on transnationals and transnational businessmen. By contrast, as Juanita Elias has noted, the turn within International Political Economy (IPE), for example, is towards approaches that stress the discursive production of globalization in the everyday practice of international politics. The important point here is that, in this literature, discourses are viewed as having both ideational and practical material effects. The discursive turn considers the notion of globalization as a self-evidently economic imperative and the multinational firm as globalization's primary agent, not as unproblematic facts but as framed in relation to neoliberal discourses.[66] In this kind of approach it becomes important to unravel how discourses of globalization constitute gender relations. In this context, feminist and other critical globalization scholars expose certain potential shortcomings of the masculinities writings on globalization by suggesting how these writings may take for granted and indeed reiterate assumptions about globalization and the role of transnationals that precisely require debate. The existing distance between critical globalization and masculinity approaches seems to me unhelpful.

Reconsidering hegemonic masculinity as a discursive political ideal involves taking up conceptions of the discursive which are not estranged from the material world, nor discrete from it, without assuming that this amounts to a strategy of dematerialization or a refusal of persistent even enduring systemic patterns in social relations. This kind of re-thinking of the term usefully opens up a dialogue between Masculinity Studies and critical globalization scholars, in that the influence of transnational business masculinity may be viewed as operating at a discursive level—as a powerful ideal that has played an important role in shaping material processes associated with globalization.[67]

EXPANDING THE TAXONOMY OF THE TERM

Having outlined the case for a narrowed clarification of the meaning of the term of the term, I will now attend to my second argument regarding the advantages of its taxonomical expansion. The first argument regarding a narrowed clarification of meaning to focus the concept of hegemonic masculinity on its meaning as a political mechanism can work against problematic slippages in its usage and can enable a useful questioning of Connell's assumptions regarding the critical status of the economic and his account of globalization. Nevertheless, de-massification and greater specification of plural hegemonic masculinit*ies* under the rubric of this newly narrowed meaning enables a more nuanced analysis of gender order and gender identity in the contemporary globalizing world. Current approaches in Masculinity Studies have multiplied the term "masculinity" but have tended to retain the notion of "hegemonic masculinity" as a singular monolith, which is insufficiently specified even to do justice the existing range of Masculinity Studies writings. Hegemonic masculinity, I would argue, also needs to be de-massified.

Connell and Messerschmidt in their recent clarification of the term acknowledge that hegemonic masculinity is not singular in the sense that it may take different forms in different geographical/cultural locations, its effects on particular men are variable, and there will contesting "claimants" to the status of hegemon.[68] They also acknowledge that global does not necessarily "overwhelm regional or local."[69] However, Connell and Messerschmidt reassert the singular character of hegemonic masculinity, as precisely about that which is deemed *the* pinnacle of a pyramid of masculinities.[70] By contrast, I consider that the term hegemonic does not require an indivisible mono-type, and indeed an insistence upon such a monolithic conception may partially explain the inclination in Masculinity Studies writings to drift into equating hegemonic masculinity with mere social dominance rather than focusing on the issue of political mobilization.

Further elaboration of this key term within masculinity theory is likely is to be helpful in analyzing contemporary gender relations and a range of politically significant masculinities. Therefore, following Judith Halberstam's "taxonomical impulse,"[71] I propose that more terms may be required, enabling recognition of what I would call "*supra*-hegemonic" and "*sub*-hegemonic" masculinities.[72] As an illustrative instance here, I would suggest that my earlier discussion of the "every-bloke" of the Holden Rodeo advertising campaign presents a local *sub*-hegemonic masculinity—a powerful Australian legitimating ideal—which is nevertheless similar to other working-class inflected manifestations in many other countries,[73] invoking as it does masculine solidarity and complicity even though it lacks institutional power. Importantly, this is a legitimating ideal shaped against *and* in concert with more global forms.

This instance reveals why taxonomical expansion matters, why it is important to talk not only about hegemonic masculinities but additionally about hierarchical relations between them. Connell describes the "globalization of gender" in ways which indicate an interaction between globalised hegemonic masculinities and localized masculinities in a globalizing world. Nevertheless, there is also an inclination in his work to understand globalization (conceived as substantively gendered) in terms of a singular, monolithic hegemonic masculinity acting on a world scale. Transnational business masculinity is presented as the hegemonic form for the world as a whole. This account is useful in highlighting that masculinities are not all the same, but does not discuss the relationship between different hegemonic masculinities. Moreover, in simply assuming that there is always only one form "at the top," Connell asserts that what he thinks is the case at a local level—a single hegemon—is also what happens in the global setting. Yet it may be argued, as my example of the working class every-bloke suggests, that the political legitimating function of hegemonic masculinity is unlikely to be left to one idealized model alone. Hegemonic masculinity, even at the local level, may be seen as hierarchical and plural. It seems even more likely that there is not one single hegemon on the global scale.

To conceive, as Connell does, that hegemonic masculinity is monolithic on a world scale, restricts analysis of globalization to a framework which presents globalization as a one-way uniform process and focuses upon how the global hegemon touches down at the local level. However, as Randall Germain has pointed out, there are significant problems attached to conceiving globalization as a uniform and all-encompassing process.[74] What is lost in Connell's emphasis upon the singular hegemonic authority of transnational business masculinity is a more nuanced account of how local cultures may also contribute to the formation of globalizing gender, let alone enabling an account of the role of the state and of the impact of differentially powerful cultures and states in the global context.[75]

By contrast, a de-massification of hegemonic masculinity, a taxonomical expansion of it to include *supra* and *sub* hegemonic forms, permits discussion of hegemonic masculinit*ies* in vertical as well as horizontal terms. The taxonomical expansion envisaged allows for a more nuanced analysis that can attend to both the unevenness of globalization in different settings and more detailed awareness of interactions between global and local/cultural/state imperatives. Such a de-massification aims to move away from conceptualizations of globalization and hegemonic masculinity that are exceptionally top-down towards an analysis of the contested and shifting nature of gender identity at the global as well as the local level, to highlight the ways in which different hegemonic masculinities are negotiated, and even resisted. To give space in our analyses to this resistant creativity is surely to refuse the ongoing inevitability of gender hierarchy.

Taxonomical expansion has a further advantage. In giving space to the plural and uneven character of gendered globalization it can work against the limits of existing scholarship rather than accepting them. Bob Pease has, for instance noted that "theorizing about masculinity in Australia has tended to be derivative of overseas literature," even though Connell's internationally influential work involves theoretical generalizations drawn from Australian men and Australian gender relations. Pease points out that Australian masculinities have a specific history that may be insufficiently recognized in more global generalizing about western masculinities.[76] I would add that limited analyses of specific cultures and states not only reiterates aspects of globalization itself, but may produce inadequate assessments of gendered globalization in terms of its multiple contexts. The location of Australian masculinities in a settler colony in between the metropolitan First World and the Third World of occupied colonies produces particular responses to gendered globalization which are likely to be different from those even in other English-speaking countries.[77] This broadly "post-colonial" analysis is encouraged by expanding the terms associated with hegemonic masculinity, enabling a more rigorous and culturally specific evaluation of globalization as an uneven process entailing complex forms of accommodation and resistance. This might also open the door to an account of globalization which entails more detailed reference to women and femininities.

CONCLUSION

Masculinity Studies writers, and Connell in particular, have made crucial contributions to gender analysis at a local, national level, and at the level of the global their work alerts us to the ways in which supposedly gender-neutral global processes are linked to the politics of masculinity. Nevertheless, like Connell, I believe, it is timely to reconsider the concept hegemonic masculinity.

In re-thinking the term I aim firstly to narrow its characterization in order to focus on its meaning as a political mechanism involving the bonding together of different masculinities in a hierarchical order, and to differentiate this meaning from a usage dealing with the authority of socially dominant men. Such a distinction also enables a re-thinking of assumptions which give rise to overly economistic interpretations of globalization. Secondly, I propose to expand the instances under the narrowed rubric of understanding hegemonic masculinity as a political mechanism—as a discursive ideal mobilizing legitimization. In particular, while retaining usage of the overall term hegemonic masculinity

when appropriate, I wish to attend to plural hegemonic masculinities within this by employing the language of "supra"
and "sub" hegemonic. De-massification of the term hegemonic masculinity is called for in order to avoid insufficiently nuanced and uniform top-down analyses of gendered
globalization.

I do not assume that Connell or other Masculinity
Studies writers will not be amenable to further re-thinking
of the term. Connell, for example, has, after all, developed
concepts that encourage intellectual flexibility and discussion and has indeed actively promoted exchanges on the
topic of hegemonic masculinity. Moreover, in my view the
term continues to have much to offer. However, I would also
suggest that it is not enough to say, as Connell does, that it
needs work but is "still essential."[78] Rather the usage of the
term in the global arena shows up certain earlier limits of
term all the more clearly. These limits have research and
political implications. Re-thinking the concept, hegemonic
masculinity, is therefore an important aspect of better
understanding and working towards transforming gender in
the contemporary global context.

Chapter 8

GLOBALIZATION AND ITS MAL(E)CONTENTS
The Gendered Moral and Political Economy of the Extreme Right

Michael S. Kimmel

"The chief social basis of radicalism has been the peasants and the smaller artisans in the towns. From these facts one may conclude that the wellsprings of human freedom lie not where Marx saw them, in the aspirations of classes about to take power, but perhaps even more in the dying wail of a class over whom the wave of progress is about to roll."

—Barrington Moore, 1966[1]

In the first lines of his 1978 song, "The Promised Land," Bruce Springsteen described the growing frustration and anger of a young guy who tries so hard to "live the right way," but finds the system so overwhelming that he says he feels "so weak I just want to explode"—and take everybody with him in an explosion of class-based rage.

Globalization changes masculinities—reshaping the

arena in which national and local masculinities are articulated, and transforming the shape of men's lives. Globalization disrupts and reconfigures traditional, neocolonial, or other national, regional or local economic, political and cultural arrangements. In so doing, globalization transforms local articulations of both domestic and public patriarchy.[2] Globalization includes the gradual proletarianization of local peasantries, as market criteria replace subsistence and survival. Local small craft producers, small farmers, and independent peasants traditionally stake their definitions of masculinity in ownership of land and economic autonomy in their work; these are increasingly transferred upwards in the class hierarchy and outwards to transnational corporations. Proletarianization also leads to massive labor migrations—typically migrations of *male* workers—who leave their homes and populate migrant enclaves, squatter camps, labor camps.

Globalization thus presents another level at which hegemonic and local masculinities are constructed. Globalization was always a gendered process. As Andre Gunder Frank pointed out several decades ago in his studies of economic development, that development and underdevelopment were not simply stages through which all countries pass, that there was no single continuum along which individual nations might be positioned. Rather, he argued, there was a relationship between development and underdevelopment, that, in fact, the development of some countries implied the specific and deliberate underdevelopment of others. The creation of the metropole was simultaneous and coordinated with the creation of the periphery.

As with economic development, so too with gender—the

historical constructions of the meanings of masculinity. As the hegemonic ideal was being created, it was created against a screen of "others" whose masculinity was thus problematized and devalued. Hegemonic and subaltern emerged in mutual, but unequal interaction in a gendered social and economic order. Colonial administrations often problematized the masculinity of the colonized. For example, in British India, Bengali men were perceived as weak and effeminate, though Pathas and Sikhs were perceived as hypermasculine—violent and uncontrolled.[3] Similar distinctions were made in South Africa between Hottentots and Zulus, and in North America between Navaho or Algonquin on the one hand, Sioux, Apache, and Cheyenne on the other.[4] In many colonial situations, the colonized men were called "boys" by the colonizers.

Today, although they appear to be gender-neutral, the institutional arrangements of global society are equally gendered. The marketplace, multinational corporations and transnational geopolitical institutions (World Court, United Nations, EU) and their attendant ideological principles (economic rationality, liberal individualism) express a gendered logic. The "increasingly unregulated power of transnational corporations places strategic power in the hands of particular groups of men," while the language of globalization remains gender neutral so that "the 'individual' of neoliberal theory has in general the attributes and interests of a male entrepreneur."[5]

As a result, the impact of global economic and political restructuring is greater on women. At the national and global level, the world gender order privileges men in a variety of ways, such as unequal wages, unequal labor force participation, unequal structures of ownership and control of property, unequal control over one's body, as well as cultural and sexual privileges. What's more, in the economic south, for example, aid programs disproportionately target women (as in population planning programs that involve only women), while in the metropole, attacks on the welfare state generally weaken the position of women, domestically and publicly. These effects, however, are less the result of bad policies or, even less bad policymakers, and more the results of the gendered logic of these institutions and processes themselves.[6]

HEGEMONIC MASCULINITY AND ITS DISCONTENTS

In addition, the patterns of masculinity embedded within these gendered institutions also are rapidly becoming the dominant global hegemonic model of masculinity, against which all local, regional and national masculinities are played out and increasingly refer. The emergent global hegemonic version of masculinity is readily identifiable: You can see him sitting in first-class waiting rooms in airports, or in elegant business hotels the world over, wearing in a designer business suit, speaking English, eating "continental" cuisine, talking on his cell phone, his laptop computer plugged into any electrical outlet, while he watches CNN International on television. Temperamentally, he is increasingly cosmopolitan, with liberal tastes in consumption (and sexuality) and conservative political ideas of limited government control of the economy. This has the additional effect of increasing the power of the hegemonic countries within the global political and economic arena, since everyone, no matter where they are from, talks and acts like they do.

The processes of globalization and the emergence of a global hegemonic masculinity have the ironic effect of increasingly "gendering" local, regional, and national resistance to incorporation into the global arena as subordinated entities. Scholars have pointed out the ways in which religious fundamentalism and ethnic nationalism use local cultural symbols to express regional resistance to incorporation.[7] However, these religious and ethnic expressions are often manifest as gender revolts, and include a virulent resurgence of domestic patriarchy (as in the militant misogyny of Iran or Afghanistan); the problematization of global masculinities or neighboring masculinities (as in the former Yugoslavia); and the overt symbolic efforts to claim a distinct "manhood" along religious or ethnic lines to which others do not have access and which will restore manhood to the formerly privileged (white militias in the United States and skinhead racists in Europe).

Thus gender becomes one of the chief organizing principles of local, regiona,l and national resistance to globalization, whether expressed in religious or secular, ethnic or national terms. These processes involve flattening or eliminating local or regional distinctions, cultural homogenization as citizens and social heterogenization as new ethnic groups move to new countries in labor migration efforts. Movements thus tap racialist and nativist sentiments at the same time as they can tap local and regional protectionism and isolationism. They become gendered as oppositional movements also tap into a vague masculine resentment of economic displacement, loss of autonomy, collapse of domestic patriarchy that accompany further integration into the global economy. Efforts to reclaim economic autonomy, to reassert political control, and revive traditional domestic dominance thus take on the veneer of restoring manhood.

To illustrate these themes, one could consider several political movements of men, in North America or elsewhere. Indeed, Promise Keepers, men's rights and fathers' rights groups all respond to the perceived erosion of public patriarchy with an attempted restoration of some version of domestic patriarchy. The mythopoetic men's movement responds instead to a perceived erosion of domestic patriarchy with assertions of separate mythic or natural space for men to experience their power—since they can no longer experience it in either the public or private spheres.[8]

In this paper, I examine the ways in which masculinities and globalization are embedded in the emergence of extremist groups on the far right in Europe and the United States, with a final discussion of the Islamic world. Specifically I will discuss the ways in which globalization reconfigures certain political tendencies among different class fractions. In the economic north, the members of the far right White Supremacists in the United States and Scandinavia tend to be from a declining lower middle class—traditionally the class basis of totalitarian political solutions like socialism or fascism. They are movements of the far right. It is the lower middle class—those strata of independent farmers, small shopkeepers, craft and highly skilled workers, and small-scale entrepreneurs—who have been hit hardest by the processes of globalization. "Western industry has displaced traditional crafts—female as well as male—and large-scale multinational-controlled agriculture has downgraded the independent farmer to the status of hired hand."[9] This has resulted in massive and uneven male displacement—migration, downward mobility. And it has been felt the most not by the adult men who were the tradesmen, shopkeepers, and skilled workers, but by their sons, by the young men whose inheritance has been seemingly stolen from them. They feel entitled and humiliated—and they are furious.

In the economic south, however, the sons of the rising middle classes, whose upward mobility is thwarted by globalization, join the downwardly mobile sons of the lower middle classes. The terrorists of Al Qaeda, or other Middle East terrorist cells like Hezbollah, tend to be highly educated young men, trained for professional jobs that have been choked off by global economic shifts. Historically, this rising middle class, as Barrington Moore noted, were the backbone of the bourgeois revolutions; today the rising middle class is no longer rising, and in its descent, the young men who trained for upward mobility seek enemies upon whom to heap their rage, and alternate strategies of mobility.[10] These are movements of the ultra-left. Both of these groups of angry young men are the foot soldiers of the armies of resentment that have spring up around the world. They are joined in the new ways in which masculine entitlement has become gendered rage.

In this essay, I discuss White Supremacists and Aryan youth in both the United States and Scandinavia as my two primary case studies, and conclude with a brief comparative discussion of the terrorists of Al Qaeda who were responsible for the heinous acts of September 11.[11] All use a variety of ideological and political resources to re-establish and reassert domestic and public patriarchies. All deploy "masculinity" as a symbolic capital, as an ideological resource (1) to understand and explicate their plight; (2) as a rhetorical device to problematize the identities of those against whom they believe themselves fighting; and, (3) as a recruitment device to entice other, similarly situated young men, to join them. These movements look backward, nostalgically, to a time when they—native born white men, Moslem men in a pre-global era—were able to assume the places in society to which they believe themselves entitled. They seek to restore that unquestioned entitlement, both in the domestic sphere and in the public sphere. They are movements not of revolution, but of restoration.

TYPES OF PATRIARCHIES

In this essay, I describe the transformation of two forms of patriarchy. It is important to note that patriarchy is both a system of domination by which men dominate women, and also a system by which some men (older men, fathers, in the classic definition of the term) dominate other men.

Public patriarchy refers to the institutional arrangements of a society, the predominance of males in all power positions within the economy and polity, both locally and nationally, as well as the "gendering" of those institutions themselves (by which the criteria for promotion, for example, appear to be gender-neutral, but actually reproduce the gender order). *Domestic patriarchy* refers to the emotional and familial arrangements in a society, the ways in which men's power in the public arena is reproduced at the level of private life. This includes male-female relationships as well as family life, child socialization, and the like.

Both public patriarchy and domestic patriarchy are held together by the threat, implicit or explicit, of violence. Public patriarchy, of course, includes the military and police apparatus of society, which are also explicitly gendered institutions (revealed in their increased opposition to women's entry). In the aggregate, rape and domestic violence help sustain domestic patriarchy.[12]

These two expressions of men's power over women and other men are neither uniform nor monolithic; they vary enormously, are constantly under flux. Equally, they are not coincident, so that increases or decreases in one invariably produces increases or decreases in the other. Nor are they so directly linked that a decrease in one automatically produces an increase in the other, although there will be pressures in that direction. Thus women's entry into the work force or increased representation in legislatures undermine public patriarchy and will likely produce both backlash efforts to reinforce domestic patriarchy (covenant marriage, tightening divorce laws to restrain women's exit from the home, increased domestic assault) or even a virulent resurgence of domestic patriarchy (the Taliban). At the same time, women's increased public presence will also undermine domestic patriarchy, by pressing men into domestic duties they had previously avoided (such as housework and parenting).

All of these movements exhibit what Connell[13] calls "protest masculinity"—a combination of stereotypical male norms with often unconventional attitudes about women. Exaggerated claims of potency are accompanied by violent resistance to authority, school and work, and engagement with crime and heavy drinking. In such a model, the "growing boy puts together a tense, freaky façade, making a claim to power where there are no real resources for power," Connell writes.[14] "There is a lot of concern with face, a lot of work keeping up a front." However, those groups in the economic North claim to support women's equality (in varying degrees) while those in the Islamic world have made women's complete re-subordination a central pillar of the edifice of their rule.

By examining far right Aryan white supremacists in the United States, and their counterparts in Scandinavia, we can see the ways in which masculinity politics may be mobilized among the some groups of men in the economic North, while looking at the social origins of the Al Qaeda terrorists, we might merely sketch how they might work out in Islamic countries. Although such a comparison in no way effaces the many differences that exist among these movements, and especially between the movements in the economic South and North, a comparison of their similarities enables us to explore the political mobilization of masculinities, and map the ways in which masculinities are likely to be put into political play in the coming decades.

THE "WHITE WING" IN THE UNITED STATES: RACISM AS MASCULINE REASSERTION[15]

In an illustration in *W.A.R.*, the magazine of the White Aryan Resistance, for 1987, a working-class white man, in hard hat and flak jacket, stands proudly before a suspension bridge while a jet plane soars overhead. "White Men *Built* This nation!!" reads the text, "White Men *Are* This nation!!!"

Most observers immediately see its racist intent. But rarely do we see the deeply gendered meaning of the statement. Here is a moment of fusion of racial and gendered discourses, when both race and gender are made visible. "This nation," we now understand, "is" neither white women, nor non-white.

The White Aryan Resistance that produced this illustration is situated on a continuum of the far right that runs from older organizations such as the John Birch Society, Ku Klux Klan and the American Nazi Party, to Holocaust deniers, neo-Nazi or racist skinheads, White Power groups like Posse Comitatus and White Aryan Resistance, and radical militias, like the Wisconsin Militia or the Militia of Montana. The Southern Poverty Law center cites 676 active hate groups in the United States, including 109 Klan centers, 209 neo-Nazi groups, 43 racist skinheads groups and 124 neo-Confederate groups, and more than 400 US-based web sites.[16]

These fringe groups of the far right are composed of young white men, the sons of independent farmers and small shopkeepers. Estimates of their numbers range from an "improbably modest" 10,000 to an "improbably cautionary" 100,000,[17] while the number of far-right extremists and Patriots of any sort is estimated to run to between three and four million who "believe themselves victims, real or intended, of an international plot to destroy their freedom and their faith and pollute their blood."[18] Buffeted by the global political and economic forces that have produced global hegemonic masculinities, they have responded to the erosion of public patriarchy (displacement in the political arena), domestic patriarchy (their wives now work away from the farm), with a renewal of their sense of masculine entitlement to restore patriarchy in both arenas. Ideologically, what characterizes these scions of small-town rural America—both the fathers and the sons—is (1) their ideological vision of producerism, threatened by economic transformation; (2) their sense of small-town democratic community, an inclusive community that was based on the exclusion of broad segments of the population; and (3) a sense of entitlement to economic, social, and political and even military power.

(It is, of course, true that women play an important role in many of these groups, ranging from a Ladies' Auxiliary to active participants as violent skinheads.[19] Yet while their activities may range from holding a Klan bake sale, using Aryan cook books, and helping their children with their racist coloring books to active physical violence and participation in hate crimes against immigrants, blacks, Jews, and gays, their gender ideology remains firmly planted in notions of unchallenged domestic patriarchy.)

To cast the middle class straight white man simply as the hegemonic holder of power in the United States would be to fully miss the daily experience of these straight white men. They believed themselves to be *entitled* to power—by a combination of historical legacy, religious fiat, biological destiny, and moral legitimacy—but they believe they do not have power. That power has been both surrendered by white men—their fathers—and stolen from them by a federal government controlled and staffed by legions of the newly enfranchised minorities, women, and immigrants, all in service to the omnipotent Jews who control international economic and political life. "Heaven help the God-fearing, law-abiding Caucasian middle class," explained Charlton Heston to a recent Christian Coalition convention, especially

> Protestant or even worse evangelical Christian, Midwest or Southern or even worse rural, apparently straight or even worse admittedly [heterosexual], gun-owning or even worse NRA card-carrying average working stiff, or even worst of all, male working stiff. Because not only don't you count, you're a downright obstacle to social progress.[20]

Downwardly mobile rural white men—those who lost the family farms and those who expected to take them over—are squeezed between the omnivorous jaws of capital concentration and a federal bureaucracy which is at best indifferent to their plight, and at worse, facilitates their further demise. What they want, says one is to "take back what is rightfully ours."[21]

In many respects, the militias' ideology reflects the ideologies of other fringe groups on the far right, from whom they typically recruit, especially racism, homophobia, nativism, sexism, and anti-Semitism. These discourses of hate provide an explanation for the feelings of entitlement thwarted, fixing the blame squarely on "others" who the state must now serve at the expense of white men. The unifying theme of these discourses, which have traditionally formed the rhetorical package Richard Hoftsadter labeled "paranoid politics" is *gender.* Specifically, it is by framing state policies as emasculating and problematizing the masculinity of these various "others" that rural white militia members seek to restore their own masculinity.

Contemporary American white supremacists tap into a

general malaise among American men who seek some explanations for the contemporary "crisis" of masculinity. Like the
Sons of Liberty who threw off the British yoke of tyranny in
1776, these contemporary Sons of Liberty see "R-2," the
Second American Revolution as restorative—to retrieve and
refound traditional masculinity on the exclusion of others.
The entire rhetorical apparatus that serves this purpose is
saturated with gendered readings—of the problematized
masculinity of the "others," of the emasculating policies of
the state, and of the rightful masculine entitlement of white
men. As sociologist Lillian Rubin puts it:

> It's this confluence of forces—the racial and cultural
> diversity of our new immigrant population; the claims on
> the resources of the nation now being made by those
> minorities who, for generations, have called America their
> home; the failure of some of our basic institutions to serve
> the needs of our people; the contracting economy, which
> threatens the mobility aspirations of working class fami-
> lies—all these have come together to leave white workers
> feeling as if everyone else is getting a piece of the action
> while they get nothing.[22]

One issue of *The Truth at Last* put it this way:

> Immigrants are flooding into our nation willing to work
> for the minimum wage (or less). Super-rich corporate
> executives are flying all over the world in search of cheaper
> and cheaper labor so that they can "lay off" their American
> employees. . . . Many young White families have no future!
> They are not going to receive any appreciable wage
> increases due to job competition from immigrants. . . .[23]

White supremacists see themselves squeezed between global capital and an emasculated state that supports voracious global profiteering. NAFTA took away American jobs; the eroding job base in urban centers led many African Americans to move to formerly all-white suburbs to find work. As a result, what they see as the "Burger King" economy leaves no room at the top so "many youngsters see themselves as being forced to compete with nonwhites for the available minimum wage, service economy jobs that have replaced their parents' unionized industry opportunities."[24]

That such ardent patriots as militia members are so passionately anti-government might strike the observer as contradictory. After all, are these not the same men who served their country in Vietnam or in the Gulf War? Are these not the same men who believe so passionately in the American dream? Are they not the backbone of the Reagan Revolution? Indeed they are. Militia members face the difficult theoretical task of maintaining their faith in America and in capitalism, and simultaneously providing an analysis of an indifferent state, at best, or an actively interventionist one, at worst, coupled with a contemporary articulation of corporate capitalist logic that leaves them, often literally, out in the cold—homeless, jobless, hopeless.

It is through a decidedly gendered and sexualized rhetoric of masculinity that this contradiction between loving the nation and hating its government, loving capitalism and hating its corporate iterations is resolved. First, like others on the far right, militia members believe that the state has been captured by evil, even Satanic forces; the original virtue of the American political regime deeply and irretrievably corrupted. "The enemy is the system—the system of international world dominance" according to the Florida Interklan Report.[25] Environmental regulations and policies dictated by urban northern interests are the outcomes of a state now utterly controlled by feminists, environmentalists, blacks, and Jews.

In their foreboding futuristic vision, communalism, feminism, multiculturalism, homosexuality, and Christian-bashing are all tied together, part and parcel of the New World Order. Multicultural textbooks, women in government, and legalized abortion can individually be taken as signs of the impending New World Order. The "Nanny State" no longer acts in the interests of "true" American men, but is, instead, an engine of gender inversion, feminizing men, while feminism masculinizes women. White men not involved in the movement are often referred to as "sheeple," while feminist women, it turns out, are more masculine than men are. Not only does this call the masculinity of white men into question, but it uses gender as the rhetorical vehicle for criticizing "other" men. Typically, problematizing the masculinity of these others takes two forms simultaneously: other me are both "too masculine" and "not masculine enough" both hyper-masculine—violent rapacious beasts incapable of self-control—and hypo-masculine—weak, helpless, effete, incapable of supporting a family.

Thus in the logic of white supremacist organizations, gay men are both promiscuously carnal and sexually voracious and effete fops who do to men what men should only have done to them by women. Black men are seen both as violent hypersexual beasts, possessed of an "irresponsible sexuality," seeking white women to rape[26] and less-than fully manly, "weak, stupid, lazy."[27] In *The Turner Diaries*, the apocalyptic novel which served as the blueprint for the Oklahoma City bombing and is widely read and peddled by militias, author William Pierce depicts a nightmarish world where white women and girls are constantly threatened and raped by "gangs of Black thugs." Blacks are primal nature—untamed, cannibalistic, uncontrolled, but also stupid and lazy—and whites are the driving force of civilization. "America and all civilized society are the exclusive products of White man's mind and muscle," is how *The Thunderbolt* put it.[28] "[T]he White race is the Master race of the earth...the Master Builders, the Master Minds, and the Master warriors of civilization. What can a black man do but "clumsily shuffle[s] off, scratching his wooley head, to search for shoebrush and mop."[29]

Most interesting is the portrait of the Jew. One the one hand, the Jew is a greedy, cunning conniving, omnivorous predator; on the other, the Jew is small, beady-eyed, and incapable of masculine virtue. By asserting the hyper-masculine power of the Jew, the far right can support capitalism as a system while decrying the actions of capitalists and their corporations. According to militia logic, it's not the capitalist corporations that have turned the government against them, but the international cartel of Jewish bankers and financiers, media moguls, and intellectuals who have already taken over the US state and turned it into ZOG (Zionist Occupied Government). The United States is called the "Jewnited States" and Jews are blamed for orchestrating the demise of the once-proud Aryan man.[30]

In white supremacist ideology, the Jew is the archetype villain, both hypermasculine—greedy, omnivorous, sexually predatory, capable of the destruction of the Aryan way of

life—and hypo-masculine, small, effete, homosexual, perni-
cious, weasely. In the White Wing cosmology, Jews are both
hypermasculine and effeminate. Hypermasculinity is
expressed in the Jewish domination of the world's media and
financial institutions, and especially Hollywood. They're sexually omnivorous, but calling them "rabid, sex-perverted" is
not a compliment. *Thunderbolt* claims that 90 percent of
pornographers are Jewish. At the same time, Jewish men are
seen as wimpish, small, nerdy, and utterly unmasculine—
likely, in fact, to be homosexual. It's Jewish *women* who are
seen as "real men"—strong, large, and hairy.

In lieu of their brawn power, Jewish men have harnessed
their brainpower in their quest for world domination. Jews
are seen as the masterminds behind the other social groups
who are seen as dispossessing rural American men of their
birthright. And toward that end, they have co-opted blacks,
women, and gays and brainwashed and cowardly white men
to do their bidding. White supremacists cast the economic
plight of white workers as being squeezed between non-
white workers and Jewish owners:

> It is our RACE we must preserve, not just one class. . . .
> White Power means a permanent end to unemployment
> because with the non-Whites gone, the labor market will
> no longer be over-crowded with unproductive niggers,
> spics, and other racial low-life. It means an end to infla-
> tion eating up a man's paycheck faster than he can raise it
> because *our* economy will not be run by a criminal pack
> of international Jewish bankers, bent on using the White
> worker's tax money in selfish and even destructive
> schemes.[31]

Since Jews are incapable of acting like real men—strong, hardy, virtuous manual workers, and farmers—a central axiom of the international Jewish conspiracy for world domination is their plan to "feminize White men and to masculinize White women."[32] *The Turner Diaries* describes the "Jewish-liberal-democratic-equalitarian" perspective as "an essentially feminine, submissive worldview."[33]

War echoes this theme: "One of the characteristics of nations which are controlled by the Jews is the gradual eradication of masculine influence and power and the transfer of influence into feminine forms."[34]

Embedded in this anti-Semitic slander is a critique of white American manhood as soft, feminized, weakened—indeed, emasculated. Article after article decries "the whimpering collapse of the blond male," as if White men have surrendered to the plot.[35] According to *The Turner Diaries*, American men have lost the right to be free; slavery "is the just and proper state for a people who have gown soft."[36] Yet it is there that the militias simultaneously offer White men an analysis of their present situation and a political strategy for retrieving their manhood. As *National Vanguard* puts it:

As Northern males have continued to become more wimpish, the result of the media-created image of the "new male"—more pacifist, less authoritarian, more "sensitive," less competitive, more androgynous, less possessive—the controlled media, the homosexual lobby and the feminist movement have cheered . . . the number of effeminate males has increased greatly . . . legions of sissies and weaklings, of flabby, limp-wristed, non-aggressive, non-physical, indecisive, slack-jawed, fearful males who, while still heterosexual in theory and practice, have not even a vestige of the old macho spirit, so deprecated today, left in them.[37]

It is through participation in these White Aryan movements that American manhood can be restored and revived—a manhood in which individual white men control the fruits of their own labor, and are not subject to the emasculation of Jewish-owned finance capital, a black- and feminist-controlled welfare state. It is a fantasy of "the Viking warrior who comes to rescue his people from the 'evil Jews and subhuman mongrels'"; a militarized manhood of the heroic John Rambo—a manhood that celebrates their God-sanctioned right to band together in armed militias if any one—or any governmental agency—tries to take it away from them.[38] If the state and capital emasculate them, and if the masculinity of the "others" is problematic, then only real White men can rescue this American Eden from a feminized, multicultural androgynous melting pot. "The world is in trouble now only because the White man is divided, confused, and misled," we read in *New Order*. "Once he is united, inspired by a great ideal and led by real men, his world will again become livable, safe, and happy."[39] The movements of the far right seek to reclaim their manhood gloriously, violently.

WHITE SUPREMACISTS IN SCANDINAVIA

While significantly fewer in number than their American counterparts, white supremacists in the Nordic countries have also made a significant impact on those normally tolerant social democracies. Norwegian groups such as Boot-boys, NS 88, the Norsk Arisk Ungdomsfron (NAUF), Varg, and the Vikings, the Green Jacket Movement (Gronjakkerne) in Denmark, and the Vitt Ariskt Motstand (VAM, or White Aryan Resistance), Kreatrivistens Kyrka (Church of the Creator, COTC), and Riksfronten (National Front) in Sweden have exerted an impact beyond their modest numbers. While some of these groups have disappeared (VAM disbanded in 1994) the most readily identifiable group today is Blood and Honour, a spin-off of the notorious British skinhead group that is an amalgam of right-wing zealots and drunken soccer hooligans spoiling for a fight. The Nationell Ungdom (National Youth Movement) and National Socialist Party are also important groups in Sweden.

Norwegian groups number a few hundred, while Swedish groups may barely top 3000 adherents, and perhaps double that number is supporters and general sympathizers. The Salem march in the southern suburbs of Stockholm on December 11 draws between 1000 and 1200 annually in the largest annual demonstration of the movement.

Most come from lower middle class families; their fathers are painters, carpenters, tiller, bricklayers, and road maintenance workers. Some come from small family farms. Several fathers own one-man businesses, are small capitalists or self-employed tradesmen.[40] In her life-history analysis of your young Norwegian participants, Katherine Fangen[41] found that only one claimed a working class identity, and his father owned his own business; another's father owned a small printing company, another was a carpenter, and the fourth came from a family of independent fishermen.

All the sons are downwardly mobile; they work sporadically, have little or no control over their own labor or workplace, and none owns his own business.[42] Almost all members are between sixteen and twenty.[43] Youth unemployment has spiked, especially in Sweden, just as the numbers of asylum seekers has spiked, and with it attacks on centers for asylum seekers. They struggle, Fangen notes, to recover a class identity "that no longer has a material basis."[44] All Scandinavian participants I interviewed are from divorced families.

Over the past three years, I have interviewed "clients" at EXIT, a government-sponsored group founded in 1998 by Ken Lindahl, himself a former Nazi. The program is designed to help members of Nazi and skinhead organizations leave the movement and reclaim their lives. EXIT has also established offices and groups in Norway and Denmark.

The clients range in age from between thirteen and twenty-three; the average age is between sixteen and seventeen. About 25 new young guys are actively participating at any one time, and one new one comes to EXIT every week. They largely fit the profile described above: their parents are divorced; their fathers are lower middle class; they describe themselves as searchers who did not fit in with any of the available cliques in middle school. Often targeted by bullies they describe their first flirtation with Nazism as a way to both express their growing sense of anger and also to entertain fantasies of revenge. "Being a Nazi in a country like Sweden is probably the worst thing you could be," said Lasse, an eighteen-year old former skinhead. "And since I wanted to be bad—really bad—I decided to be a Nazi."

Like the American white supremacists, Scandinavian Aryans understand their plight in terms of masculine entitlement and humiliation which is eroded by state immigration policies, international Zionist power, and globalization. All desire a return to a racially and ethnically homogenous society, seeing themselves, as one put it, as a "front against alienation, and the mixing of cultures."[45] Yet because of their age, many Scandinavian neo-Nazis are less committed to political ideologies and see their activities more in terms of adolescent masculinity. In both cases—the American and the Nordic—the participants exhibit what Connell calls "protest" masculinity, in which the project of asserting gender identity is linked to some form of gendered anger at institutional or interpersonal forces of emasculation. The emphasis of the protest may be different—the Americans are more fully ideologically committed and politically analytic; the Nordics are more dedicated to an adolescent identity project.

Let me illustrate this with a couple of cases drawn from the interviews in Stockholm.

Andrew[46] is a relatively small boy, with short, streaked dyed-blond hair tucked under a black baseball cap. His eyes are bright and blue, and his round prepubescent face gives him an androgynous sweetness to his features. He wears a black hooded sweatshirt that says, in English, "Go Fuck Yourself" and a black nylon bomber jacket over that. He sits, slouched, his buttocks barely touching the edge of the seat as he strains to lean back as far as the chair will allow. His arms are crossed over his chest in an edgy mix of defiance and resignation as he describes to me what first brought him into the Nazi movement, what he believes and how he left the movement several months ago. Andrew is thirteen.

Andrew is from Varmedo, a working-class Stockholm suburb. His father is in construction and his mother is a housewife who formerly worked as a kindergarten teacher.

Andrew also felt marginalized—in third grade. By fourth grade he had discovered white power music, like Screwdriver, and that was his point of entry into the White Power movement. He spent his time going to parties, putting up posters, drinking and driving around in a car with several other kids, yelling obscenities at immigrants. Unlike all the others, Andrew says he was not the target of bullies. "Not at all," he states calmly and flatly. "I was the bully."

"I liked the fighting and the attention," he says of being part of the movement. He doesn't see himself as a Swedish nationalist. When asked what it means to be Swedish he said, "Dunno. I'm white." Being a Nazi "means I'm part of something, part of a group. It gives me a chance to express my hate."

Still living at home, Andrew has lots of conflicts with his parents about his beliefs. His mother has a friend who is Jewish and was in a concentration camp. "She's OK, I guess," he says. "My mom likes her. It's OK." But it isn't so "OK" with his mother, who has taken down the Nazi flag he hung in his room and burned it, along with his storm trooper uniform—even in its rather small size.

Ironically, although Andrew had been the bully in his school, as a visible, and visibly small Nazi, he has now become the target for others. He is constantly harassed and beat up by violent anti-Nazi groups—"which is really just other kids my age who hate just like I do." The ritual purity of the Nazi movement held no appeal. "I drink all the time," he says casually. Addicted to the videogame "Counterstrike," Andrew now says he likes gaming more than fighting. This past summer, he "jumped." The group's leader, twenty years old, was furious and threatened him. "But my mother's boyfriend knows some Hell's Angels, and I just told him [the leader of the group] that if he messes with me, I'll tell my mom's boyfriend. Now he's incredibly nice to me, and said 'Cool, whatever.' He even offers to drive me home from school." Andrew hopes to become a fireman.

David is a bit older; he's seventeen, and he "jumped" from the Nazi movement two years ago. He's bigger and pudgier, with two studs in his right eyebrow and a labret just below his lower lip. His smile reveals serious over-bite and his glasses are a bit smudged and crooked. Each of his forearms is tattooed; one is of Bart Simpson, smiling demonically, his shorts around his ankles as he moons the viewer.

David is from Uppsala, and his father worked as a foreman in a warehouse of a pharmaceutical company; his mother is on disability. His stepfather works in a photocopy shop. At seventeen, he has dropped out of school, but plans now to return. Chubby, academically disinterested, and feeling marginal, David was a target for bullies in primary school. By sixth grade, though, he, and many of his classmates, were increasingly drawn into neo-Nazi ideology and affect, and they began to wear the clothing, offer the various salutes, and identify as Nazis. He had a few friends who were into Blood and Honour or the National Youth (NU) "We spent all our time drinking and fighting," he explains, which was the primary draw for him as well.

In seventh grade, his school was so alarmed by the number of kids who were getting interested in Nazism that the administrators called in a member of EXIT to give a presentation. But the life was too much fun. He'd go to meetings of more than 100 and sometimes upwards of 200 kids—with a pretty even gender split. "The meetings would become parties, and then everyone would go out afterwards. The girls used to start the fights, provoking some immigrants or something, but then they'd run away, leaving me to clean it up. But it was OK, and there were plenty of girls."

David felt that the Nazis "had the right idea about unifying the country and unifying the people." He sees Sweden as divided and the politicians as corrupt. He wants them to act, to bring Sweden together again. He would target immigrants "because we hate them. They have no reason to be here. They keep saying they don't like Sweden. So what are they doing here?"

Arrested three times, but never convicted, David had his share of injuries, but none serious. Gradually, he began to feel that movement participation was losing its fun. "I began to think that the people I was hanging out with were not living up to the ideals of the movement, weren't living up to what they were saying. They were drinking and smoking and one of the leaders was actually dating a Thai woman! And it started to get boring, always going to the same parties with the same people." Although he also continued to drink and smoke, David began to drift away. He came to EXIT one year ago, and for a while lived in a safe house. "They said they were going to kill me," he said of his former comrades. He has gone back to school, now has a regular girlfriend and is about to take his first holiday with her. "I just want to have a good life," he says.

DYNAMICS OF ENTRY

Above, I described how the young men of the extreme right experience their downsizing, outsourcing or economic displacement in specifically gendered ways: they feel themselves to be emasculated. This political-economic emasculation is accompanied by a more personal sense of emasculation: all but one of the Scandinavian participants (Andrew) I interviewed had been bullied in school. The only other interview-based study, *Smaka Kanga* (literal translation: "Kiss the Boot!") found that bullying was a common unifying theme among the participants.[47] Typical is this EXIT client: "It was common knowledge that you could beat me up without risk. And my parents thought I should stay submissive. I didn't get the support I should have had. They did nothing."[48]

Pelle and Robert, Exit's staffers, also described themselves as having been small, skinny and easily targeted. Robert says now he was a "searcher," which is "a young kid looking for an identity, a place to fit in." "I felt like a nobody," he says, picked on by gangs of immigrants in his school and neighborhood. First, he hung out with some soccer thugs, later he got into death metal music. "Then the 'Viking wave' sort of hit Scandinavia in the early 1990s, and I became really interested in Vikings, and I had a necklace of Thor's hammer. The Vikings were such strong men."

Insecure and lonely at twelve years old, and utterly alienated from his distant father, Pelle met an older skinhead who took him under his wing and became a sort of mentor. Pelle was a "street hooligan" hanging out in street gangs, brawling and drinking with other gangs. "My group actually looked down on the Neo-Nazis," he says, because "they weren't real fighters." "All the guys had an insecure role as a man," says Robert. They were all asking 'who am I?'"

Markus, eighteen, also an EXIT staffer told it this way:

As a child I had friends, sometimes, but I was completely left out at times. I got beat up a lot, both at home and at school. And I was always told I was stupid. When I was 11 I started looking up to my stepbrother, he was 18 and he was a skinhead. He took care of me, he cared. Once when I got beat up by five blokes (three Swedes and two immigrants,) he started going on about "those bloody foreigners." Being only 11, I had no racist opinions but I was affected by what he said. And when I walked around with him, I suddenly got my revenge for everything that had happened to me. Everyone I was afraid of was suddenly afraid of me. It felt great. My stepbrother started giving me white supremacy records, a T-shirt with some nationalist slogan on it, and eventually a bomber jacket. I went straight from listening to boy bands to listening to white supremacy music.[49]

Already feeling marginalized and often targeted, the boys and men also described themselves as "searchers" or "seekers," kids looking for a group with which to identify and where they would feel they belonged. "When you enter puberty, it's like you have to choose a branch," said one ex-Nazi. "You have to choose between being a Nazi, anti-Nazi, punk, or hip-hopper—in today's society, you just can't choose to be neutral."[50]

Of course, not all boys who have been bullied in school, or who have divorced parents, or distant and perhaps abusive fathers become neo-Nazis. Some drift into other identities, and some may even become violent *anti*-racists, as their profiles often seem very similar. But that, in a way, underscores my argument that it is other dynamics, besides the lure of the ideology that brings these guys into the movement. Points of entry into the movement included social activities such as parties and drinking with other kids. Many also described relationships with older guys who were already in the movement, who served as mentors and guides. An older cousin or brother, or an older friend, is often the gateway to choosing Nazism over other forms of rebellion.

> Then I joined my cousin to go meet his skinhead friends, drink beer and listen to white supremacy music. And it just went on from there. The music got harder and harder. You'd sit there, not knowing you were a racist. You'd get your boots, your flight jacket and peel off your hair.[51]

For others, it was a sense of alienation from family, and especially the desire to rebel against their fathers. "Grown ups often forget an important component of Swedish racism, the emotional conviction," says Jonas Hallen.[52] "If you have been beaten, threatened, and stolen from, you won't listen to facts and numbers."

One must not underestimate the power of White Power music on these young prepubescent boys decision to "go Nazi" instead of the variety of other rebellious identities on offer. Music by such bands as Skrewdriver, Arvingarna, and especially Ultima Thule offer angry, hardcore, punk-inspired, metal-inflected driving rock—almost deliberately amateurish, loud and raucous, with a pounding simple beat and nearly indecipherable lyrics screamed out over the thundering rhythm section. Every song seems to be a contrived anthem. In short, just the sort of music that an enormous number of young suburban boys find irresistible. "The music reinforces the feelings that I am righteous and outside of society," says one.[53] As the purveyor of the largest White

Power music website on the Internet proclaims, "music that is hard, music that awakens the warrior spirit in these white people, within these white youth, which stirs up barbarian rages in them—is healthy."[54] Their "concerts" also provide a sort of instant community, a place to meet friends, get drunk slam dance and take out all of one's frustrations and rage.

It is at the concerts, in modes of dress and affective styles that one can best see the dynamics of gender as they play out for these young guys.

NEO-NAZISM AS EMBODIED GENDERED PRACTICE

Alienated young adolescent boys, searching for a masculine identity, targeted by school bullies, whose family ties are attenuated at best and diffident and abusive at worst—easily a recipe for adolescent rebellion. Indeed, many of the ex-Nazis in EXIT see their behavior exactly in these terms, more as efforts to secure a masculine identity and experience community than as commitment to ideology. A wide variety of affective styles—posture, clothing, drinking, fighting—all were engaged in with consciously masculinizing effects.

"Before I joined, I felt like a nobody, I felt like a loser, I felt like, worthless," says Robert. "Their world offered me a world where I was better—just because I was white." "When I was with VAM, I felt dangerous, violent, in control," says another. "People respected me and were scared of me. I felt like a man."[55]

Another former skinhead recounted his experience of masculine transformation as he joined up:

When I was 14, I had been bullied a lot by classmates and others. By coincidence, I got to know an older guy who was a skinhead. He was really cool, so I decided to become a skinhead myself, cutting off my hair, and donning a black Bomber jacket and Doc Martens boots. The next morning, I turned up at school in my new outfit. In the gate, I met one of my worst tormentors. When he saw me, he was stunned, pressing his back against the wall, with fear shining out of his eyes. I was stunned as well—by the powerful effect my new image had on him and others. Being that intimidating—boy, that was a great feeling![56]

For Pelle, it was a "pure power trip":

I really wanted to fight and the best way to start a fight is to say "Seig Heil." I wanted to fight, to release all that anger and hatred. I think it was a good way for me to rebel against my father, he is a legitimate politician, and the worst thing a legitimate politician's son could be is a Nazi.

In the end, Pelle said, "I held the opinions to get the more personal feelings I wanted."

The cultural practices of White Power culture were also masculinizing. White Power music was both "visceral and emotional," says Robert. Drinking also made them feel like real men. All the guys I interviewed described drinking between twenty and thirty beers, listening to White Power music, or watching certain videos (*Romper Stomper* or *Clockwork Orange*) to get themselves ready to go out and look for fights. "By the time we'd downed twenty beers and watched the movies, we'd be banging into each other, butting our heads together, and screaming," recalls Pelle.

On the other hand, many of these rituals were also deeply intimate and caring. Pelle describes how the skinheads in his group would shave each other's heads as they bonded for "war," and how their physical affection during and after fights was the source of the most physical intimacy he had ever had to that point. "I was hugged very seldom as a kid," he remembers. "I guess now looking back, some of the things we did would look pretty gay."

Becoming a soccer supporter was also a dominant theme. In Scandinavia, as in Britain, being a "fan" is different from American adherence to a sports team, no matter how passionate. For some British and Scandinavian fans, fandom is the occasion for indulging in massive quantities of alcohol and engaging in serious brawling. In one survey, half of all Swedish Nazis were serious soccer hooligans.[57] All of the guys I interviewed were avid soccer fans, and were making the transition from soccer hooliganism to simple fandom.

THE ROLE OF IDEOLOGY

Thus far, I have described the points of entry into Nazism as embedded within a developmental psychological trajectory of response to marginalization and the effort to establish and sustain a hyper-masculine identity as a hedge against feelings of psychological emasculation. And I have said nothing about the ideology—the role of anti-Semitism, racism, nativism, and xenophobia. Such an omission is deliberate.

Among the ex-Nazis of EXIT, white supremacist ideology played a relatively minor role, both while they were in the movement and today. Being a boy, growing up to be a man, these were important in their developmental process, and occasionally the ideology would serve as a sort of theoretical prop for their masculinity. On the other hand, racist ideology served to underscore the taken-for-granted aspect of their entitlement. "We believed we were superior," says Robert, and "that we had the right to beat up other people because we were white."

EXIT's promotional material underscores the minimal role of political ideology and instead emphasizes the developmental trajectory for young boys:

> Political opinions have little to do with it, but many of them have been abused early on in their lives. They have felt unwanted or pushed aside, sometimes by "friends" and teachers, sometimes by ethnic youngsters and occasionally by their own parents. They are used to being picked upon, and find themselves at the bottom of their social hierarchy.[58]

Only one of fifteen neo-Nazis interviewed by Arnstberg and Hallen denied the Holocaust or used any other catch phrases from National Socialism; in my interviews, none of the young men did. In fact, those who expressed any political opinions at all might just as well have been categorized as liberal or progressive, supporting the environment, a strong regulatory state that restrains greedy corporations and promotes environmental stewardship.[59]

Perhaps the only central component of ideology that seems consistent among members is "an idealized view of the male as a strong defender of the family and nation."[60] They maintain a fairly traditional understanding of male-female relations, especially in the absence of positive male role models in their development.

They believe that wild young immigrant boys have been foisted on their schools by a seemingly beneficent, but ultimately blighted government, and they look on with dismay as "free" Swedish girls are attracted to immigrant boys, who, in turn see them as "easy" or "tramps." Swedish boys are cowardly "wimps" who must unite to protect Swedish "girlhood" and reclaim the mantle of masculinity.[61]

"Swedish men are such wimps," says Robert. "That's what we believed. They're soft, so easily pushed around. We looked up to the police, the military. We looked up to strength."

Nazism as a masculinizing project is also easily observed in the symbology of the movement. In addition to Nazi paraphernalia, the single most common symbolic tropes among Scandinavia Nazis are references to the Vikings. Vikings are admired because they lived in a closed community, were fierce warriors, feared and hated by those they conquered.[62] Vikings also represent an untrammeled masculinity, an "armed brotherhood" of heroes and martyrs.[63] "The Vikings were real men, all right," explains Lars, now eighteen. "They were so strong and powerful, and they never gave up. They also knew who was boss in the family." "Viking destroyed all those other cultures, conquering them and subjecting them," notes Thomas. "That's what we need to be: Vikings."

Another interesting symbol that unites many Scandinavian Nazis is the Confederate battle flag, the Stars and Bars. Outside of the American South, where it is celebrated as the hallmark of tradition and loyalty to the "lost cause," the Confederate flag is the universal symbol for racism. Scandinavian

Nazis sport T-shirts, tattoos, and hats with Confederate insignias, and hang flags in their rooms or from their apartment windows.

A few also described their decision to leave the movement in ideological terms. They noted—as did *none* of the American Aryans—that being a Nazi requires a significant amount of discipline, since one is obligated to purify the body as well as the nation. Nazis are required to be pure in body—to abstain from alcohol, steroids, drugs, and tobacco, to be vegetarian, and to avoid pornography.

Like their American counterparts, these Nordic groups experience significant support from young women, since the males campaign on issues that are of significance to them; i.e. they campaign against prostitution, abortion, and pornography because they are seen as degrading to women.[64] On the other hand, many of these same women soon become disaffected when they feel mistreated by their brethren, "unjustly subordinated" by them, or just seen as "mattresses."[65]

Often sexualized images of women are used to recruit men. In one comic strip for Vigrid's newspaper, a topless woman, with exaggerated breasts is hawking the newspaper on the streets. "Norway for Norwegians!" she shouts. She's arrested by the police for "selling material based on race discrimination"; meanwhile caricatures of blacks and Pakistanis burn the city and loot a liquor store.

One significant difference between the American and the Scandinavian Aryan movements concerns their view of the environment. While American Aryans support right-wing and conservative Republican efforts to discard environmental protection in the name of job creation in extractive industries, and are more than likely meat-eating survivalists, Nordic White Supremacists are strong supporters of a sort of nostalgic and conservative environmentalism. Many are vegetarians, some vegan. Each group might maintain that their policies flow directly from their political stance. The Nordics groups claim that the modern state is "impure," "perverted," and full of "decay and decadence" and that their environmentalism is a means to cleanse it. As Matti Sundquist, singer in the Swedish skinhead group Svastika puts it:[66]

> Well, it's the most important thing, almost, because we must have a functioning environment in order to have a functioning world... and it's almost too late to save the earth, there just be some radical changes if we are to stand a chance.[67]

NEO-NAZISM AS A MASCULINE RITE OF PASSAGE

According to those who have left the movement, participation in neo-Nazi groups was a rite of passage for alienated and insecure adolescent males. Their commitments were to a masculinizing project, not a National Socialist ideology. Ex-Nazis in Scandinavia appear to be far less interested in ideology than in action.

Yet, while less committed to the ideological project of Nazism than their American counterparts, it is also, of course, likely that this is the result of my interviewing two different groups of men. While the American White Supremacists I interviewed were still in the movement, the Scandinavia men were all *ex*-Nazis, and they would, undoubtedly, engage in a sort of revisionist recreation of their participation—one that would underplay the role of ideological commitments and, perhaps, even over-estimate the developmental tasks of becoming adults. Their descriptions of their activities rarely, if ever, referred to ideology; indeed it was very difficult to extract the sorts of racist comments from them that came so casually and effortless out of the mouths of the American Aryans. It is no doubt the case that I would hear a greater commitment to the ideology from those Scandinavia Nazis who have remained in the movement.

I believe, though, that the difference in their ages was at least of equal importance in understanding their relative emphasis on ideology. The American Aryans entered later, in their late teens and early twenties, while by age twenty, every one of the Scandinavian Nazis were out of the movement—some for more than five years. Their years of participation were, on average, from thirteen to sixteen, with some beginning as early as ten but none of them remaining beyond age twenty. So the Scandinavia Nazis were leaving just as the Americans were entering.

Perhaps Pelle expressed this rite of passage best. Becoming a skinhead and a neo-Nazi enabled him to express his rage and, eventually, he says, to put it behind him. In leaving, he was forced to examine who he was and who he wanted to be, to delve into the lineaments of identity and discard those elements that were destructive. Now twenty-seven, and ten years out of the movement, Pelle is, like many of the long-time ex-Nazis I met, soft-spoken, thoughtful and deliberate in speech. "I'm a better man for having been a Nazi," he says.

Fortunately, for most men, in Scandinavia and elsewhere, there are other routes available to become "better men."

232   MASCULINITIES IN A GLOBALIZED WORLD

CODA: THE RESTORATION OF
ISLAMIC MASCULINITY AMONG AL QAEDA

Although it is still too soon, and too little is known to
develop as full a portrait of the terrorists of Al Qaeda, certain
common features warrant brief comment. For one thing, the
class origins of the Al Qaeda terrorists appear to be similar to
these other groups. Virtually all the young men were under
twenty-five and well educated. Some were lower middle
class, downwardly mobile; others were sons of middle classes
whose upward mobility was blocked.

Other terrorist groups in the Middle East appear to have
appealed to similar young men, although they were also
organized also by theology professors—whose professions
were also threatened by continued secularization and westernization. For example, Jamiat-I-Islami, formed in 1972,
was begun by Burhannudin Rabbani, a lecturer in theology
at Kabul University. (Another leader, Ahmed Shah Masoud,
was an engineering student at Kabul University.) Hisb-e-
Islami, which split off in 1979 from Jamiat, was organized by
Gulbuddin Hekmatyar, also an engineering student at Kabul
University.[68] This group appealed particularly to relatively
well-educated radical students, most of whom were studying
engineering. Ittihad-I-Islami was formed by Abdul Rasoul
Sayyaf, former theology lecturer at Kabul University. One
study of 129 Lebanese members of Hezbollah found them to
be better educated and far less impoverished than the
Lebanese population of comparable age. Another study of
149 suicide bombers offers a fascinating portrait. Over two-
thirds (67.1%) were between seventeen and twenty-three;
almost all the rest were between twenty-four and thirty. Over

one-third (37.6%) had high school educations, while another 35.6% had at least some college. Nearly nine of ten were single.[69]

Of course, it's well known that several of the leaders of Al Qaeda were quite wealthy. Ayman al-Zawahiri, the fifty-year-old doctor who was the closest advisor to Osama bin Laden, was from a fashionable suburb of Cairo; his father was dean of the pharmacy school at the university there. And bin Laden, himself, was a multimillionaire. By contrast, many of the hijackers were engineering students, for whom job opportunities had been dwindling dramatically. (Form the minimal information I have found, about one-fourth of the hijackers had studied engineering.) Kamel Daoudi studied computer science at a university in Paris; Zacarias Moussaoui, the first man to be formally charged with a crime in the United States for the events of September 11, took a degree at London's South Bank University. Marwan al-Shehhi, a chubby bespectacled twenty-three year-old from the United Arab Emirates, was an engineering student, while Ziad Jarrah, a twenty-six year-old Lebanese had studied aircraft design.

The politics of many of these Islamic radical organizations appear to have been similar. All were opposed to globalization and the spread of Western values; all opposed what they perceived as corrupt regimes in several Arab states (notably Saudi Arabia and Egypt), which were merely puppets of US domination. Central to their political ideology is the recovery of manhood from the devastatingly emasculating politics of globalization. Over and over, Nasra Hassan writes, she heard the refrain "The Israelis humiliate us. They occupy our land, and deny our history."[70] The Taliban saw the Soviet invasion and Westernization as humiliations. Osama bin Ladin's 7 October, 2001, videotape describes the "humiliation and disgrace" that Islam has suffered for "more than eighty years." Even more telling is his comment to the Arab television network Al Jazeera in December 1998, in which the masculinity of the American is set against that of the Muslim:

> Our brothers who fought in Somalia saw wonders about the weakness, feebleness and cowardliness of the US soldier. We believe that we are men, Muslim men who must have the honor of defending [Mecca]—We do not want American women soldiers defending [it]. The rulers in that region have been deprived of their manhood and they think that the people are women. By God, Muslim women refuse to be defended by these American and Jewish prostitutes.[71]

This fusion of anti-globalization politics, convoluted Islamic theology and virulent misogyny has been the subject of much speculation. Viewing these through a gender lens, though, enables us to understand the connections better. The collapse of certain public patriarchal entitlement led to a virulent and violent effort to replace them with others, fore example in the reassertion of domestic patriarchal power. "This is the class that is most hostile to women," said the scholar Fouad Ajami.[72] But why? Journalist Barbara Ehrenreich explains that while "males have lost their traditional status as farmers and breadwinners, women have been entering the market economy and gaining the marginal independence conferred even by a paltry wage." As a result, "the man who can no longer make a living, who has to depend on his wife's earnings, can watch Hollywood sexpots on pirated videos and begin to think the world has been turned upside down."[73]

When these groups have gained some political power, such as the Taliban, they have moved quickly to enact deliberately gendered policies, designed to both remasculinize men and to re-feminize women. "The rigidity of the Taliban gender policies could be seen as a desperate attempt to keep out that other world, and to protect Afghan women from influences that could weaken the society from within."[74] Thus, not only were policies of the Afghani republic that made female education compulsory immediately abandoned, but women were prohibited from appearing in public unescorted by men, from revealing any part of their body, or from going to school or holding a job. Men were required to grow their beards, in accordance with religious images of Mohammed—but also because wearing beards has always been associated with men's response to women's increased equality in the public sphere. Beards especially symbolically reaffirm biological natural differences between women and men, even as they are collapsing in the public sphere. Such policies removed women as competitors and also shored up masculinity, since they enabled men to triumph over the humiliations of globalization, and well as to triumph over their own savage, predatory and violently sexual urges that would be unleashed in the presence of uncovered women.

Perhaps this can be best seen paradigmatically in the story of Mohammed Atta, apparently the mastermind of the entire operation and the pilot of the first plane to crash into the World Trade Center Tower. The youngest child of an ambitious lawyer father and pampering mother, Atta grew up a shy and polite boy. "He was so gentle," his father said. "I used to tell him 'Toughen up, boy!'"[75] Atta spent his youth in a relatively shoddy Cairo neighborhood. Both his sisters are professionals—one is a professor, the other a doctor.

Atta decided to become an engineer, but his "degree meant little in a country where thousands of college graduates were unable to find good jobs."[76] His father had told him he "needed to hear the word 'doctor' in front of his name. We told him your sisters are doctors and their husbands are doctors and you are the man of the family." After he failed to find employment in Egypt, he went to Hamburg, Germany, to study to become an architect. He was "meticulous, disciplined, and highly intelligent," yet an "ordinary student, a quiet friendly guy who was totally focused on his studies" according to another student in Hamburg.

But his ambitions were constantly thwarted. His only hope for a good job in Egypt was to be hired by an international firm. He applied and was constantly rejected. He found work as a draftsman—highly humiliating for someone with engineering and architectural credentials and an imperious and demanding father—for a German firm involved with razing lower-income Cairo neighborhoods to provide more scenic vistas for luxury tourist hotels.

Defeated, humiliated, emasculated, a disappointment to his father and a failed rival to his sisters, Atta drifted into an increasingly militant Islamic theology. By the time he assumed controls of American Airlines flight 11, he evinced a gendered hysteria about women. In the message he left in his abandoned rental car, he made clear what really mattered to him in the end. "I don't want pregnant women or a person who is not clean to come and say good-bye to me," he wrote.

"I don't want women to go to my funeral or later to my grave."[77]

MASCULINE HUMILIATION AND THE FUTURE OF TERRORISM

Of course such fantasies are the fevered imagination of hysteria; Atta's body was without doubt instantly incinerated, and no funeral would be likely. But the terrors of emasculation experienced by the lower middle classes all over the world will no doubt continue to resound for these young men whose world seems to have been turned upside down, their entitlements snatched from them, their rightful position in their world suddenly up for grabs. And they may continue to articulate with a seething resentment against women, "outsiders," or any other "others" perceived as stealing their rightful place at the table.

The common origins and common complaints of the terrorists of 9-11 and their American "comrades" were not lost on American White Supremacists. In their response to the events of 9-11, American Aryans said they admired the terrorists' courage, and took the opportunity to chastise their own compatriots. "We could work with those Islamic guys," one Klansman from Alabama said. "You know, when I see those nation of Islam guys at rallies, I go right yup to them and tell them I'm in the Klan and most often they give me the thumbs up." "Those Islamic guys," he concluded, "all feel the same way we do about who controls the world."

Bill Roper of the National Alliance publicly wished his members had as much "testicular fortitude."[78] "It's a disgrace that in a population of at least 150 million White/Aryan Americans, we provide so few that are willing to do the same," bemoaned Rocky Suhayda, Nazi Party chairman from Eastpointe, Michigan. "A bunch of towel head/sand niggers put our great White Movement to shame."[77] It is from that gendered shame that mass murderers are made.

CODA

I began my paper with an epigraph from Barrington Moore about the declining lower middle classes as the shock troops for populisms of the left and the right, as well as a reference to Bruce Springsteen, America's poet laureate of the dispossessed white working class. In his 1978 song, "The Promised Land," Springsteen explains how gendered humiliation can be so easily translated into violent rage. The last two lines of that song's chorus, in which the voice proclaims his manhood ("I ain't a boy") and his belief in a "promised land," provide perhaps a poignant epitaph to frame this discussion.

The assertion of manhood—a homosocial assertion since he assumes the listener is also a man—is followed by a declaration of faith in the Promised Land. To some men facing global displacement, that Promised Land is a heavenly garden of virginal delights; to others it's a purified material world. But in both cases, it's a world that will let men be men. And in a globalizing world of cynical consumerism, these men might be last of the true believers.

Chapter 9

CLOTHING AS AN IDENTITY RESOURCE FOR MEN
A View of the Italian Fashion Industry

Emanuela Mora

INTRODUCTION

I began wondering about the role of clothing in male identity construction during a lesson on the theme of "Consumption behaviors and cultures." While I was discussing about dress with my students, a gender dispute arose with males on one side and females on the other.

The matter of issue was the one that usually goes along with reflections on the value and meaning of fashion: ambivalence between being and appearing, and the greater importance given to authenticity over image.

Men reject the idea that clothing may actually represent who or what a person is, a person's authenticity. Women, instead, acknowledge the role of dress and the way one appears as a communicative tool, as an expression of one's self. However, while I was observing my students discussing, all of them appeared to be accurately dressed, such as one usually expects of university students (and particularly those of the Università Cattolica): blue jeans or sport trousers, decorated t-shirts, pullovers and sweatshirts, designer sneakers, etc. In that group, in particular, nobody distinguished him- or herself through accessories or details that might be associated with a particular youth subculture (hair cut, stressing particular colors, piercings or showy tattoos, etc.).

My surprise over this sharp gender dispute was followed, in both male and female students, by a partial awareness of the process that had taken place. A clear difference in the spontaneous attitudes and discursive regime driving men and women was established with clothing and its symbolic values, a relation based on the gender to which one belongs. However, as soon as this argument occurred, all students, whether male or female, did not only agree on conceptually attributing a supremacy to being over appearing, but also on recognizing that they used dress for communicative purposes.

This brief experience led me to personally reflect on gender relations and their (non-?) correspondence with the evolution of dressing practices in a particular category of persons, namely, white educated male and female young adults.

In particular, I wonder why young men who make a conscious use of clothing as a relation and communicative tool—both with their peers and with the other generations—need to theorize the supremacy of being over appearing and the futility of fashion, considering it a superficial phenomenon. Why is this need not felt equally by girls of the same age, but is instead replaced by a desire to show the many ways it is possible to use clothing to reveal one's authenticity and express one's preferences and belonging?

Obviously, there is a ready-made answer available, circulated over the whole history of industrial society, which can be summarized as follows: men produce, and women consume.[1] Though based on the acknowledgement of phenomena so well-rooted in Western societies as to appear now as a natural fact, this answer obviously cannot be taken seriously. It limits itself to repeating and fossilizing the effects of a process, whose causes it does not recognize. A great deal of contemporary literature has wondered about the changes having occurred in gender relations, as well as the particular dressing practices of men and women.[2] The experience I had with my students, however, leads me to limit my reflection to a particular social category, that consisting of white educated young adult males and their female counterparts. It is obviously a central category in society, since it has available the requisite cultural, material, social, and hence, symbolic resources[3] to control the stabilization of its position during the critical transition from youth to adult life and the process of taking on social responsibilities (in jobs, in private and public interpersonal relations, in cultural preferences, in orienting policy, etc.).

By acknowledging, in terms of discourse, the supremacy of being over appearance, these young men implicitly reassess their social central position. They show that they are sharing the representation, according to which men—who comprise the central social category given with power and responsibilities—are those who deal with important, actual things.[4] This centrality is never questioned, as well as its being "naturally" an expression of a dominant cultural paradigm, which foresees male gender superiority in social and political life. As Berger[5] argues, men act, and women show themselves.

In this paper, I try to show how the men's fashion industry in Italy contributed to construct the hegemonic masculinity that has developed in the twentieth century and around the end of the century partially changed its characteristics (with the representation of the so-called new man). This is also due, in part, to the international role played by the Italian brands of prêt a porter. Hegemonic masculinity is quite a complex concept, and probably also one that is often questioned. It is interesting to me from several different points of view:

1. The concept of hegemonic masculinity allows us to describe the behaviors and attitudes of the people who occupy the best positions in the society (economic resources, networks of relationships to people who have influence in the fields of politics, culture, business, etc.).
2. It is useful to recognize the unwritten rules and habits to which men are supposed to conform in order to play their social role.
3. It helps to identify specific groups of men who are subject to the representation of hegemonic masculinity (as is the case of my students) or tend to adopt its prescriptions in order to be included in the central and dominant strata of society.

In the following pages I'm going to sketch some features of the masculine image, which are historically part of the hegemonic representation of masculinity, underlining especially those aspects that have more to do with clothing practices. I will contend that in this representation we can find some apparently contradictory aspects that have to do with different ways of life, all of which are very common among the more central strata of the Western societies during the last two centuries. The Italian men's fashion industry has been playing an enormous role in the building of the prominence of the white western bourgeoisie and in stratifying the different meanings in the images' stock through which "central men" express themselves in Western societies.

In the following pages, I will try to illustrate how the emphasis on being and the devaluation of appearance is coherent within the roots and the formation of Western culture during the modern age. In the following two parts I will give some elements of the visible features of the hegemonic masculinity: the man of the great renunciation, the dandy, and the new man. Finally, in the fourth section, I will say some words about the roles of different types of fashion firms that give worldwide visibility to marks of the lifestyles of white bourgeois men. The thesis that I am promoting (if not yet evident) is that Italian men's fashion served the aim of innovating the clothing practices of the central strata of masculine population, while English men's fashion played the role of emphasizing classical male clothing. As a corollary to this thesis, the Italian consumption practices have not been as innovative as the industry has shown to be. The sociological argument is that, in Italy, an autonomous culture of consumption, which is independent from the advertizing and marketing campaigns has not yet developed and spread. The media hasn't been playing the independent, institutional role[6] one might expect from them. Media and industry have always been strictly bound to each other. Media hasn't been able to represent the cultural, economic, and political interests of consumers. Even if we are speaking about a long lapse of time during which the consumers' cultures have changed, one can say that Italian consumers are, generally speaking, geared toward social inclusion and are always seeking the best ways to obtain social acknowledgement from the dominant social groups, even when they adopt the most innovative styles the brands are proposing.

EASIER SAID THAN DONE...

Historically, clothing practices have always been a powerful tool aimed at providing visibility, and symbolically assessing gender separation, as well as the superiority of one gender over the other.[7] This gender superiority has quite often coincided with life-sphere specialization. To women private, reproductive life, and to men public, productive life—along with the corresponding wardrobes.[8]

In the past, social work division and its representation in dressing practices reproduced a social order and built personal male and female identities with clear, sharp contours.

Today's insecurity and precariousness concerning gender identities seem to be heavily associated with the difficulty of finding a correspondence between the level of the clothing practice (that is very expressive and communicative) and the level of the theoretical discourse about the function of clothing.

The ways to overcome this insecurity have become the

subject of many sociological studies focused on different social categories (migrants, women, young people, persons ousted from the labor market, etc.). The field of cultural consumption—and particularly the one referring to clothing practices, which involves both men and women—may then become a fertile ground for testing new ways of considering oneself in one's relations with the others, with things, and institutions. It is not by mere chance that studies and inquiries focusing on social inclusion opportunities and the risks of exclusion produced by consumption, are increasingly spreading.

From a certain point of view, it seems that men continue to adopt the typical discourse and justification regimes[9] of the Greek-Christian Western society. As regards the theme we are examining in these pages, the most visible outcomes of this approach are the following two: on the one hand, persistence of a dualist vision of reality, which opposes being to appearing, where image is a mask concealing an underlying reality[10]; on the other hand, stabilization of a natural power relation in which the man dominates the woman.[11] As we know, male domination shows itself also through the action that is perceived as the real life, while women are entrusted with managing and taking care of appearances by showing themselves. This has occurred in modern Western societies, at least since the age of industrial revolution.[12]

According to a very practiced current of thought in twentieth-century philosophy, we might even say that the whole Western culture is based on the opposition between being and appearing, whose archetype can be found in Plato's myth of the cave.[13] Furthermore, it is useful to remind (as several researchers who deal with consumption and material culture have done) that this basic matrix has been reproduced in two of the most influent cultural constellations of modern Western society, Christianity and Marxism. Though much more recent than the Christian faith, Marxism has rapidly shaped and conditioned, over the whole twentieth century, scientific interpretations and explanations, political decisions, and everyday practices, thus evidencing a greater modeling power on reality than any other social theory. Its power can be compared only to the power of morals derived from religious beliefs. Both constellations propose, in fact if not in their basic constitution, morals that privilege work rather than consumption, making rather than showing, being rather than appearing— in other words, all the social functions, which in Western history have always been a male prerogative. If in the Christian religion this can be explained by the fact that the exclusive right of exegesis and theological elaboration has been always granted to a clergy exclusively formed by men,[14] in Marxism this may be attributed to a radical criticism related to the production of goods, in which the expropriation process of the most typical value of the "homo faber" bereaved of his own work, and consequently of his own human nature, becomes visible.[15] The widespread growth of Marxism and Christianity in all social classes and their guidance roles in people's actions has strengthened and made invisible an entire power system, which had risen along with the development of nineteenth- and twentieth-century industrial society. Appearance devaluation, however, is not a universal phenomenon covering the entire history of the West. If the role played by ornaments and clothing in the history of rigidly stratified traditional societies[16] is clear (such as in modern age when they encouraged trade and arts[17]), their function becomes as much important in that particular transition age represented by eighteenth century, marked by the French revolution and the birth of the modern middle-class. According to D. Roche, for example, in eighteenth-century France (but to be more exact, we could say in all European countries with old traditions), clothing continued to play a major role in representing the social spaces that were undergoing a re-definition process in that period: the public sphere was rising, and the private one was changing. "In a society based on inequality, the hierarchy of representations must coincide with the social hierarchy. . . . If a noble is, first of all, what he represents, and a bourgeois is what he produces, as a consequence, the former must seem, and the latter, first of all, must be. When there is confusion between these two registers, when anyone can have his say, there is chaos."[18] Clothes have always had the social value of making the social structure visible, as well as its internal stratification, and a corresponding attribution of honor and respectability. However, it is particularly in modern age that appearance becomes a tremendously serious matter, because the classes which aim at receiving the same rewards double. Middle-class persons' entry in society produces a great deal of confusion, because it questions all traditional respectability attribution standards. Those who in those years are charged with creating confusion between registers are in fact the *nouveaux riches* who, thanks to their money, usurp appearances that belong to other social groups, changing them into pretences.[19]

Focusing on a similar social and cultural context, the English industrial revolution, C. Campbell studies the birth of consumer society, identifying its origin in the Romantic culture, which comes alongside the ascetic ethics of Puritan Protestantism from which production ethics had originated,[20] the latter being a totally male prerogative, just as the former is totally feminine.

Women create a bridge between aristocratic honor and bourgeois respectability. The aesthetical forms through which the latter expresses itself derive, however, from the aristocratic repertoire,[21] and introduce in middle-class life a dichotomy between reality and appearance, as well as an associated gender specialization. By producing, men deal with reality. By working for the social image of respectability, whose legitimate forms belong to aristocracy, women deal, instead, with appearance. Though women's work is aimed at stabilizing the new class, exactly in the same way as the directly productive men's one, it is nonetheless considered a second-rate function. This most likely depends on the social imperative of authenticity, which crosses over the whole modern age, from Rousseau onwards[22] to today, keeping its normative ideal role.

The historical origins of men's cultural and social domination on the one hand reveal the contingent and arbitrary nature of this cultural constellation, and on the other hand teach us the performing power of representations, which provide social actors with powerful interpretation and evaluation patterns, in compliance with which they behave.

Therefore, getting rid of the question of masculinity, such as MacInnes does,[23] and considering it a false problem, since it would not be an actual reality, but only a representation, is in my opinion a misleading approach. In fact, the author himself acknowledges the normative character of such a representation, which would show men how to behave.[24] It is actually the normative nature of representations that opens the way, as L. Boltanski explains, to a discursive regime that justifies and legitimates behavior forms. "Actually, it is just in the inter-space that separates reality, such as it is, from what we would like it were, that morals unfold, and with them, criticism and justifications unfold either."[25] Furthermore, this French scholar explains how actors' justificatory and discursive argumentations confront reality (and I would add, also the reality of their actions and interactions), and how, through confirmations provided by "often institutionalized devices…deeply rooted in the world of objects,"[26] persons are able to acknowledge and affirm the legitimacy and foundation of their own claims. Throughout the 1980s, Boltanski and his colleagues used this approach to study persons' critical competences in disputes over justice. It seems, however, more useful, in general, for understanding the ways in which persons strive to explain, both to themselves and to the others, their own preferences, beliefs, and actions, or at least what they consider right and appropriate.

Here we come to the kernel of the problem from which we started, that attests to the complexity of the representation of hegemonic masculinity. The young men in my class (and by extension, I daresay, all the educated, white, young men belonging to our advanced societies, or at least the Italian ones) exhibit a discrepancy between the justification regime they have adopted and their clothing practices. They behave as "new men" are supposed to do; but they think to themselves as prescribes the traditional view of modern man. Based on a representation we might consider taken for granted—the primacy of being over appearing—for criticizing a kind of object (clothing) associated by definition to appearance, they in fact reproduce an actual discursive regime, the one referred to as male domination, through which an entire social order is ruled. The most interesting aspect, however—and possibly foreboding new developments in terms of gender relations—is that they actually test behavior forms, which belong to a reality level, that disavow the discursive regime confirmed with their words. And even more interesting is, in my opinion, the fact that female students—their companions in sharing privileges in age, class, and race—avail themselves of a justification apparatus (or at least of some propositions) potentially in the position to water down the strength of the discursive regime based on male domination, and on the primacy of being over appearing. Which, then, are the normative representations of masculinity these young adults have to confront?

HISTORICAL FORMS OF URBAN MASCULINITY

There are two historical models of masculinity to which we usually refer when considering men's relations with clothing in the modern age. One of them is "the dandy," a man who keeps with his body and his aspect a close, careful relation, which is still related to the one of pre-modern aristocrats, whether men or women, and therefore does not seem completely assimilated into and standardized by middle-class society. The second one is the bourgeois, the middle-class man who plays a major role in the development of industrial society, who would have made the "great renunciation" of appearance and decoration splendor in favor of a sobriety more consonant with an everyday life spent in job and business routines.[27] Both models have become, more or less implicitly, the reference points to which the clothing styles and the behavioral codes that have crossed the twentieth century had to be anchored, the former—at least until recent years—as a dull, or niche tendency, and the latter as a dominant and normative representation. If both models may be considered expressions of cultural constellations deeply rooted in the life of the continuously expanding nineteenth- and twentieth-century cities, it is also true that during the twentieth century, and particularly in the second half of it, other marginal models of masculinity entered into competition with them, embodied by social categories, which have found in the adoption of an alternative style codified by a strategy aimed at making visible and, consequently, claiming one's social legitimization (the young, the black, the gays, the feminists, etc.).[28]

But how do the dandy and the "great renunciation" bourgeois present themselves?

Usually, the dandy is described as a man who attributes particular importance to physical appearance, to a sophisticated language and amusing hobbies, and adheres to aristocratic values, even when he is not an aristocrat by social origin. The most outstanding example is Lord Brummel, who in late eighteenth-century London laid down the laws of the most innovative and elegant fashion:

> . . . a buttoned jacket tight in the waist, with two tails dropping back to the knees, lapels (perhaps supported by little whalebones) rising up to the ears, which revealed the waistcoat line and the tie folds. Under his waistcoat, he

252   MASCULINITIES IN A GLOBALIZED WORLD

wore long trousers, which followed the leg line, rather than adhere to it, and slipped into the large Hessian boots that came up to his knees. The colors he used were only two: deep blue for his jacket, and a light biscuit hue for his waistcoat and chamois leather trousers, which brought out the snow-white of his shirt and the raven black of his boots. The only ornaments he allowed himself were the brass buttons of his jacket and a heavy golden watch chain, only two links of which were however visible.[29]

The "great renunciation" man is, instead, the one who, after the French Revolution, realizes that in Europe radical changes are taking place in relation to both the legitimate structure of social stratification and the social value of work:

[In late eighteenth century] one of the most striking events in clothes history took place . . . : men renounced their right to have the most brilliant, magnificent, eccentric and elaborate decoration forms, and handed it over to women, thus making men's clothing one of the most sober and severe arts. . . . Men abandoned their claims on beauty and began being only concerned about practicality.[30]

According to this German psychologist, the causes of the "great renunciation" may be sought in the progressive spreading of the values promoted by the revolutionary spirit, freedom, equality, and fraternity, ideals incompatible with a clothing style whose major social function was to underline census and status differences. Furthermore (and this is, in my opinion, the conclusive element), the social evaluation of work began to change. In fact, until then, any economic

activity connected to consumer good production and distribution was considered a degrading activity incompatible
with social respectability. The revolutionary ideals reversed
this situation and, consequently, a rather simple way of
clothing (long trousers, a waistcoat, and a jacket) demanded
of those who were working in offices and shops soon became
the mark of respectability.[31]

Though dandyism underwent different historical stages
and achieved different social values, differences that
occurred in relation to the variety of places in which it made
its appearance (particularly and obviously, in England and
France),[32] it seems to be a phenomenon that marked the age
in which modern fashion assumed the role of an exemplary
social practice of the dominant cultural climate (e.g.
increased attention to aesthetics, to pleasure, to individual
expression). With the first industrial revolution, the sphere
of public life parted from the sphere of private life, and the
public asceticism displayed by businessmen was counterbal-
anced by the private romanticism of their wives. Therefore,
it does not seem incorrect to acknowledge the political role
of the dandy, such as C. Breward[33] does when criticizing, on
the other hand, the more radical position of those who[34]
believe that the cultural model embodied by the dandy has
been used in late nineteenth-century to describe some
emerging sexual roles considered transgressive, both on the
level of behaviors and on the level of images, such as those of
the so-called new woman and the homosexual. According to
this interpretation, the first signs of a crisis of masculinity
would have become visible in those years, which, however,
should be read as a crucial point in the development of
modern forms of sexuality. Breward, instead, claims that

those who identify the dandy style with a sexual dissonance, risk overshadowing the sense of merely stylistic choices made by men who, on the other hand, perfectly identify themselves with the status quo. Dandyism is not transgressive in itself,[35] since it embodies one of the major characteristics of modern fashion: ambivalence. On the one hand, a sober style, which emphasizes male body naturalness, and, on the other hand, a waste of economic and time resources dedicated to the care of one's outward appearance; An exclusive lifestyle, which only aristocrats could afford,[36] and, at the same time, a model which anticipated behaviors and attitudes that would have become typical again by the end of twentieth century. The image of the dandy, interested in learning about everything happening on the globe, fairly corresponds to the image of the contemporary man, who is not concerned at all about being a victim of product fetishism, such as Marx thought of those who used to devote a great deal of energy to dressing staging.[37]

CONTEMPORARY HEGEMONIC MASCULINITY AND THE NEW MAN

The debate on contemporary masculinity, though now including several different voices, which underline a plurality of themes,[38] unanimously agrees on underlining two aspects, which only apparently clash. In the first place, the fact that there is a variety of masculinity representations, corresponding to different categories of men and to their lives and experiences. In the second place, the fact that only some of these representations can be considered socially normative, and namely, those incorporating and shaping attitudes and behaviors approved and hoped for by the persons who hold central positions in society. C. W. Connell,[39] pointing out the coexistence of those phenomena, also underlines the complexity of social expectations to which men are exposed, particularly when they hold marginal social positions, from which they can exert only a limited control on their own life. As the author's inquiry demonstrates, men find themselves obliged to cope with the expectations of the women they meet, the judgment of men with whom they share their social destiny, and the emulation of those who more successfully embody the hegemonic model. In addition, the pressure exerted by mass media and advertising weighs considerably by pointing out one or more masculinity models to which a man should correspond.

Over the twentieth century, the representation of masculinity that was to become dominant was the one that best complied with men's general interests, as it allowed them to keep their privileges, disregarding any actual difference in social position, education, geographical origin, political belonging, etc., insofar as they were just men. In this way, a representation strongly consistent with the typical virilistic culture of fascisms asserted itself, which was in fact accepted also by those who did not identify themselves with the fascist ideology and political practices.[40]

In the period between the last two to three decades of nineteenth century and the 1970s, a normative representation of masculinity, which may be defined as the "twentieth-century masculinity," formed and imposed itself, affecting all gender relations over the past century.

During the first half of twentieth century, several factors

accelerating progress (industrialization, urbanization, education, mass media, transports, trade, advertizing, and scientific discoveries) began to spread, which, along with women's
claims for a reduction of inequalities, led to a crisis of the
traditional masculinity model based on values, such as
strength, health, and male beauty. The rising mass society
seemed to acquire some characteristics traditionally associated with femininity. However, since the female gender was
generally considered subordinate, this tendency looked like
an involution in the development of humankind, and particularly the masculine gender considered universal up to that
point in time. In the mid-decades of the past century, as soon
as women's visibility and social role began to grow, the two
forms of dominant culture that in Italy accompanied the
modernization process, namely the Catholic and the Marxist
cultures, committed themselves to strengthen the representation of a rigid social work division, that is, the man as a
worker, and the woman as a wife and mother.[41]

The dominant virilistic model, to which Bellassai refers,
seems therefore softened through man's representations as a
worker-father-husband. Gradually, as soon as wealth began
to spread in a country, the hegemonic model adopts the features of the respectable middle-class man, the "great renunciation" man, to be clear, and extends them to increasingly
large groups of citizens, that is, the rising lower-middle class
including employees, self-employed workers, retailers, etc.

Consequently, far from being a homogeneous and integrated body, the so-called twentieth-century hegemonic
masculinity embodies contrasting ambivalences and value
precepts. It is, however, interesting to note that there is an
inverse proportionality relation between the limited norma-

tive effectiveness of the real man model, the "macho," who is widely represented in twentieth-century popular literature,[42] and the definitely greater pervasiveness of particular behavioral models, in which male power is not the subject matter, but is in fact exerted and implicitly accepted as an unavoidable, naturalized event, both by men and by women. It is the so-called male invisibility. According to T. Polhemus, it is man's great renunciation of being beautiful and his self-condemnation to follow a utility and rationality imperative. Having renounced his body in order to completely identify himself with a disembodied intelligence, twentieth century man has become invisible.[43] In a less intense but sociologically acute way, M. Kimmel[44] explains men's invisibility in terms of representing performing power. Normal masculinity—the one La Cecla calls[45] "mean masculinity," between the excesses of the "macho" and the Peter Pan's syndrome—forms as a natural glance cast at the world, a non-thematized zero point, which establishes the rule. It is not visible, because it does not need to be represented. In other words, normal masculinity is what both men and women imperceptibly absorb from the moment of their birth, and whose functioning they learn in the same way they learn their mother-tongue.

In the case of primary learning, we learn at the same time to speak a language (which presents itself only as something in progress, in our or other people's words) and to think *in* that language (rather than *through* that language). The ignorance of all what is tacitly granted through one's *investment* in the field and the *interest* in its existence and perpetuation are the more complete, the most imperceptibly and back in time the entry in the game and the learning associated with it take place. The limit obviously consists in being born in the game, in being born with the game.[46]

Women's movements and feminism have further complicated the framework of masculinity models. By claiming and building femininity representations independent of the male gaze, they have in fact established a symbolic space, in which they have begun to think about a normal, and at this point de-naturalized, masculinity[47] and have assigned to men the same task, that is, thinking about their own gender identity.[48]

The discourses about twentieth-century hegemonic masculinity, and the discourse about its crisis, are some of the representations that have occupied that symbolic space. Until the 1970s, only Adorno,[49] with his study on the authoritative personality, had tried to focus the hegemonic masculinity image from a strongly critical point of view. Along with the full expansion of the consumer society and mass communication, the communication market (media, advertizing, and marketing) began circulating a new representation of masculinity which, instead of making a synthesis, or making a choice among available models, uncritically absorbed them in a syncretic way. It is the birth of the image of the so-called new man,[50] who is able to provide scope to emotions and private sphere activities,[51] and is no longer afraid of his affective manifestations, homosexual ones included (which means not only being gay, but also giving importance to heterosexual friendship with men[52]).

According to F. Mort, the "new man" rhetoric, which went across the Anglo-Saxon media during the 1980s, and was fostered by them, is the product and one of the drives of the new consumer culture, which was just developing in those years. In particular, uncertainties about oneself and one's own social roles made a significant segment (significant also because of their buying power?) of the male population become the target market for the new products of the cultural industry—and particularly, of the fashion industry—destined to suggest new images and new possible identities. Not just by chance in those years, some men's magazines appeared, providing a consumer society vision not very different from the one provided by the women's press.[53]

The debate on twentieth-century hegemonic masculinity and the coming on the media stage of this "new man" obviously go along with the breaking of sexual and gender stereotypes and the acquired social visibility of homosexual persons. A decade of "gay" policies led the gatekeepers of public culture (journalists, artists, opinion makers, etc.) to acknowledge and legitimize them. The interest in the new man's appearance, style, and body, an interest strongly functional to consumer culture, is surely fostered by this dissident reading of gender identities and sexual roles, against which, however, a strong resistance is exerted by the popular mainstream culture, which is still firmly anchored—because its followers so believe—to the most traditional roles, and to a hegemonic representation of twentieth-century masculinity.[54]

Since the 1980s, the use of men, of their bodies as passive sexual objects, began spreading in advertisements. This phenomenon becomes particularly visible in three markets: men's wear, toiletries, and men's magazines. These three markets build the new man's code as a new version of masculinity.[55]

Commenting on the representation of masculinity in some fashion reports of the late 1980s and the early 1990s, S. Nixon emphasizes that the staging of the elements of novelty in masculinity (in particular, an enhancement of corporeity, through a more visible sensuousness) is mostly carried out through the choice of models that cannot be inscribed on traditional masculinity patterns (namely, the typical white, middle-class man), or through the choice of models with exotic characteristics (black persons with fair complexion, Italo-Americans), "sensuousness and harshness, or a soft-hard mix within the same picture."[56]

The author adds that the representation of masculinity in those fashion reports is not filtered through a feminine lens, which mediates man's representation of his masculinity. The representation is specifically designed for the male perspective, and Nixon interprets this fact in a quite peculiar way:

> Images are placed on a thin line, which on one side stimulates an observer's identification with the represented look, and on the other side, emphasizes the pleasure one can get from the vision of the model himself, who in this way becomes the object of a longing glaze. This ambivalence between identification with the model and the pleasure one can get from seeing him is strongly encouraged by the particular male sensuousness coding in images and by the way in which some images draw from gazing forms, which historically were a gay men's prerogative—without making that gaze pathological.[57]

Dominant masculinity thematization, to which, as we have seen, mass-media has definitely contributed, has also produced a rather paradoxical result, namely a normalization of subordinate or marginal forms of masculinity, which in the arena of our mostly commercialized imagination, have lost the great part of their transgressive power and resistance meaning. These forms—under the comprehensive label of the "new man"—end by simply playing the role of possible options, identities, or images to be used at pleasure as a provisional reference model. In this, the self-representation one can provide risks becoming devoid of any political value and reduced to a mere consumption game, particularly by the central members of society.

The uneasiness shown by my students seems to be consistent with this overall picture. They limit themselves to play with clothes, certainly in a competent and communicative way, without, however, putting forward particularly deep meanings for both their self and their authenticity. Perhaps inasmuch as they neither have anything to prove, nor anything to claim as to their own social protagonism, they do not expect anything other than entertainment and pleasure from clothing.

MASCULINITY MODELS IN THE ITALIAN FASHION INDUSTRY

Since the end of World War II, the men's fashion industry in Italy has embodied, in an exemplary way, the typical tensions and contradictions in the twentieth-century hegemonic model of masculinity described in the previous pages. The textile, clothing, and fashion system, such as we know it today, was taking shape just in those years and included very different kinds of manufacturing companies:

1. Tailors manufacturing made-to-measure suits with high-quality materials they initially purchased from England, later on buying from wool factories based in the district of Biella (Piedmont), which had succeeded in specializing in the production of very fine fabrics celebrated all over the world. These tailors' fashion houses manufacturing made-to-measure suits had often been established already in late nineteenth century or in the first decades of twentieth century. It was particularly in Naples, Rome, and in the small towns of Abruzzo, that tailoring abilities, skills, and knowledge spread, accumulated, and settled, giving birth to real tailoring schools placed out of any traditional educational process, and following the Renaissance craftsman's workshop model. Beginning in the post-war period, many of them began achieving international visibility, thanks to cinema and to the exceptional intermediary role played by some Italian and foreign cosmopolitan personalities who travelled and spent long periods of time in foreign countries. The tailor Caraceni, for example, learned the secrets of British high tailoring, by undoing and dismantling the suits of a Italian composer, his countryman (Francesco Paolo Tosti), who lived in London and forwarded to his siblings and relatives his cast off suits, which were to modify.[58]

2. Standard-size garment industries. These manufacturers can be placed at a middle level of the market. Some of them began specializing in a medium-high market segment interested in fine-quality products, while other firms specialized in the medium-low

market segment. The major characteristic of these manufacturers—who became the decisive factor in laying the foundations of the industrial fashion system in Italy, and in the 1970s allowed stylists to invent the prêt-à-porter and successfully competed with France—was the industrialization of cutting and tailoring processes, enabled by the adoption of a size system through which it was possible to standardize the manufacturing of ready-to-wear items, which did not require fittings. The post-war development of the clothing industry mostly depended upon relations with the United States and the injection of capitals and goods (often processing machinery) established by the Marshall Plan.[59] The discovery of the importance of a standard-size system was also made possible by Italy's special relations with the United States. In the 1960s, one of the major textile industrial groups, GFT based in Turin, which with its trademark Facis had become the market leader, commissioned a sample inquiry. This inquiry carried out the measurement of 9,000 Italian men, and developed a complex size system in the position to combine "different heights, forms and drops, which try combining in consumers the feeling of wearing a suit especially tailored for them."[60] These technical features, as well as the reasonable price policy carried out by the Italian economic and industrial system, which was still in a settling-down stage, surely contributed to the international achievements of Italian men's wear, but also allowed gradually improving "off-the-peg" wear quality standards, and consequently, the birth of labels and production lines dedicated to more demanding consumer segments, in competition with tailors' made-to-measure suits.[61]

3. There is also a third kind of firm, which began to develop in the 1950s, trying to join high-level style, manufacture, and material contents with industrial production, though limited to small series or even custom-made items.[62] Some of the most outstanding firms in this area, such as D'Avenza, though still aspiring to the English tailoring tradition, introduced important stylistic innovations, which are visible particularly in details, combinations, and final wearability. According to some critics, these manufacturers remain ambiguously placed between tailored suits and industrial ready-to-wear clothes. Tailor's made-to-measure suits, in fact, involve a direct, personal relation between tailor and customer. Made-to-order suits, though allowing greater personalization and contribution to stylistic innovation than standardized "off-the-peg" clothes, would in any case imply an only apparently free relation between manufacturer and consumer, since the latter would be obliged to make his choice within an already defined collection.[63] As a matter of fact, this ambivalence lays, in my opinion, the conceptual foundations that in the 1970s led to the birth of the Italian prêt-à-porter, a phenomenon that at the beginning was typically connected with women's wear, but actually brought in itself a contamination between stylistic innovation and industrial standardization.

All these different kinds of fashion firms actually concur to the consolidation process, all over the century, of the twentieth-century hegemonic masculinity, particularly as to its seriousness, sobriety, and self-control features. This process is carried out by rigorously complying with a men's elegance standard explicitly inspired by the British model, which provides for a limited variety of suit models and typologies, and for a rather precise codification of colors, material and accessories to be used. The correspondence of the look of a suit with the prescribed circumstances in which it should be used, contributes to confirm a widespread social representation of men's centrality in tasks and activities that allow society reproducing.

In my opinion, there are three major aspects that deserve being emphasized concerning the particular declination of twentieth-century hegemonic masculinity made by men's fashion in Italy.

First of all, the dominant model, which after World War II removed the features of pure bodily strength and virilism embodied by the different European fascisms, circulates a man's image corresponding to the middle-class businessman. In the early 1960s, the American sociologist E. Goffman properly summarized the characteristics of the typical social actor in the United States, but also, broadly speaking, in the whole industrialized Western world. "For example, we can say that in America there is only one kind of man who does never have to blush: this man is young, married, white, city-dweller, originating from northern states, heterosexual, Protestant, father, with a university education, a good job, fine complexion, right weight and height, and practicing several sports."[64] In those years, in Italy, some of the characteristics identified by Goffman are unimportant, because they practically do not exist or are almost completely invisible from a social point of view (persons belonging to a religion other than Catholicism, homosexuals, colored). The characteristics referring to civil status, place of residency, educational degree, and professional typology are instead those that form the carrying structure of the normative masculinity model. The rising clothing industry, articulated in different kinds of firms addressing different population class targets, through its marketing strategies and its production lines, helps consolidate and spread this model in all social strata, and plays an important role in quickly, and at least apparently, releasing the population masses from the rural culture that had dominated until recent years in a country that only in the post-war years began to see a significant development of its industrial structure. In the quickly developing cities, the typical professionals' and middle-class workers' suit became the clothing style in leisure time and social events for the workers who formerly wore overalls, smocks, and uniforms at their jobs. As a matter of fact, this has happened everywhere and in all times. The aristocratic way of dressing, and later on, the middle-class one, have always been the reference normative model for all the other classes, which in their (though very limited) non-working activities have always tried to adopt the aesthetic standards of the ruling classes.[65] Italy's peculiarity, in my opinion, consists in the fact that, through the industrial structure of clothing production—which actually begins as a production particularly addressed to a medium-low consumer target—the inter-personal relation between the local tailor and the customer is replaced by an impersonal relation in which the customer finds him- or herself in the position of a passive consumer undergoing the dictates of fashion. Since this process accompanies the process of modernization (Italy passes from an agricultural economy to an industrial economy centered in cities), it happens that brands, firms, and producers represent the petition of society. City-dwellers, following fashion, feel that they correspond to what "the society" actually expects of them. Even if firms are in fact merely private economic actors, they are received by citizens as normative/institutional actors. This has relevant consequences on the development of real consumer culture. In fact, in those years, we cannot find a parallel criticism, increasing awareness in consumers, such as it seems to have happened in other industrial contexts, particularly the United Kingdom and in the United States, where people would use personal critical thought and develop a theoretical suspicion of brands. On the contrary, in Italy people seem to accept being guided and/or manipulated by firms in exchange for a social visible image. People offer their loyalty, their acceptance of the mainstream, in exchange for social recognition.

The opinion shared in Italy by several representatives of fashion studies is that in our country the relation between fashion-makers and fashion-users (between producers and consumers) has been a relationship based on authority since its origins.[66] Furthermore, instead of elaborating on a critical discourse about the position to catch, on the one hand, stylistic and artistic innovations, and on the other hand, the signals of an existential innovation in the lifestyles of new social groups, and interpret them as a case of in-progress popular cultural production,[67] the specialized press seems to have over-emphasized the economic value the fashion industry contains, and to have acted as a business and advertizing resonance box of trends imposed on consumers from the top. In other words, the Italian press has renounced the role of encouraging the formation of a real public sphere (or simply couldn't play such a role). In the case of men's fashion, it continued to assess the hegemonic masculinity model, at least until the moment in which prêt-à-porter stylists and their men's collections began rediscovering the body, colors, and decorations, and a flourishing market for sportswear began developing. But this happened only in the 1980s, when the signals of a crisis in twentieth-century masculinity were already extensively visible and widespread beyond the boundaries of fashion and clothing.

A second element to be considered is the following: Firms operating in the highest segments of the fashion system and targeting people in search of exclusiveness and distinction contribute to the success of the dominant masculinity model, but introduce in their fashion items and in their relationships with consumers such a great deal of attention to details, forms, material, and tailoring quality, as to recall also the peculiar features of the normative masculinity model that in twentieth-century industrial society had somewhat lost, that is, the dandy. In the tailor's tradition of Naples and Abruzzo, as well as in the high-profile firms that have been inspired by it, the aim is to join British rigorous and classical style with the typical smooth shapes of the Mediterranean style. It is a clothing philosophy, which, instead of stiffening the body within a framework of wadding, stiff fabrics, and canvasses, geometric forms aim at following it, revealing it, and making the clothed body look natural. This clothing style, which particularly strikes the imagination of the American public, accustomed and sensitive to practicality and comfort in clothes,[68] became famous thanks to its popularity among Hollywood stars working in Rome, in the Cinecittà studios (such as, for example, Gregory Peck and Clark Gable), or among some Italian actors, such as Marcello Mastroianni, who became an icon of the sensuousness and physicalness of the Italian male.[69] Compared to the two hegemonic models of other industrialized countries such as England, the Italian style actually provides an alternative representation, whose socially innovative value, however, is not acknowledged in Italy. This non-acknowledgement depends on the scarce attention anthropological and sociological studies paid in those years to customs and clothing as important examples of material culture at play in the deep social changes that taking place, and to the deep influence of Catholicism and Communism on the Italian culture, as both of them were strongly critical towards the political and social role of appearances.

According to Polhemus, "the particular style of dresses which evolved in postwar Italy was aesthetically appropriate to its historical moment. The sharp, short jackets and trim tapered trousers which looked so right on a vespa signified an easy, carefree, lighter approach to life." Through the movies, through some products, such as the Vespa or the first design products, through the traditional association of Italy to holidays and tourism, Italy's image that asserts itself abroad is the image of a leading country in the Leisure Age, emerging in the industrialized world. "Italy also offered to the world the role model of the *pavoneggiarsi* (peacock male) . . . Italian men had never participated in the renunciation of masculine finery which had followed the French and industrial revolutions."[70]

In terms of clothing styles, Italian men's wear can actually represent a lucky synthesis of the two opposed British models, the middle-class and aristocratic model, and the peasant one. J. Berger[71] masterfully describes this: "Traditional peasant working or ceremonial clothes respected the specific character of the bodies they were clothing. They were in general loose and only tight in places where they were gathered to allow for freer movement. They were the antithesis of tailored clothes, clothes cut to follow the idealized shape of a more or less stationary body and then hang from it."

Finally, looking at the Italian man's clothing image from an international point of view, we might even say that includes some of the roots for the new man model that developed in consumer society beginning in the 1980s. But viewing things from inside Italy, we are able to observe a contradiction, or at least a discontinuity in this process. If in women's fashion Italy's leading role began to develop in the 1970s, men's fashion achievements began much earlier, at least as early as the 1950s, due to the international visibility attained by the tailoring school of Naples and Abruzzo, and also to the role of some manufacturers producing top-quality and more innovative products than the British versions, which, however, are still considered as a regulatory reference for all. Above all, Italy's leadership influences the global imagination of masculinity,[72] while domestic consumption remains mostly conventional,[73] the result of a lack of a widespread consumer culture in the position to encourage independent judgment and bottom-up practices.

On the other hand, as soon as the Italian prêt-à-porter begins to change consumers' relationships to fashion, special competences will begin to spread among consumers, as well as choice abilities, which have made Italian consumers more and more sophisticated, more inclined to give increasing importance to their body and to their leisure time by surrounding themselves with objects and garments that may allow them to express a wider range of self-representations than in the past. In particular, the literature focused on this sector proposes, since the early 1980s, a man's representation that tries to abandon the conventionality and the formalism of the previous years, and drives consumers to regain possession of their body, their leisure time, and their emotionality. Lifestyles, relationships between genders, and social situations have nevertheless continued to confirm for many years a consumers' more traditional vision, since they still consider men's fashion collections as scarcely wearable, funny provocations. It is only in recent times that the levels of imagination and practice seem to be closer, even though (such as the different gender approaches I noticed in my class have demonstrated) a hegemonic representation of masculinity still has great relevance in the cognitive and interiorization processes of gender identities, if not in everyday practices and in consumption rituals.

CONCLUSION

According to the complexity of the concept of hegemonic masculinity, one can dare to draw some provisional conclusions from the disparate elements gathered in the previous pages.

Since the early second post war, the Italian men's fashion industry covered a wide range of market segments with a production of suits that satisfied the different (conventional and innovative) needs of different social groups. Alongside the whole social pyramid, each Italian man had a model to follow in order to assess his social position or to achieve a better one.

Thanks to the innovative technical and stylistic skills of tailors and entrepreneurs (especially in the highest level of the production system), the Italian men's fashion industry has been contributing to the widening of the semantic area of hegemonic masculinity: attention to the body and aesthetical care have become daily attitudes for many business men, politicians, and intellectuals at different levels of the social pyramid. We can say that men are aware of their consumption and don't behave as "cultural doped," but, at the same time they neither advance criticisms toward the fashion system nor develop suspicion toward brands. On the contrary, they show trust in the well-organized cultural industries' system.

In Italy there are social groups, such as my students, who possess cultural, economic, and relational resources useful in exploring the multiple facets encompassed in the latest versions of hegemonic masculinity. As I have shown elsewhere, these groups are becoming aware of their new power, but the strength of social habits and shared discourses reinforces the taken for granted naturalness of the traditional gender relationships and makes it difficult to develop new representations of gender identities.

GENDER GLOBALIZATION AND AN ETHICS OF CARE

Chapter 10

NATIONALISM, BELONGING, GLOBALIZATION, AND THE "ETHICS OF CARE"

Nira Yuval-Davis

INTRODUCTION

The focus of this exploratory paper is on the relationship between constructions of nationalism and belonging and the feminist "ethics of care." I explore this as an illustration of some of the problematics that arise in the interrelationships between the political, the economic and the emotional in a contemporary neo-liberal globalized world, as well as a link between feminist and political theory.

In his sixteenth-century book *Utopia* Thomas More speaks on one certain kind of inhabitants of that utopian society:

Another type of slave is the working-class foreigner who, rather than live in wretched poverty at home, volunteers for slavery in Utopia. Such people are treated with respect,

275

and with almost as much kindness as Utopia citizens, except that they're made to work harder, because they're used to it. If they want to leave the country, which doesn't often happen, they're perfectly free to do so, and receive a small gratuity.[1]

Joan Tronto is using this quote from More as a description of the social, economic, and political situation of contemporary migrant domestic workers. Tronto, one of the main feminist scholars who are promoting "ethics of care" as the alternative feminist ethics to that of liberal ethics, believes that the solution to their situation is to give them citizenship in the countries in which they work.

Although such a solution is often a necessary step and might help to alleviate some of the most horrendous aspects of the lives of these workers, I doubt that it touches all, or even most of the issues involved. The situation highlighted in this quotation by More relates to some of the complex features of contemporary politics of belonging and changing the legal state of these migrants might be a necessary but definitely not sufficient condition to resolve their situation.

CITIZENSHIP AND BELONGING

Tronto's recommendation raises some of the more general issues about the construction of national collectivities, the relationship between citizenship and belonging to a nation as well as the relationship between the suggested citizenship of the workers in the country where they work and their country of origin in which usually their families continue to live.

Nationalist ideologies usually include an immutable relationship, which is sometimes called "the holy trinity" of people, state, and territory.[2] There is an automatic assumption that the boundaries of civil society overlap the boundaries of the nation, that is the "homeland" territory, controlled by the nation-state.

This mythical relationship has never been completely true. There were always members of the civil society who were not members of the dominant national collectivity, they were members of "the nation" who lived outside the state, and often there were disputes and contestation where the "real" borders pass between one homeland and another. And this relates to the minority of national and ethnic collectivities in the world that were not ruled by other states and empires and in times before the contemporary "age of migration," to use Castle's and Miller's terminology.[3]

Tronto suggests citizenship as a solution to the situation of migrant domestic workers. And indeed, citizenship might give these women some legal rights and minimum wage that otherwise they would not have. Formal citizenship can bestow not only civil, political and social rights but what I've called elsewhere, spatial rights.[4] By this I mean the right to enter the territory of a state, and once entered, the right to stay there as long as one wants—in other words, the right to plan a future and not to be afraid every day of the knock on the door and the order of deportation. Spatial rights also involve the spatial freedom to move in the country and from one employer to another, as often migrant workers, especially domestic care workers, depend on their employers for the right to stay legally in the country. This enslavement has caused a lot of abuse and suffering.

However, as members of racialized minorities in Britain and elsewhere know, formal citizenship does not equate the Marshallian definition of citizenship which defined it as "full membership in the community, with its rights and obligations."[5] The Norman Tibbet "cricket test"[6] which has been mirrored by some of Blunkett's[7] writing on football, make very clear the differentiation between formal citizenship and belonging to the national collectivity. Moreover, in the days of "global war on terrorism," the milder exclusionary discourse of multiculturalism and tolerance[8] has been replaced by a "clash of civilizations" discourse that essentializes "the other" as long as s/he is not prepared to completely assimilate.

This assimilation is not only—or even mainly—cultural. It is about loyalty and belonging. The cricket test constructs belonging as a zero-sum game—you're either one of us or you're the enemy, as president Bush likes to state. More and more states, including Britain, have passed laws that enable them to take away not only people's permit to stay in a country but also their citizenship, even if they were born and grew up in the country, as long as they also have another citizenship (so as not to break some of the international human rights covenants that forbid making people stateless). Even if no formal act of withdrawal of citizenship takes place, often states, let alone societies, sharply differentiate between those who belong and those who do not. An illustration of this principle took place during the western evacuations from Lebanon in the summer of 2006, in which those who had western citizenship but also a Lebanese one were not, at least initially, evacuated.

For this reason, Tronto's suggestion to solve the hardships in the lives of the migrant care workers by endowing them formal citizenship falls far short from tackling in any serious way their situation. However, her suggestion recognizes the fact that social and cultural citizenship and belonging of most people on the globe today is not a zero-sum game but is actually multi-layered, including local, ethnic, national, religious, regional, cross- and supra-national collectivities—and this is true of people of hegemonic majorities and not just of racialized minorities and migrant populations. These multi-layered citizenships and belonging affect and construct each other and dictate access to a variety of social, economic, and political resources. This has been recognized by Wendy Sarvasy and Patrizia Longo[9] who embedded the citizenship status as suggested by Tronto in a more complex multi-layered citizenship structure in which such citizenship is a necessary facet of an anti-colonial world citizenship. Unfortunately, however, they anchored their suggestion in a critical use of the Kantian notion of "hospitality." Hospitality, like the notion of tolerance mentioned above, assumes pre-given boundaries of belonging that guests, like tolerated minorities, cannot transgress.

In order to analyze these complex issues, I have moved from working on citizenship to work on belonging and the politics of belonging.

Belonging is about emotional attachment, about feeling "at home" and, as Michael Ignatieff points out,[10] about feeling "safe." Belonging tends to be naturalized and become articulated and politicized only when it is threatened in some way. The politics of belonging comprises specific political projects aimed at constructing belonging in particular ways to particular collectivities that are, at the same time, themselves being constructed by these projects in very particular ways. The politics of belonging encompass the participatory dimension of citizenship and the identificatory dimension of individual and collective identities but crucially also assume and promote particular emotions of attachment, solidarity, loyalty, and often love to one or more of the triad components of people, state and territory. As Adrian Favell said,[11] the politics of belonging is all about "the dirty work of boundary maintenance"—of who is in and who is out—and it at best relates only partially to the status of formal citizenship.

The politics of belonging is, therefore, where the sociology of power and the sociology of emotions get together. As more and more people who study politics and societies, let alone nationalism, recognize, the theorization of the relationship of the emotional and the political needs to be at the heart of this scholarship. Some political theorists assume emotional bonding as the normative principle of the relationships between people (or, rather, citizens) and their national community.[12] Some feminist scholars, however, put an "ethics of care" at the heart of their alternative vision of all social, economic and political relations. It is for this reason that it might be useful to study their approach to the issue and to evaluate their potential contribution to this field of study.

CARE AND THE "ETHICS OF CARE"

Feminists have made important contributions to the study of social and political relations in general and nationalism in particular. In my own work,[13] I have pointed out some of the major gendered dimensions of nationalisms and nations.

Women are constructed in ambivalent ways in nationalist discourse. On the one hand they are members of the nation as all others, but on the other hand they are constructed and controlled in specific ways as symbols of the nations, its biological and cultural reproducers as well as borderguards of the symbolic boundaries of the nation. However, the large number of feminists who've been working on issues of care and "ethics of care" have not usually referred in their work to issues of nationalism, although a growing number has started in recent years to look at issues of globalization and even international relations.[14]

However, when examining the feminist literature on care, there seem to be some inherent problematics and paradoxes in the approach.

The main problematic is that there is a central ambiguity in the notion of "care" and the "ethics of care" as to whether "care" means "to take care of," and/or "to care about." The two meanings are connected in the sense that caring work assumes a certain emotional regime of labor[15] and that emotional attachments involve performativities and practices as well as narratives, but they cannot be reduced to each other. This ambiguity is of central importance in relation to the great body of feminists and others who study care workers, although some of these writings[16] carefully distinguish between the different components—emotional, cognitive, and practical—of care work. However, I would argue that this is an important distinction that is not made clear enough in all the recent debates on social cohesion and integration (a point which is beyond the scope of this paper but which I hope to be able to expand at some future time).

In this paper, however, I want to examine two related

paradoxes. One paradox relates to the fact that care ethics is constructed—by both neo-liberals and by their opponents, especially feminists—as the anti-thesis of neo-liberal ethics which sees in the pursuit of self-interest the proper mode of human behavior. And yet—care work has come to be pivotal to the functioning of local as well as global economy.

The second paradox relates to the fact that the "ethics of care" has been developed by feminists such as Gilligan,[17] Ruddick,[18] and others, as a feminine mode of viewing the world. And yet, nationalism and all other identity projects of politics of belonging, often considered as masculinist, if not actually patriarchal, are actually dependent upon particular kinds of ethics of care.

These two paradoxes have their own social, political, and economic dynamics and yet interrelating them can highlight to us some of the impasses of contemporary "global" lives.

CARE AND GLOBALIZATION

Neo-liberal ethics consider the pursuit of self interest, more or less within the strictures of law, not only as legitimate and natural (hence the popularity of the theme of the "selfish gene"[19]) but also as the best regulator, not only of the free market's supply and demand but also of social order as a whole. As a recent series of programs produced by Adam Curtis for the BBC have shown,[20] neo-liberal ethics and understanding of social relations, have been constructed by the discourse of rational choice developed by computer simulation games during the cold war period and sanctioned by the mathematical equations of Nash,[21] whose dictum that every one has to be suspicious of everyone all the time was constructed, as he now admits, during the time he was suffering from paranoid schizophrenia.

Minimalist state; denial of the "public good," definitely of "public interest"; maximizing profit—these are the dictates of this extreme form of capitalism in action.

When Marx and Engels tried to theorize the working of capitalism, as motivated by profits extracted from the surplus value of productive labor, there was one kind of labor that resisted incorporation into the paradigm—that of reproductive labor. When Marxist feminists in the 1970s and 1980's tried to analyze domestic labor in a way which would fit and explain women's oppression, they failed as well.[22] The domestic labor debate is one of the glorious impasses of feminist literature.

It can be argued that care work is the form of reproductive labor that has defied to a great extent attempts to incorporate it into the neo-liberal globalized model of the economy, and yet it is pivotal for its sustainability.

Saraceno,[23] Hochschild,[24] Tronto[25] and others have pointed out the emergence of what they call "the care gap" and the resulting "global chains of care." Second wave feminism and the needs of the economy allowed women fuller and more equal access to the workplace. This removed women, at least partially, from their role as primary carers of nuclear families. At the same time, the nature of work itself changed and as Harvey pointed out,[26] globalized, "restless capitalism" under conditions of space/time compression, has created demands of more physical availability of service-oriented workers (the infamous 24/7). The establishment of the practice of flexitime, especially for women workers, did not mean the reduction of work but rather more work from different spaces. This created, as Tronto points out,[27] "a huge gap in the care work that they used to do (especially for women but also for men)." The care worker crisis has created a commodification of care work in a "pink collar ghetto" with less attractive work conditions.

There were not enough local women attracted to these jobs, hence "the care drain" of care workers, skilled and unskilled, from the Third World.

The microchip, communication, and transportation revolutions have meant that most of the productive work with unattractive work conditions, in order to defeat organized workers demands for more attractive work conditions, could often be exported. This is one of the reasons that the relative success of labor movements in curtailing the power of capitalists via resistance and organizing which resulted in the establishment of welfare states in which citizens became entitled to social as well as political and civil rights, could become subverted, and the power of multinational corporations could not be upheld by specific nations states.

However, although certain sectors of the service industry as well as that of industrial labor could be exported—call centers, health tourism etc.—note all labor demands can be exported: reproductive and other kinds of care work have much greater spatial constraints. No virtual presence can replace cleaners, nannies, carers for the elderly and the disabled—at homes and in institutions—as well as the more skilled labor of nurses, doctors and teachers.

Care work does not only have specific spatial constraints, it usually also demands a specific emotional regime which is very different to that of other sectors in the labor market. To carry out care work, the workers have to care—or, at least, to perform their work as if they care. Often caring—as in the case of migrant nannies who have left their own children to the care of relatives or care workers from even less privileged parts of their countries or the globe—is the only thing that makes their work bearable. However, even if this is not the case, and the women have migrated as a way of escaping bondage of traditional gender relations,[28] it is the emotional regime of these jobs which is crucial. Often, in attempts to regulate the labor market and especially to make it more attractive to local workers, there are attempts to profession-alize, at least the more skilled care jobs. However, as is often reported, this results with either the transfer (usually partial and inefficient) of care duties—e.g. when the cleaners rather than the nurses in hospitals are the ones on whom often the patients depend on the caring aspects of their stay, or the cre-ation of new kinds of "care gaps" altogether. Hanne Marlene Dahl also points out that the attempts to professionalize care work are often accompanied by a counter discourse of "New Public Management" that articulates care giving as a simple, manual function and therefore de-professionalizes care-giving work.

This is not surprising, as caring for others is the opposite of neo-liberal ethics which does not recognize and is cynical about notions such as "public good" or "public interest." Feminists have developed the "ethics of care" as an ideolog-ical and moral alternative to this. Moreover, in the work of feminist scholars like Gilligan and Ruddick, care, if not "innate" in women, is part of their universal construction. Others, like Joan Tronto and Fiona Robinson, have con-structed the "ethics of care" as a feminist, rather than as a feminine, ideology. However, given the above, it can be argued that the adoption of an "ethics of care" by women, especially those who work in the care sector, facilitates and oils, rather than obstructing and resisting, the smooth working of globalized neo liberalism.

CARING AND BELONGING

As mentioned above, caring, as constructed by feminists who developed the "ethics of care," is often seen by them as a specific feminine characteristic. I would argue, however, that when analyzing various political projects of belonging, especially nationalism, caring and the ethics of care (although very different from the usual feminist version of it), while deeply gendered, are constructed as constituting the heart of collectivity membership and are at the heart of modern masculinities.

The probably obvious, and yet groundbreaking at its time, element in Benedict Anderson's theory of nationalism in his book *Imagined Communities*[29] has been a recognition that nationalism, although modern and correlative of the age of enlightenment, is not based on rationality. Like other "modernist" theorists of nationalism,[30] Anderson linked the rise of nationalism to a particular stage of the rise of industrialization and capitalism (print capitalism in his case), and saw it as replacing religion. In this respect he was wrong, as we can see that most contemporary nationalist ideologies incorporate, rather than fully replace, religious belonging. However, he was right to emphasize the passion which is at the base of the nationalist sentiment which, like religious or familial attachment, there is no actual rational reason and self interest involved.

There can be no clearer sign that men care about their nations than their traditional readiness to perform the ultimate citizenship duty—to sacrifice their lives for the sake of the nation.

As Cynthia Enloe pointed out,[31] fighting for the nation, often was constructed as fighting for the sake of "womenand-children" as one word. More concretely, it has been shown that men care not only for the abstract notion of home and homeland but for the other men in their unit with whom they are fighting. One of the main worries of including women in combat military unit has been the worries of the commanders that their presence will disturb the male bonding which is at the heart of military performance. On their side, women as carers are not only the biological and cultural reproducers of the nation, but are also the men's "helpmates"—their roles in the formal and informal labor market have been usually defined according to the range of duties demanded from the men, fulfilling, in addition to their traditional reproductive duties, all the tasks the men left when called to fulfill national duties in times of war and other crises.[32]

Caring, in its different gendered forms, therefore, has been at the heart of the performativity, a well as narratives of national belonging.

Nowadays, in many states, serving in the military is no longer a male citizenship duty. Just when women started to be allowed to join the military formally in a more equitable manner, the military was transformed from a national duty into a form of career, like other agents of national external and internal security which are gradually being privatized as part of the growing domination of neo-liberal market forces. This is also a time in which usually in these states, women bear fewer children and the national population as a whole starts to age.

This is also the time in which women come to participate in higher and higher percentages in the national labor market, just when, due to neo-liberal globalized economy demands, the nature of service work itself changes and becomes more demanding. This is when the "care gap" appears, not only in the domestic sphere, but in the national sphere as well, and when the growing dependence on migrant and immigrant workers in various sectors of the economy (but especially the care one), raises issues of racialized boundaries of the nation and the various inclusionary and exclusionary political projects of belonging.

However, maybe even more importantly, this is the time in which, in many countries, the percentage of citizens who vote in the elections falls beyond any previous known rate. On the one hand, the neo-liberal morality of the "selfish gene" seem to be celebrating at the same time that growing global social movements concerned with war, poverty, and global warming transcend borders and boundaries, promoting common human values rather than ethnic and national belonging.

GLOBAL CARING

The complexity of the contemporary globalized world, the time/space compression, the development of non, cross and supra-national political communities and multi-layered belonging/s have brought about greater cosmopolitan discourses of human, rather than just citizenship, rights and duties. They have strengthened the sphere of rule of international law while at the same time endowed probably unprecedented powers to non-state multinational corporations.

There is an ongoing debate whether, under these conditions, emotions of attachment and caring for the nation, especially in the West, have been weakened, remained constant or become more specific and/or localized.[33] Cosmopolitanism—this time, however, formulated in more "rooted,"[34] vernacular,[35] visceral, and situated[36] ways—has become a fashionable label to encompass international, transnational and global social movements and networks. However, at the same time, we see the rise of ethnic and religious fundamentalist movements and others which Manuel Castells[37] has called "defensive identity communities" throughout the world. Not since the time of the rise of fascism in the 1930s, have there been as many and as strong extreme right wing movements and parties.

I would argue, however, that these defensive identity political projects of belonging, are not motivated, primarily, by love and care for their ethnic and national communities, but are ruled by another strong emotion, that of fear. The same conditions that have given rise to globalized multi-layered belongings, have also created conditions of deep insecurity and existential crisis of meaning in many people's lives. People are not sure what work they'll do, where they'll live and with whom they'll live under the conditions of late modernity. This is when they start to feel insecure, unsafe and uncared for and desperately search for fixed, if not primordial identities, belonging and meanings. The so-called structural adjustment demanded by international financial agencies, the dismantling of the welfare state and the privatization of more and more agencies that used to be controlled by the public sector, has hastened this process.

The "care gap," then, is not just a question that relates to individuals, families or communities, but lies at the heart of the local and global rise of ethnic and religious strife. It affects us all, but especially the countries of the South in which most of the population, as Zygmunt Bauman[37] has argued convincingly, constitutes no more than "human waste." As we have seen in the recent G-8 summit, a cosmopolitan anti-poverty movement which promotes a global ethics of care (which demands to "make poverty history") can achieve very little if there is no accompanying political and economic power and structures to achieve this.

We need to develop a way of analyzing the interrelationships of the cultural, political, economic and emotional[38] rather than compartmentalizing them.

Chapter 11

GENDER, GLOBAL ETHICS, AND HUMAN RIGHTS

Victor J. Seidler

DISCIPLINES

Within philosophy and the human sciences an Enlightenment rationalist tradition can still foster a distinction between the "descriptive" that is taken to be factual and so can be described as a matter of fact and the "normative" that has to do with values that we might, or can be brought, to share. Sometimes this is taken to be a distinction between the social sciences, which are taken to be concerned with the empirical world and so with describing relations as they are, and philosophy, whose concern is with the normative. Philosophy can have as its task to show that some issues pertain to a shared value, for instance, a value of respect or not shaming others that we might not have originally appreciated or that can be brought under a principle that we find that we can agree to. As Virginia Held explained in conversations at the Social Trends Institute seminar,[1] it might be difficult to draw a clear distinction

For Virginia Held

between the descriptive and the normative but it is still a significant distinction that has proved its value over time in settling a number of theoretical and practical claims.[2]

At some level she holds to an influential Kantian ethical rationalist tradition that accepts that you can think about morality as somehow similar to law. This is a view that I contested in *Kant, Respect, and Injustice: The Limits of Liberal Moral Theory* where I try to show a tension between a Kantian rationalist tradition and a more relational ethics that can learn from feminism and sexual politics.[3] Though Virginia Held acknowledges a shift in her own work towards a more relational view, as was demonstrated in her paper for the conference, "Gender Identity and the Ethics of Care," written out of a liberal premise that identifies history with progress. As she says, "I start with an assumption that slowly and unsteadily, with periods of sometimes violent backlash, women will progress towards greater equality." But she also acknowledges the significance of men in renegotiating a more equal gender contract and challenging gender relations of power and subordination when she says, "Gradually, men will have to share more in the work of care giving. . . . And as men are pressed to do caring work by women demanding greater equality as they do other work as well as caring work, men will come to value care in ways they have often not. They will identify more as fathers who do fathering labor, not just as men who 'father' children in the send of impregnating women."

For Held seems firm in her conviction that "there will increasingly be a recognition that gender identity is much less a given that has been thought, and need not and should not determine the shape of a person's life except as persons develop their own identities and decide in relation with others how to organize their lives around it." This is where Held shows her commitment to an ethics of care as a specific ethical tradition that Second wave feminisms have helped to identify that can more helpful than other ethical traditions in illuminating issues around gender equality: "The newly developed moral theory known as the ethics of care is well suited to reflect and guide these trends. It is more promising for dealing with the issues involved than are the standard, dominant moral theories of recent decades. The ethics of care is compatible with and capable of promoting the equality of gender identities, and to do so in appropriate ways."

Held surmises, "That men cannot themselves give birth is probably the deepest source of men's desires to control women and thereby their own capacity to reproduce. It seems to support the anxiety about gender identity that affects men much more strongly than women." This helps establish Held's suspicion about a postmodernism that would depend upon a view of social or cultural construction and which would tend to assume that we can only know nature through the categories of culture, so leaving nature as inert. As she explains, "I believe the biological fact that only women can create new human beings is significant. To say that this aspect of human reality is socially or culturally con- structed would often be, I think, misleading. What clearly is socially or culturally constructed is what human beings make of this biological fact, such as holding that women are unsuited for social leadership because they give birth."

This helps explain Virginia Held's sympathy for Seyla Benhabib's view that "the strong theses of postmodernism can undercut feminist critique: How is the project of women's emancipation even thinkable, she asks, without regulative principles of agency, autonomy, and selfhood? Yet postmodernism can be thought to reject the idea of an autonomous self, a subject beyond what relations of power in society produce. And it can be thought to reject the possibility of justifying norms and concepts beyond those established by the social and cultural relations with which persons have been constituted. To Benhabib, if we have no discourses of justification, social criticism becomes impossible and only can only describe "regimes of discourse and power as they succeed each other."[4]

At the same time Held is able to "appreciate the advice of Judith Butler that any given conceptual or normative schemes remain open to an examination of the power relations that have led to its acceptance, and open to appropriate reformulation." "The critique of the subject," she writes, "is not a negation or repudiation of the subject, but, rather a way of interrogating its construction as a pre-given or foundational premise." But issues remain open and awaiting further investigation when Held says following this, "Perhaps we can agree that although the facts of biology as well as the norms of social organization and individual action all require interpretation, there are significant differences between how these interpretations should proceed."

Held seems to think that often it is a matter of establishing claims of justice within specific spheres and regions that exist as if they were bounded areas of social life within which specific claims and counter-claims can be settled. She acknowledges a significant shift in her own work away from a liberal individualism that was influenced by Rawls' *A*

Theory of Justice that saw justice in distributive terms. The last sections of Rawls' early text go beyond the terms of thinking about respect, dignity, and self-worth simply as "moral goods" that need to be more equally distributed and there is some recognition given of the workings of social relations of power but these are never really integrated into the theory and they tend to fall away as Rawls makes a move towards a more political conception of justice that focuses upon the overlap that might exist between different national conceptions of justice.[5] Virginia Held was always clear in her work that it was not enough to have rights over certain physical and moral goods unless you also have access and so control over goods that can help you realize these rights. She has always been concerned with more substantive notions of respect and equality.

Held shared in conversation how she has mainly taught working class students in New York who have had direct experience of exploitation in their working lives and so who could develop a critique of the capitalist idea that is framed through the "American dream" that "everyone, if they work hard enough and have the necessary talents, will be able to succeed and become successful." Even if the students she has taught over many years in New York have not direct trade union or socialist awareness, they do sense the exploitation in the jobs they are obliged to do, even if they initially have difficulties in articulating its sources. With her background in Marx's critique of capitalism, she appreciates that work can be an important means of self-realization and so not just a means to wages. This also helps her to a feminist awareness of a conception of the self as relational and that gender identity, like other aspects of identity, deeply involves our relations with other people. She is open to exploring the range of possibilities that can be open to people and with facets of identity that individuals can transform as they change and transform their lives.

This helps Held question "the oppressive features of thinking in traditional ways about gender identities. To start 'reproduction' is an unfortunate term for all but the most purely biological aspects of giving birth. It suggests that all that goes on in bringing up children and with the caring labor of households is mere repetition…," while Held insists, "The reality is that the care and upbringing and education of children are potentially among the most creative and historically transformative activities in which human beings engage, for they create new persons. Both women and men should engage in this kind of work, and in the full range of other kinds of work, so that gender identity is not a determinant of occupation, and occupations are not structured by gender."

Virginia Held insists, "Identities are constructed, and construct themselves, in the midst of social conditions." She readily agrees with Nancy Hartsock, "My body certainly carries the marks of, and is in many important ways created by, the social and power relations within which my subjectivity constitutes itself and is constituted."[6] But if these formulations remain somewhat generalized, they help Held insist, "At the same time we can resist the social order as established, and bring about change in it. Understanding that we are embodied subjectivities, and that these are shaped within networks of social relations, our identities emerge as a combination of influences acting on us and of resistances and initiative which we marshall." But if there is a willingness to recognize that we are "embodied subjectivities," the terms in which this is framed, I argue, can make it difficult to really appreciate what this could mean.

Feminism has helped to question Marx's focus upon work as means of self-fulfillment and also the terms in which Engels argued that it would be through gaining access to paid work that women would find liberation. Second wave feminisms also recognized the significance of the personal *as* political while at the same time acknowledging *how* intimate relations were also a source of meaning and value that had to be balanced along with the opportunities for paid work outside of the home. Within the new capitalism this involved a process of careful negotiation as young people sought out workplaces that had what has become known as "family friendly policies." But they are also wary of declaring an interest in these issues because they know it could count against them in the competition for jobs. Often these policies are used to sustain an image of a modernizing company and though these policies might well exist, it can be a difficult matter for people to take advantage of them, because this can so easily be made to count against them in the eyes of their colleagues who can show their dedication to the firm and their ambition by working long hours and constantly being available in the office. This is a tension that young women and men can feel within the corporate world as they feel judged for taking advantage of policies that a company might publicly pride itself in. Learning to identify with their careers and not wanting to lose their position on the ladder of promotion, couples can find themselves competing with each other. Both can present themselves as sacrificing in the present to ensure the future for their families.[7]

Though traditionally in sociology work and family were framed through discrete sub-disciplines of the "the sociology of work" and "the sociology of the family," it was the turn towards Marx in the late 1960s that upset disciplinary boundaries. Those who came to reading Marx through Hegel tended to rethink relationships between state and civil society and were influenced not only to interpret the world in different terms but also to change it. There were resonances between Marx, Wittgenstein, and feminist theories that in different ways brought together ways of understanding with social practices.[8] There was, for a time at least, a cultural appreciation that it was through efforts to *change* lives that people made visible some of the social relationships of power they were up against and helped to transform the ways they understood their lives in social and historical context. As the later Wittgenstein came to understand it, language was not an autonomous structure through which the world was to be conceptualized, but was an aspect within social practices. In the way that he explored the meaning of statements through the use that was made of them in particular circumstance, Wittgenstein was questioning the terms of a "philosophy of language" that often governed the ways he was to be interpreted. He was questioning the ambitions of a "linguistic turn" and insisting that we return to the context in which we first come to use certain concepts if we are to grasp their meaning.[9]

But some of these insights were lost as the disappointments that accompanied the efforts to change in the 1970s fostered a turn towards Althusser's more reading of a structuralist Marxism that framed Marxism as a theory of history and politics and insisted upon a sharp distinction between the "humanism" of Marx's early work and the "science" of his later analyses of capitalism.[10] It was through Althusser that discourses were to be framed as articulating the "objects" of discrete disciplines. Through the notion that the "economic" was determining "in the last instant" and the idea of the "relative autonomy" of different areas of social life, there was a return to disciplinary boundaries. If Althusser helped question a rigid economic determinism, so seeming to open up new spaces to explore the workings of politics, ideology and culture, it tended to foster a vision of "theoretical practice" that was to shape an intellectual generation. It was to shape the ways that people would read Marx but also the ways they would go on to read Foucault as a theory of governmentality.

THEORY / EXPERIENCE

Though there is a recognition in Marx that theoretical reflection cannot be separated from attempts to change the world through engaging in practical activities, so making connections between theory and politics, this tended to be broken within a post-structuralist tradition that, at least in the United Kingdom, was largely framed through a critical relationship with Althusser and Lacan. There was also a tension between Second wave feminisms that tended to coalesce around notions that "the personal is political" and so grounded its thinking in relation to the dilemmas and contradictions of lived experience within a patriarchal society and the ways a post-structuralist tradition was wary of the category of experience and assumed experience was discursive. Through framing the issue in relation to whether there was experience "prior to" language, it became difficult to acknowledge tensions between language *and* experience and so recognize resonances between feminist philosophies and the later Wittgenstein.

But there was also a tension between philosophical traditions that were rationalist and felt unsettled in their relationship with personal and emotional life that was deemed to be "subjective" and "anecdotal" and so sat in uneasy relationship with philosophy conceived as a matter of sound and rigorous argument. As Cora Diamond and Stanley Cavell recognized in different ways, the nature of argument was a critical issue for the later Wittgenstein, for he was concerned with the ways that, for example, in an arithmetical series people could learn "how to go on" when there were different "rational" possibilities and it was partly as a matter of convention that logic was to be established. This involves recognizing the *difficulties* of description and so the philosophical issues that can be at work in deciding upon one description rather than another. But for a rationalist, even one informed by feminism, it can seem as if a paper is "too empirical" and will be framed as "sociological" or "political" if it does not explore the "normative" seemingly "in its own right." But it is this very distinction between the "descriptive" and the "normative" that often needs to be brought into question. This distinction also continues to frame the ways Virginia Held frames an ethics of care.

Held tends to contrast her theoretically developed position of an ethics of care that is directed to a particular sphere of social life—and so which can be seen as supplementing in some way a Rawlsian distributive conception of justice—with earlier theories she associates with Carol Gilligan and

Nell Noddings that can seem to have an aspiration to replace theories of justice with an ethics of care. But this formulation can miss a strength in Gilligan's work (I am less familiar with Noddings) that was to recognize the ways in which women's voices were silenced and a sense of *how* the complexity of their lived experience is limited. Gilligan was not concerned to replace a vision of justice which was framed through a language of rights but to give due *recognition* to the moral concerns of women that were often articulated through an ethics of care. Though she was challenged for gender essentialism, what was more significant for her was the validation of women's moral experience that had been traditionally invalidated within distributive theories of justice.[11]

There could be a helpful connection between some of Gilligan's attempts to validate women's moral experience that had too easily been silenced and trivialized within traditional masculine ethical tradition, with some of the critical insights Simone Weil develops in her seminar essay "Human Personality" in which she insists through her own example of a young woman being dragged into a brothel against her will, that the "moral reality" of rape and sexual abuse *cannot* be adequately understood in terms of a discourse of the infringement of rights. This shows that it is not an issue of linguistic construction. Rather we need to learn to recognize the inadequacy of certain moral traditions that insist on understanding justice in distributive terms. Weil insists that while justice as distribution has its place—say, in her example to do with the unequal distribution of a birthday cake where some children are offered bigger pieces—in the case of the young women this is injustice as *violation* and she argues that it has to be a prior conception of justice since it underpins claims towards individual autonomy and independence that distributive theories of justice tend to take for granted.[12]

Though a rationalist tradition might want to insist that the narratives, say to do with rape and domestic violence, can seem to be "mere descriptions," so that they cannot "add much" to the argument about the nature of the injustice involved and can in any case be open to being interpreted in different ways. Those philosophers who want to insist upon a clear division being upheld between the "descriptive" and the "normative" and so between a description of facts and values will often want to insist on an "autonomy" of argument. They want to insist that the moral arguments *can* be presented as a matter of reason alone and that even if it helps to have examples that can be illustrative of the issues involved, it is on the basis of the strength of the arguments that the moral issues need to be resolved. Somehow this structure of argument can seem to remain intact for Held, at least in the ways she presents her shift in moral theories away from a liberal individualism she learns from Rawls towards an ethical theory of care that involves a *relational* understanding of care and relationships. She is concerned with developing an adequate moral theory of care but at times it can seem as if she threatens to lose connection with aspects of injustice that have traditionally been done to women, and which Gilligan recognizes in the invalidation of their moral experience. Though Held helps us grasp how and why this experience is "moral" she can be less clear how it involves a concern with justice.

Held seems to want to think that there has already been a lot of discussion of the relationship of an ethics of care to justice and that there were those like Nel Noddings who were mistaken in thinking that an ethics of care could somehow *replace* and not just *renew* a concern with justice. But Held tends to think that theories of justice remain more or less "in tact" within their own region where it can give an adequate account of the kind of claims that are made and the "cluster of values" around it such as equality, respect, fairness, and human rights. She thinks these theories have proved their worth and they do not really need to be renewed. They can do the philosophical work that is required of them. But the mistake, according to Held, that theorists of justice make is in thinking this designates the whole sphere of morality. Rather, she insists that there are *other* fields of moral concern that need to be illuminated through an ethics of care and that have to do with care, vulnerability, dependency, connection, and love. She also appreciates that the asymmetry these relationships often start with often allows for recognition of unequal relationships of power. These unequal relationships allow us to learn about how *not* to care for others.[13]

There is also an awareness that unless we know how to care for ourselves and so give due recognition to ways that we feel vulnerable, it can be difficult for us to care well for others. If we have learn to assume that it is always a matter of dealing with misfortune as if it has never happened, so never learning *how* to register the pain, unease, and humiliation we might have felt, then it can be difficult to develop a sensitivity towards others. Often we also learn that you either have these qualities of care and concern or you do not so we never learn to appreciate a need to grow and develop these qualities in ourselves. We do not recognize *how* these are qualities that it can take time and attention to develop in ourselves. Often within different cultures there is a fear of vulnerability that is associated with dominant masculinities that can work to make men not only insensitive to others but also to themselves. They can feel a need to show that they are strong, as if they are surrounded by a box that cannot be penetrated so that whatever they might be beginning to feel inside they are determined not to show to the outside world. Traditionally men have learnt that they show their care for their families through acting as breadwinners and providers. They might think they have a particular responsibility to make their sons strong and independent so learning to conceal whatever vulnerabilities they feel. As men they are expected to be strong so that in heterosexual relationships they can allow their female partners to depend upon them. Since heterosexual masculinities are framed through a fear of homosexuality that is identified with feelings and vulnerability, they are affirmed often through a suppression of emotional life that comes to be defined as "feminine."[14]

ETHICS / GENDER / INSTITUTIONS

Virginia Held wonders whether an increasing global recognition, at least in theory, of the importance of gender equality will mean that, at least in the West, gender identity will wither away as relatively unimportant. Even if this seems to be happening for a younger generation that appears to be taking gender equality for granted—at least before they have children and find they are left with responsibilities they had not anticipated—Held identifies some factors that explain why this might not be happening more generally. She recognizes that in the continual need to combat patriarchy and compulsory heterosexuality, gender identities "are revalued and asserted in the face of denigration." Sometimes they are also emphasized in the context of parody and playfulness "to bring about awareness of stereotypes and reconsideration of what behavior is acceptable or to be changed."

She also suggests that another "important factor causing the non-decline of strong gender identity may be that bodies have become increasingly sites of commercial exploitation as well as of self-expression." Not only does she recognize how "the use of sexuality to promote more and more what is marketable expands" but, she argues, "The effects of the increasing marketization of everyday life are greatly magnified by the expansion and reach of media images and forms of entertainment. With sexualized bodies offering yet another site for economic exploitation, gender identity seems to be increasingly a product of commercial manipulation."

The reach of the global media has meant that the international circulation of images of Western sexualized bodies has had an effect on diverse global audiences. For example, in Thailand this has fostered a norm of whiteness as identified with beauty and modernity in relation to thin bodies which has led to an expanding market in products that promise to whiten the skin. Whiteness becomes presented as an achievable goal that you have to be prepared to work for if you want to approximate the celebrity bodies that are presented as ideals of beauty. Sexuality also becomes a powerful tool to market a whole range of other consumer goods where it is the celebrity lifestyle that is being consumed through the mediation of objects. For years we have witnessed the ways that cars have been advertised using sexualized images of women. Increasingly these media images and advertisements have been tied to visions of technological control that have also been offered in post-feminist consumer cultures in the West to young women who have also become part of the target consumers. Shifting gender relations are both reflected in and help to shape generational expectations of relationship and desire.

With the increasing dominance of neo-liberalism as framing developments in global capitalism, as Held recognizes, "more and more of what there is in the way of activities and ways of being are being pushed into the market. Aspects of reproduction such as surrogate pregnancy or promotions of fertility are seen as marketable services, along with commercial child care, health care, and education, or 'privatized' security or military services." Within a neo-liberal economy there has been an attack on public services and the ethos that has inspired them that has been fought out in Britain with New Labour in relation to education and health. Thatcherite attempts in the 1980s to privatize the National Health Service were resisted but more and more of its services have been privatized in the name of improving patient care and financial efficiency. Through the use of targets, the government has sought to internally shape Health service reforms since hospitals were obliged to reorganize in order to meet these targets even when these had negative impact on the provision of other services. Since these targets were nationally set they sometimes worked to skew local provision. But they had to be followed, for it was in relation to these particular performance targets that the hospitals, like the schools, were to be evaluated and placed on public league tables. If they did not perform well in meeting these targets budgets would suffer and they would be "named and shamed."

As Held recognizes, "The ethics of care has developed out of feminist thinking and can be a morality with universal appeal. It rests not on divisive religious traditions but on the experience every person has had of being cared for, and on the experience many persons have had of caring for others." This is to ground a potential universal appeal on a shared experience of care even if this can be difficult to reach for men who have been brought up within dominant masculinities that are affirmed through disavowing care. Defined through notions of independence and self-sufficiency within European modernities, as investigated in *Unreasonable Men: Masculinity and Social Theory*, we have to explore relationships between masculinities and an ethics of care.[15] Held argues, "The ethics of care examines the values implicit even in existing care, unjustly structured as it usually is, and the ethics of care provides guidelines for improving care and extending its values. It focuses on the cluster of values involved in fostering caring relationships, values such as trust, empathy, mutual consideration, and solidarity. It appreciates the importance of the emotions in understanding what morality requires, and the importance of cultivating caring emotions, not only of carrying out what reason dictates."

But to what extent do we need to think of these values as gendered? There seems to be a reluctance to do so in Held and this partly relates to her assumptions about what is involved in framing an ethics of care as a potentially universal ethics that can be set against a Kantian or utilitarian tradition. Though when it comes to thinking about the relationship between an ethics of care and justice she is careful to question those who might claim that an ethics of care is needed to set different terms for our discussions of justice, as Weil might also contend, she tends to think in terms of "moral theories" in quite general terms. Of course, when we talk about trust, empathy, and mutual consideration we can acknowledge that these values can be equally significant for men from diverse class, "race," and ethnic backgrounds. But at the same time we can recognize, for example, that being brought up to be self-sufficient and to feel that needing help is a sign of weakness that is often experienced as a threat to male identities, can mean that men often find it difficult to feel emotionally that others can really be there for them at times of need. Even in intimate relationships you can find that sometimes men find it easier to care than to be cared for themselves. Their partners in heterosexual relationships might feel it is difficult for them to make their own emotional demands when their middle class partners so rarely do themselves and this can creating an uneasy inequality in relationships. But again we need to be explore the diverse dynamics in intimate relationships and be careful not to generalize.

Often a younger generation of men and women brought up to take gender equality for granted and to identify themselves as being independent and self-sufficient within the corporate cultures of new capitalism can be quite unaware of what they feel emotionally and can feel without a language that adequately articulates what they are living through. This can make it difficult to trace the new lines of gendered emotional life. Often young men are still brought up finding it difficult to trust that they are loveable and at some unspoken level fear they will be rejected if they dare to make themselves vulnerable. For so long they have learned to distrust others and to be "on guard" emotionally just in case things collapse emotionally around them, that it can take time to learn *how* to trust within an intimate relationship. Sometimes men find personal contact difficult and this can explain why they feel easier seeking advice on the Internet where they feel more protected and less exposed personally. They might visit sites and seek information they would never ask for directly. I also recall conversations in Stockholm in the 1980s where cancer specialists were concerned that men who had been through treatment were not making use of services that the hospitals had made available to them. Research showed that men who had been through an operation were often concerned to prove to themselves that "life could return to normal" and this was achieved through returning to work. Even though a caring service was available, it needed to learn how, when, and where to provide services that men would welcome.

Though it might also be important, as Held recognizes, for men to cultivate "caring emotions, not only of carrying out what reason dictates," we have to develop a gender aware-ness that allows us to understand the sources of male reluc-tance. People will show that they care in different ways and within Protestant cultures there is often wariness about emo-tional expression that emerges out of a fear of interfering in the lives of others. This can help to share particular caring practices that can also be gendered in significant ways. Research also shows that men who had fought in the Second World War often felt a duty to protect their families from what they had witnessed and lived through. They often kept their own council for years and sometimes it was only at the

very end of their lives that they might share themselves emotionally with their families. Men often share how important it
was to be able to spend time with their fathers as they lay
dying in hospital and how they had known at some level their
father's love for them, but that it was so important to hear it
spoken, even if was indirectly. Men grow up with their own
codes of emotional expression and often they can feel a particular obligation to "be strong" and so set an example to their
sons. Often sons cherish the time they spend with their
fathers, recalling how, for instance, helping them stack shelves
in the shop or hand tools to them while they were working
were practices of intimacy. Sometimes memories of such
moments sustain men years after their fathers have died.

An ethics of care can help us question institutional practices that seem to be efficient and effective in utilitarian
terms. As Held recognizes, "Where such other moral theories
as Kantian morality and utilitarianism demand impartiality
above all, the ethics of care understands the moral import of
our ties to our families and groups. It evaluates such ties, dif-
fering from virtue ethics in focusing on caring relations
rather than simply on the virtues of individuals." But as she
also recognizes, an ethics of care can easily become a rhetoric
that becomes part of the institutional self-presentation of
organizations. When we think about how such ties are to be
evaluated, it is helpful to be reminded, as Held explains in
The Ethics of Care: Personal, Political and Global, that an
ethics of care does not imply that the discourse of rights is
dispensable, "but it does suggest arguments for limiting the
reach of law and legalistic thinking rather than imagining
that law is the suitable model for all thinking about
morality." She argues in *The Ethics of Care* "for caring

between fellow human beings as the wider network of relations within which we can agree to treat people as if they
were liberal individuals for the limited purpose of legal and
political interactions." She thinks it can also be defended
"against the requirements presumed by dominant moral
theories that universal principles of impartiality and reason
must always be accorded priority over partial attachments."

An ethics of care allows for a challenge to those would
argue that corporate and market ways of conducting a range
of activities and institutions should be expanded through
privatization "since it makes clear how other values than
market ones should have priority in such activities as childcare, healthcare, education, and cultural activities. Where
other theories have little to say, the ethics of care can provide
strong arguments for limiting markets." Held recognizes that
while "Kantian moral theory and utilitarianism differ significantly, but both are theories of justice, thought suitable for
public life, emphasizing impartiality, rationality, universal
principles, equality, and rights." But Held is clear that while
other feminist philosophers have been concerned with "how
care and justice might be meshed. In my book I consider
how we might conceptualize the fitting together of its various parts into satisfactory, comprehensive, moral theory."
While this is a significant goal, it can sometimes find it difficult to engage critically with specific traditions and the ways
their assumptions might remain gendered. While she thinks
an ethics of care "has the resources for dealing with power
and violence," it can be difficult to show *how* moral relations
are framed through relations of power.

VIRTUES AND RELATIONSHIPS

In her paper "Gender Identity and The Ethics of Care" Virginia Held argues, "In traditional virtue ethics, attention has not been paid to caring as one of the virtues. In the ethics of care, although it is virtuous to be caring, the caring person not only has the right motive or disposition, but also participates adeptly in activities of care and in cultivating caring relations. Caring relations require responsiveness to need, sensitivity, empathy, and trust. It is characteristic of the ethics of care to see persons as relational, yet capable of autonomy." Though this can be a helpful realization, the distinctions that it makes remain generalized and it can make it difficult to deal with the workings of gender relations of power at the personal, institutional, and global levels. It might be that some cultures are more adept at encouraging caring feelings and behaviors as a cultural norm. Even though Brazil is a country characterized by hideous inequalities, there is a culture that fosters human responsiveness and caring. Though people can be responsive and sharing at a personal level, this does not translate into a politics of solidarity that travels across social classes.

While it is important to recognize that an ethics of care is capable of seeing "persons as relational, yet capable of autonomy," the way that this contrast is framed is socially and historically conditioned. In Brazil, for example, people might more easily see themselves in relation to others, feeling a sense of obligation to attend ritual occasions as part of expected behaviors towards others, while in Britain this would remain a matter of individual moral choice. In Brazil, young people might find it harder to establish a sense of autonomy and independence in relation to their friendships. They might feel lonely but surrounded by a group, while in Britain people can be so concerned with not interfering with others that they can seem to be uncaring and unconcerned. This helps us recognize the ways that a discourse of values needs to be grounded within cultural relationships of power and subordination, rather than framed as individual and shared commitments. Sometimes it is difficult to identify different cultures and societies and the ways they foster *different* relationships of care and concern. Societies carry different histories and are marked by traumatic events that can echo across the generations, as for instance the trauma of slavery can impact unconsciously the psychic lives of future generations.

Within the organization of health care and education it can be difficult to appreciate the importance of individual relationships within administrative cultures that present themselves in professional terms. For example, women who are attending anti-natal clinics might really appreciate being able to see the same nurse during their different visits. They might feel recognized and the personal relationships can foster trust that can affect the ways a woman can feel about her pregnancy. But this preference might be difficult to express outside an ethics of care, since it will often be said that, because each of the nurses has been professionally trained, they are equally capable of offering the "personal and professional service" that is required. An ethics of care *can* help to empower women and men to ask for the services they require. Paradoxically, it might encourage some people to seek privatized care, since this is a setting in which they are paying for a continuity of care that might not be adequately valued within a state public medical service. Of course, there might also be issues of fairness and impartiality, in that people might resent some people being offered a service they are denied when there is no good reason for the different treatments offered. There are also issues where people go through the motions of caring behaviors because this presentation of self has become expected of them, but establish no real relationship of trust and empathy. An adequate moral theory should be able to take these different facets into account.

A crisis emerges when children are no longer offered the kind of care and attention that they might need to thrive. Refusing to reconsider the gendered division of labor and the ways that work places would need to be radically reorganized to allow a fair division of emotional labor for children between different adults, it has become assumed that it is an issue about whether women should go out to work, while they have responsibilities for childcare. If we recognize childcare as a shared responsibility then we have to think in radically new ways about the ways work is organized and the opportunities it gives for men and women to develop equal relationships of care with their children. Rather than deconstruct the terms of Kantian theory and the distinction it relies upon between reason and nature that I attempted in *Kant, Respect and Injustice*, Held tends to accept the terms in which Kantian theory offers itself. She hardly begins the critique just saying, "When there is a lack of appreciation for the caring labor women provide in addition to paid work, women fail to achieve equality. The equal respect demanded by Kantian morality would go some distance towards recommending what is needed, but the ethics of care would better handle what persons should do over and above what rights would require."

Held is convinced that "Trust, sensitivity, and mutual consideration—crucial values in the ethics of care—should replace the desire to exploit and the indifference that too often characterize both personal and social interactions at best restrained by Kantian limits." However significant this is, it is not enough to suggest that we replace one set of values with another, but we need to engage much more directly with the moral dilemmas produced through unequal relationships of power, as Shelly Wilcox was attempting to do around issues of domestic workers from the South who were working as childcare and domestic workers in the homes of the middle-class. Often it is the women who are left to negotiate these relationships that enable them to go out to work and so establish more equal gender relations with their partners. These are difficult moral and political predicaments for families to resolve and it might well be that poor women from the South welcome the incomes they can earn, especially when they are working in families that do not exploit their time unduly. But these are issues that cannot be resolved at the level of the family alone, as they involve global gender relations of power and transnational migrations.[16]

What is involved in the respect that children are due from their parents? What does this mean about the time and attention that children might need and how do we give due acknowledgment to the very different needs that individual children might have? These are issues that have been sharply raised through some of the school shootings in the United States where children have shared their anger at having been brought up by the television and through the consumer goods they were bribed with to often compensate for their parents' absence. If they complained, they were made to feel guilty, being told that their parents were working to afford the lifestyle they all wanted and to be able to get the new sound systems and computer technologies their children craved. As it has become necessary for both parents to work and as this has also been legitimated through ideas of gender equality, silence has often fallen about the place of children and the kind of time and attention they need. There has been a discourse of "quality time" that has often been invoked as a justification of how little time they can get.

These concerns show the limits of Kantian tradition that gives little acknowledgement to the respect for emotions and feelings that need to be integral to a respect for a person. Rather, Kant's writings in *On Education* show his conviction of the ways the will of the child has to be broken if they are to make a transition to adult rationality. Held thinks that an ethics of care can offer clear grounds for critique of the market exploitation of bodies and sexualities, which have reached new intensities with celebrity consumer cultures. She acknowledges: "Kantian ethics requires that persons not be used only as means, and that the rights of all persons be respected. But it has little to say about where the limits on markets should be drawn. Whether markets should expand to handle ore and more human activities or to be restricted to only such activities as appropriate is entirely unclear on such a theory." As long as the rights of all are respected, or at least this can be claimed, then there is little to be said about who is involved in childcare or how hospitals or schools should be organized or whether they should be allowed to give priority to commercial gain. She also recognizes that "while utilitarianism can recommend what is conductive to the general happiness, if the preferences of persons have been formed to favor market arrangements for given activities, utilitarianism will not assert other values in their place."

GLOBAL JUSTICE / HUMAN RIGHTS

In Carol Gould's paper for the STI conference entitled "Women's Human Rights in a Culturally Diverse World," she shows a reluctance to call upon an ethics of care because she assumes that it has to start from the caring relationship between individuals and from that basis wants to "move out" to foster caring relationships and concern for the pain of distant others. In her paper, Held had referred to a consideration of issues around gay marriage, where she talks about parents of gay children saying, "If such people are at all caring, they do not want their gay children or relatives or friends to suffer needless pain. They should not want anyone to suffer needless pain, but they may be relatively indifferent toward gay strangers, thinking their pain unfortunate but required to maintain standards of heterosexuality. How the pain is 'weighed' is likely to be different when it is the pain of strangers and the pain of one's children. To a utilitarian, this is an unfortunate fact of psychology and not of moral significance, but utilitarian impartiality is often then dismissed as too demanding. To the ethics of care, the differences can be acknowledged, however, from empathizing with the pain of those close to us persons would be encouraged by the ethics of care to empathize with those more distant."

Held does not explain how this might be expected to happen, but we can imagine that learning and coming to terms with a son or daughter's homosexuality might also encourage people to think differently about sexuality and might foster a transformation not only of personal but also of cultural and political attitudes. It might give you some understanding where formerly there had been prejudice largely based upon received traditional opinion. While Held recognizes that defending the rights of gays, lesbians, bisexuals, and transgendered persons to non-discriminatory can be achieved through a discourse of human rights and abstract principles of justice and equality offered by dominant moral theories, she thinks "the willingness to respect such rights depends on the acceptance that is fostered by caring relations more than on a rational recognition of rights."

In this way, Held makes connections between the moral and the political that can be read as helping to question a too radical split that Gould relies upon between the ethical, which she tends to identify with individual moral action, and the political. But somewhat paradoxically, this means that Gould's appeal for a discourse of women's human rights somehow disavows what was ethically significant in the feminist insight that "the personal is political," which promised for a while to open up a space in which to revision the relationship between gender, philosophy, and social theory. Gould tends to frame women's human rights as a social and political notion that encourages her to read an ethics of care as being grounded in "personal" or "psychological" notions. She frames herself as making a radical shift towards a discourse of women's human rights that can be sensitive to what women in different cultures are struggling to achieve for themselves. In this way, she questions a universalist tradition that might implicitly impose Western conceptions of human rights as if they were universally applicable.[17]

Gould it sensitive to the complex political tasks involved in creating transnational solidarities and she thinks in terms of political alliances that can be forged between different groups that emerged in different cultural settings. But there are still difficulties about the terms on which you could interfere in a culture if women's rights are being broken. Sometimes it seems as if there is need for more thought about the relations of power and empire that have shaped relationships between women's movements in the North and the South. There are difficulties of cultural translation and the different ways that feminists might conceptualize the struggle towards women's freedom and liberation and movements towards greater gender equality. This is not simply a matter of taking different paths towards the same goals, for it might be that the goals are *also* to be imagined differently. We might have to be more careful in the terms of intervention and the ways this is negotiated across cultural and religious differences.[18]

In the STI seminar, Virginia Held was more reluctant to intervene, say in relation to the complex issues around female genital circumcision. She tended to think in more evolutionary and progressivist terms that if women are given information about the health risks they will gradually give up these practices themselves. It is a matter of the education of women and recognizing that it is ignorance standing in the way. This shows her rationalism, though at the same time she recognizes that it is pressure on mothers not to shame their families and to guarantee that their daughters have a chance for marriage. But even if this seems to be a longer-term strategy that does not moderate the practice in the present, Held prefers to depend upon the hope that mothers will gradually recognize with education that it is harming their daughters to continue with the practice. As rational selves who care for the well being of their daughters, they will not want this. At the same time, they know that it hurts and that there are risks involved from their own experience, but for many this remains a risk that you take in order to preserve your traditional culture.

But difficulties with notions of cultural relativism that do not identify the assault that can be taking place against women's human rights are also sustained when we are tempted into thinking of cultures as homogeneous and when we treat them as static and unchanging. This was a feature of colonial anthropologies that had their own investments in treating traditional cultures as autonomous and unchanging, as if they were not being changed through the consequences of colonial rule. A rationalist philosophy will want to think, in contrast, that people will be persuaded if they are presented with rational arguments and that their customs, rituals, and traditions will be open to discussion and change. But too often the West has assumed itself to be the bearer of civilization, culture, and modernity that traditional societies that are deemed to be "simple," "primitive," or "backward" lack. It was assumed that they would not be able to change from resources within themselves because they were deemed to be part of nature. It was only through the external intervention of the European colonial rule that they could hope to make a transition from nature towards culture, from tradition towards modernity.

These painful histories of colonial rule continue to shape anxieties and fears in the present, so we have to show care in the ways that women's human rights are being defined and the kind of relationships that are established across different countries and traditions. Possibly, philosophical work that is sensitive to the significance of narratives might be more helpful in issues to do with cultural translation than traditions, including those to do with an ethics of care, that are concerned with developing "theories" that are often blind to some of their own implicit masculinist assumptions. Of course, the kind of philosophical traditions you can feel drawn to partly depend upon temperament and the time that you are educated into the ways of thinking within particular disciplines.

If we think in Simone Weil's terms about violation as injustice we can appreciate limits to discourses of human rights even if these are framed as women's rights. We might recognize that a strength of Second wave feminism was its recognition of the pain and suffering when bodies are violated through rape and sexual abuse. Weil was concerned to show that the harm could not be understood as "psychological" because it involved both power and morality. It was the way that patriarchy across different cultures assigned masculinities control over women's bodies and sexualities that established a global feminist conversation across cultural, religious, and social differences. It was the recognition that until the 1970s there was, across diverse cultures, a failure to acknowledge the possibility of rape in marriage that showed an injustice that was normalized within the legal codes of democratic and authoritarian regimes. It was an awareness that women's voices were silenced and their experience systematically invalidated with the supposedly advanced and democratic regimes of the West that inspired a generation of feminist activists.

I can recall a moment of difference with my thesis supervisor Richard Wollheim who could see nothing inappropriate in drawing upon a language of rights to frame what was so shocking in a young woman being dragged into a brothel against her will. Simone Weil's example did not seem to touch him and he felt that a universal discourse of rights was quite adequate to revealing the "moral reality" as Weil framed it. You could say that we had different intuitions, but still more would need to be said. If an injustice *as* violation was taking place this called for a conception of women's human rights that needed to be imagined in different terms. It needs to recognize the depth of suffering that is often involved, and the time, care, and attention that it takes for women and also men to recover from sexual abuse, rape, and sexual violence. Of course, each experience is different and has to be evaluated through learning how to listen to the people involved. But we need to develop a moral theory that *is* adequate to the task and this might go beyond many interpretations of an ethics of care. When the soul has been violated it takes a particular kind of love to heal and when the connections between body and soul have been broken it takes time to recover.

With the trafficking of so many young women across national borders for a life of prostitution and when so many men are concerned with using their wealth to finance their sexual tourism and affirm their power over young people in the South, we need to develop moral theories that can engage the realities of global power, transnational migrations, and global communications. As we are becoming aware of the depth of transgenerational losses due to slavery that still resonate in the present, so we are learning to appreciate human vulnerabilities that are so often disavowed. The powerful have always had the means to write history in their own terms, but with global means of communication we are finding that those who have suffered for so long in silence are finding the words to *speak* truth to power. We are obliged in the West to recognize that the past is continually returning to disturb the present and that, for example, those long buried in the Civil War in Spain are being recovered and their relatives are calling for different narratives that can come to terms with these traumatic histories that cross national boundaries and exist in different forms in different places. We are learning, as we learnt from the Holocaust, that the dead have rights also and that they are also demanding for justice to be done to their memory. Gender is part of these narratives and it is a story promises to shape a different relationship between philosophy and social theory.

NOTES

CHAPTER 1

1. See World Bank Staff (CB), *Gender and Development in the Middle East and North Africa: Women in the Public Sphere* (Washington, DC: World Bank Publications, 2004); see also Amanda Ellis, Claire Manuel, Mark Blackden, *Gender and economic growth in Uganda. Unleashing the power of women* (World Bank, 2006).

2. Tsjeard Bouta, *Gender, Conflict, and Development* (Washington, DC: World Bank Publications, 2004).

3. There are exceptions. See for instance the interesting book edited by Eliza W. Y. Lee, *Gender and Change in Hong Kong: Globalization, Postcolonialism and Patriarchy* (UBC Press, 2003).

4. In the meantime, the distinction between gender and sex has also been called into question. While there remains a current of feminist thought which is more interested in stressing the radical alterity of the feminine, and which stresses sexual difference, others have argued that sex itself—and not only gender—constitutes a social construction. From the 1980's onward there have been three main strands of theorising which "have influenced this radical questioning: ethnomethodology, materialist feminism, and poststructuralism/modernism." See S. Jackson and S. Scott, "The Gendering of Sociology," in S. Jackson, ed., *Gender: A Sociological Reader* (Routledge, 2001), p. 15.

5. Of course, one may wonder whether someone could actually identify him/herself as a man or woman, in this sense, in the event that others did not recognize him/her as such. To the extent that self-identification is mediated through others, this could not possibly be the case. At the same time, to the extent that self-iden-

tification incorporates elements which are not completely mediated by others, or to the extent that one's identity is mediated
through different groups of reference, there is room for discrepan-
cies between self-identification and identification by others of
oneself. Here we recognize an aspect of that "unsocial sociability of
human beings," as Kant would put it.

6. See E. Zaretski, "The Birth of Identity Politics in the
1960's: psychoanalysis and the public/private division," in M.
Featherstone, S. Lash, R. Robertson, eds., *Global Modernities*
(London: Sage Publications, 1997), pp. 244–59, p. 254.

7. See Stevi Jackson and Sue Scott, "The Gendering of Sociology," in S. Jackson, ed., *Gender: A Sociological Reader* (Routledge,
2001), p. 9.

8. Were we to pay heed to the studies conducted by Margaret
Mead in 1934 on the sexual differences in three New Guinean societies (the Arapesh, the Mundugamor, and the Tchambuli), as well
as to her later reflection on those matters, the superiority of men
over women would be a universal social fact, independent of the
content of the activities performed by men—which in some cases
are activities deemed feminine by western standards. Subsequent
work on the inequalities enmeshed in sexual roles would prepare
the contemporary conceptualization of gender. See S. Jackson, S.
Scott, "The Gendering of Sociology," in S. Jackson, ed., *Gender: A
Sociological Reader* (Routledge, 2001), pp. 6–7.

9. See S. Frank Parsons, *The Ethics of Gender* (Blackwell,
2002), p. 30.

10. E. Zaretski, "The birth of identity politics in the 1960's:
psychoanalysis and the public/private division," in M. Featherstone, S. Lash, R. Robertson, eds., *Global Modernities* (London:
Sage Publications, 1997), pp. 245–46.

11. See N. J. Chodorow, selection from "Gender, Relation, and
Difference in Psychoanalitic Perspective," in C. Gould, *Gender*
(New Jersey: Humanities Press, 1997), pp. 25–40.

12. See A. Elliot, *Concepts of the Self*, Polity (Oxford University Press, 2001), p. 126.

13. "Queer theory... has exceeded the careful examination of the specification of male homosexuality in the late nineteenth century, which was a feature of early work in gay and lesbian studies, to examine a myriad of practices, subjectivities, and readings. Queer and diasporic studies have, indeed, come together in recent work on queer diasporas, interstitial spaces of identity that resist solidifying into coherent identities. The notion of a queer diaspora, in its focus on a community beyond the nation, destabilizes nationalist ideologies that attempt to interpellate respectable sexual citizen-subjects; simultaneously, in its stress on a queer, multiply inflected identity, it questions globalizing discourses of gay or lesbian sexuality," Philip Holden, ed., *Imperial Desire: Dissident Sexualities and Colonial Literature* (Minneapolis, MN: University of Minnesota Press, 2003), p. ix.

14. See A. Elliot, *Concepts of the Self*, (Oxford University Press, 2001), p. 124.

15. N. Chodorow, "Gender, Relation and Difference in Psychoanalitic Perspective," in Carol C. Gould, ed., *Gender* (Humanities Press, 1997), pp. 25–40.

16. In speaking of conventions, I am not referring to the fact that many men have finally discovered that their responsibility as fathers goes far beyond that of making money for supporting their homes. This discovery has nothing to do with breaking conventions, but rather with developing domestic moral virtues. I am referring, rather, to those social and cultural conventions—mainly forms and manners—which used to reinforce gender differentiation. In absence of those conventions, western men seem to have lost external references to differentiate themselves from women, for in the meantime women do practically everything that men can do.

17. Philip Holden, ed., *Imperial Desire: Dissident Sexualities*

and Colonial Literature (Minneapolis, MN: University of Minnesota Press, 2003), p. xiii.

18. Z. Bauman, *Liquid Love* (Polity, 2003), p. vii.

19. See D. Perrons, *Globalization and social change. People and places in a divided world* (London, New York: Routledge, 2004). See also Jacqueline Andall, ed., *Gender and Ethnicity in Contemporary Europe* (Oxford: Berg Publishers, 2003).

20. See R. Robertson, "Glocalization: Time-Space and Homogeneity-Heterogeneity," in M. Featherstone, S. Lasch, and R. Robertson, eds., *Global Modernities* (London: Sage Publications), pp. 25–44.

21. See Anthony Giddens, 1990, 1991.

22. See M. Waters, *Globalization* (London, New York: Routledge, 2nd ed., 2002), p. 198; see also J. N. Pieterse, "Globalization as Hybridization," in M. Featherstone, S. Lasch, and R. Robertson, eds., *Global Modernities* (London: Sage Publications), pp. 45–68.

23. Against this background, some theorists have come to talk of "belonging" as "a socially constructed, embedded process in which people reflexively judge the suitability of a given site as appropriate given their social trajectory and their position in other fields." M. Savage, G. Bagnall, and B. Longhurst, *Globalization and Belonging* (London: Sage Publications, 2005), p. 12.

24. See M. Waters, *Globalization* (London, New York: Routledge, 2nd ed., 2002), p. 6.

25. For a critique of Giddens' view see R. Robertson, *Globalization. Social Theory and Global Culture* (London: Sage Publications, 1992), chapter 9.

26. See Z. Bauman, "Searching for a centre that holds," in M. Featherstone, S. Lasch, and R. Robertson, eds., *Global Modernities* (London: Sage Publications), pp. 140–54, p. 148.

27. See C. Campbell, *The Romantic Ethic and the Spirit of Modern Consumerism* (Oxford: Alcuin Academics, 2005).

28. Cf. G. Lipovetsky, *La tercera mujer* (Barcelona: Anagrama, 1999, 1st French edition, 1997).

29. G. Lipovetsky, *La tercera mujer*, p. 12.

30. Z. Bauman, *Postmodernity and its discontents* (Polity Press, 1997), p. 185.

CHAPTER 2

1. Earlier versions of this essay were presented at the Conference on Gender Identity in a Globalized Society, Social Trends Institute, Barcelona, Spain, October 13–14, 2006; to the Politics Seminar, University of Edinburgh, November 17, 2006; as the Keynote Presentation, Conference on Women in a Global World: Feminist Values and Human Rights Issues, University of Waterloo, March 9, 2007; to the Queen's University Department of Philosophy, March 22, 2007; at the American Political Science Association, Chicago, IL, August 30, 2007; and as the Keynote Address, Feminist Ethics and Social Theory Annual Conference, Clearwater, Florida, Sept. 29, 2007. I would like to thank Alistair Macleod, Margaret Moore, Tim Hayward, Janna Thompson, Shelley Wilcox and the other participants in those meetings for their helpful comments and suggestions.

2. Ronald Inglehart, and Pippa Norris, "The True Clash of Civilizations," *Foreign Policy* 135 (March/April 2003): 62–66. This article summarizes some of the findings in their authored book, *Rising Tide: Gender Equality and Cultural Change around the World* (Cambridge: Cambridge University Press, 2003).

3. Marianne H. Marchand, and Anne Sisson Runyon, "Introduction," in Marchand and Runyon, eds., *Gender and Global Restructuring* (London: Routledge, 2000), p. 13.

4. Chandra Talpade Mohanty, "'Under Western Eyes,' Revisited: Feminist Solidarity through Anticapitalist Struggles," *Signs* 28, no. 2 (2002): 499–535.

5. Arlie Russell Hochschild, "Global Care Chains and Emo-

tional Surplus Value," in ed. W. Hutton and A. Giddens, eds., *Global Capitalism* (New Press, 2001), pp. 130–46.

6. See, for example, Anne E. Lacsamana, "Sex Worker or Prostituted Woman?" in Delia D. Aguilar and A. E. Lacsamana, eds., *Women and Globalization* (Amherst, NY: Humanity Books, 2004), pp. 387–403.

7. Marianne H. Marchand, "Challenging Globalisation: Toward a Feminist Understanding of Resistance," *Review of International Studies* 29 (2003): 145–60.

8. Amartya Sen, "More than 100 Million Women are Missing," *The New York Review of Books* 37, no. 20 (December 20, 1990).

9. Alison M. Jaggar, "Global Responsibility and Western Feminism," in *Feminist Interventions in Ethics and Politics* (Lanham, MD: Rowman & Littlefield, 2005), pp. 185–200.

10. Jaggar, especially pp. 193–95.

11. Hilary Charlesworth, "Human Rights as Men's Rights," in Julie Peters and Andrea Wolper, eds., *Women's Rights, Human Rights* (Routledge, 1995), pp. 103–13.

12. See the essays in J. Peters and A. Wolper, *Women's Rights, Human Rights*, and in Robin Cook, ed., *The Human Rights of Women* (Philadelphia: The University of Pennsylvania Press, 1994), as well as Carol C. Gould, *Globalizing Democracy and Human Rights* (Cambridge: Cambridge University Press, 2004), chapter 6, and Carol C. Gould, "Women's Human Rights and the US Constitution: Initiating a Dialogue," in Sibyl Schwarzenbach and Patricia Smith, eds., Women and the US Constitution: History, Interpretation, Practice (New York: Columbia University Press, 2003), pp. 197–219.

13. Rhonda Copelon, "Intimate Terror: Understanding Domestic Violence as Torture," in Cook, ed., *The Human Rights of Women*, pp. 116–52.

14. See, for example, F. Beveridge and S. Mullally, "International Human Rights and Body Politics," in J. Bridgeman and S.

Millns, eds., *Law and Body Politics: Regulating the Female Body* (Dartmouth, 1995).

15. Amartya Sen, "Gender Inequality and Theories of Justice," in M. Nussbaum and Jonathan Glover, eds., *Women, Culture and Development* (New York: Oxford University Press, 1995); see also Martha Nussbaum, "Human Capabilities, Female Human Beings," in *Women, Culture and Development*, pp. 61–104; see also Martha Nussbaum, *Sex and Social Justice* (New York: Oxford University Press, 1999).

16. Mary Margaret Fonow, "Human Rights, Feminism, and Transnational Labor Solidarity," in Wendy S. Hesford and Wendy Kozol, eds., *Just Advocacy? Women's Human Rights, Transnational Feminisms, and the Politics of Representation* (New Brunswick: Rutgers University Press, 2005), pp. 221–42.

17. I argued a similar point in my "Cultural Justice and the Limits of Difference: Feminist Contributions to Value Inquiry," *Utopia* 21 (Athens, July-August, 1996): 131–43; and in revised form in J. G. Haber, and M. S. Halfon, eds., *Norms and Values: Essays in Honor of Virginia Held* (Lanham, MD: Rowman and Littlefield, 1998), pp. 73–85. See also my discussion of this point in *Globalizing Democracy and Human Rights*, chapter 5.

18. Sally Engle Merry, "Human Rights Law and the Demonization of Culture (And Anthropology along the Way)," *Polar: Political and Legal Anthropology Review* 26, no. 1 (2003): 55–77.

19. Ibid. See also Sally Engle Merry, *Human Rights and Gender Violence: Translating International Law into Local Justice* (Chicago: University of Chicago Press, 2005).

20. Arati Rao, "The Politics of Gender and Culture in International Human Rights Discourse," in *Women's Rights, Human Rights*, pp. 167–75.

21. Ann Elizabeth Mayer, "Cultural Particularism as a Bar to Women's Rights: Reflections on the Middle Eastern Experience," in *Women's Rights, Human Rights*, pp. 176–88.

22. Brooke Ackerly, "Culture, Gender and Human Rights: A Memorial Essay for Susan Okin," http://web.mit.edu/polisci/research/gender/ackerly_culture_gender_hr.pdf.

23. Abdullahi An-Naim, *Toward an Islamic Reformation: Civil Liberties, Human Rights and International Law* (Syracuse: Syracuse University Press, 1990), cited in Ackerly, "Culture, Gender and Human Rights," p. 17.

24. Alan Gewirth, *Reason and Morality* (Chicago: University of Chicago Press, 1978); *Human Rights* (Chicago: University of Chicago Press, 1982); and "The Basis and Content of Human Rights," in J. R. Pennock, and J. Chapman, eds., *Human Rights, Nomos XXIII* (New York: New York University Press, 1981), pp. 124–34.

25. Carol C. Gould, *Rethinking Democracy* (Cambridge: Cambridge University Press, 1988, chapters 1–3), and *Globalizing Democracy and Human Rights*, chapters 1–2.

26. Carol C. Gould, "The Woman Question: Philosophy of Liberation and the Liberation of Philosophy," *The Philosophical Forum* V, nos. 1–2 (Fall-Winter, 1973–74): 5–44, reprinted in Carol C. Gould and Marx Wartofsky, eds., *Women and Philosophy: Toward a Theory of Liberation* (New York: G.P. Putnam's Sons, 1976).

27. The recent discussion is in Gould, *Globalizing Democracy and Human Rights*, chapter 2.

28. Gould, "The Woman Question."

29. Fiona Robinson, "Care, Gender and Global Social Justice: Rethinking 'Ethical Globalization,'" *Journal of Global Ethics* 2, no. 1 (June, 2006): 5–25.

30. Herta Nagl, ed., "Philosophical Dichotomies and Feminist Thought: Towards a Critical Feminism" *Feministische Philosophie, Wiener Reihe* 4 (Vienna: R. Oldenbourg Verlag, 1990): 184–90.

31. See Carol C. Gould, "Self-Determination beyond Sovereignty: Relating Transnational Democracy to Local Autonomy," in

Carol C. Gould, and Alistair Macleod, eds., *Journal of Social Philosophy* 37, no. 1 (Spring, 2006): 44–60; and "Conceptualizing the Role of Solidarity in Transnational Democracy," forthcoming in Carol C. Gould and Sally Scholz, eds., *Journal of Social Philosophy, Special Issue on Solidarity* 38, no. 1, (Winter, 2007).

32. See Marianne H. Marchand, "Challenging Globalization: Toward a Feminist Understanding of Resistance," *Review of International Studies* 29 (2003): 145–60.

33. Fiona Robinson, "Care, Gender and Global Social Justice," pp. 13–14.

34. See Carol C. Gould, "Conceptualizing the Role of Solidarity in Transnational Democracy."

CHAPTER 3

1. Salazar Parreñas introduces this term. See *Servants of Globalization: Women, Migration, and Domestic Work* (Stanford, CA: Stanford University Press, 2001).

2. In the 1950s, most married American women quit their paying jobs upon the birth of their first child, returning if at all when their children left home. Today, more than 60 percent of all married women living with their husbands work outside the home, including those with young children. Only 13 percent of all American families fit the traditional model of husband as wage-earner and wife as homemaker. Donna E. Young, "Working Across Borders: Global Restructuring and Women's Work," *Utah Law Review* 1 (2001): 3. By suggesting that women have advanced in professional careers, I do not mean to deny that the glass ceiling persists.

3. It is estimated that married women, regardless of employment status, are responsible for 70 to 80 percent of total housework hours. Young, 2001, p. 23.

4. Pierrette Hondagneu-Sotelo, *Doméstica: Immigrant Workers Cleaning and Caring in the Shadows of Affluence* (Berkeley: University of California Press, 2001), pp. 23–24.

5. Joan Tronto introduces this term in her article, "The Nanny Question in Feminism," *Hypatia* 17, no. 2 (2002): 34–51.

6. Ibid, p. 42.

7. Ibid.

8. Pierrette Hondagneu-Sotelo, *Doméstica: Immigrant Workers Cleaning and Caring in the Shadows of Affluence* (Berkeley: University of California Press, 2001), p. 28.

9. Because I focus on the experiences of full-time private domestic workers, I do not address the growing need of working class and lower-middle class women to hire part-time domestic workers. However, the policy reforms I recommend in Section V of this paper would also improve conditions for these employers and domestic workers. For an interesting discussion of the emerging two-tiered domestic service market, see Leslie Salzinger, "A Maid by Any Other Name: The Transformation of 'Dirty Work' by Central American Immigrants," in Michael Burawoy et al., *Ethnography Unbound: Power and Resistance in the Modern Metropolis* (Berkeley: University of California Press, 1991).

10. Joan Tronto and Gabrielle Meagher, "Is it Wrong to Pay for Housework?" *Hypatia* 17, no. 2 (2002): 52–66.

11. Pierrette Hondagneu-Sotelo, *Doméstica: Immigrant Workers Cleaning and Caring in the Shadows of Affluence* (Berkeley: University of California Press, 2001).

12. Ibid; see also Mary Romero, *Maid in the U.S.A.* (New York: Routledge, 2002).

13. Ibid.

14. Ibid.

15. Mary Romero, *Maid in the U.S.A.* (New York: Routledge, 2002). For the purposes of my discussion, I will use the term "migrant" as shorthand for "migrant non-citizen."

16. Ibid.

17. Ibid, p. 57.

18. Joan Tronto, and Gabrielle Meagher, "Is it Wrong to Pay for Housework?" *Hypatia* 17, no. 2 (2002): 52–66; see also Mary Romero, *Maid in the U.S.A.* (New York: Routledge, 2002); see also Pierrette Hondagneu-Sotelo, *Doméstica: Immigrant Workers Cleaning and Caring in the Shadows of Affluence* (Berkeley: University of California Press, 2001).

19. Ibid.

20. Pierrette Hondagneu-Sotelo, *Doméstica: Immigrant Workers Cleaning and Caring in the Shadows of Affluence* (Berkeley: University of California Press, 2001).

21. Joan Tronto, and Gabrielle Meagher, "Is it Wrong to Pay for Housework?" *Hypatia* 17, no. 2 (2002): 52–66; see also Bridget Anderson, *Doing the Dirty Work? The Global Politics of Domestic Labor* (London: Zed Books, 2000).

22. Joan Tronto, and Gabrielle Meagher, "Is it Wrong to Pay for Housework?" *Hypatia* 17, no. 2 (2002): 52–66.

23. Donna E. Young, "Working Across Borders: Global Restructuring and Women's Work," *Utah Law Review* 1 (2001): 3; see also Pierrette Hondagneu-Sotelo, *Doméstica: Immigrant Workers Cleaning and Caring in the Shadows of Affluence* (Berkeley: University of California Press, 2001).

24. Ibid.

25. Pierrette Hondagneu-Sotelo, *Doméstica: Immigrant Workers Cleaning and Caring in the Shadows of Affluence* (Berkeley: University of California Press, 2001).

26. Ibid.

27. For a discussion of neo-nativist legislation and its targeting of migrant women, see Shelley Wilcox, "American Neo-Nativism and Gendered Immigrant Exclusions," in Barbara Andrews, et al, *Feminist Interventions in Ethics and Politics* (Lanham, MD: Rowman and Littlefield, 2005), pp. 213–32.

28. Pierrette Hondagneu-Sotelo, *Doméstica: Immigrant Workers Cleaning and Caring in the Shadows of Affluence* (Berkeley: University of California Press, 2001).

29. Rhacel Salazar Parreñas introduces this term. See *Servants of Globalization: Women, Migration, and Domestic Work* (Stanford, CA: Stanford University Press, 2001), p. 120.

30. Ibid.

31. Ibid.

32. Ibid.

33. Joan Tronto and Gabrielle Meagher, "Is it Wrong to Pay for Housework?" *Hypatia* 17, no. 2 (2002): 52–66.

34. Iris Marion Young, *Justice and the Politics of Difference* (Cambridge: Princeton University Press, 1990), p. 49.

35. Ibid, p. 50.

36. Ibid, pg. 49. Young is discussing MacPherson's account of exploitation here; however, she endorses this aspect of the account.

37. See Young (1990), pp.50–52. See also Christine Delphy, *Close to Home: A Materialist Analysis of Women's Oppression* (Amherst, MA: University of Massachusetts Press).

38. It is unsurprising that "dignity and respect" topped the Domestic Workers' Association of the Coalition of Human Immigrant Rights of Los Angeles list of goals, ranking above a fair salary (Pierrette Hondagneu-Sotelo, *Doméstica: Immigrant Workers Cleaning and Caring in the Shadows of Affluence* (Berkeley: University of California Press, 2001), p. 217.

CHAPTER 4

1. For an interesting discussion of the relation between Western and non-Western feminism, see Alison Jaggar, "Globalizing Feminist Ethics," *Hypatia* 13, no. 2 (1998): 7–52.

2. Iris Marion Young, *On Female Body Experience: Throwing*

Like a Girl and Other Essays (Cary, NC: Oxford University Press, 2005), p. 14.

3. cf. Virginia Held, *The Ethics of Care: Personal, Political and Global* (New York: Oxford University Press, 2006), p. 46.

4. In *Feminist Morality: Transforming Culture, Society, and Politics* (Virginia, Chicago: University of Chicago Press, 1993), p. 14, Virginia Held expresses agreement with other feminists' concerns regarding the dangers of the constructivist, post-modern conception of the self for the feminist movement. She states that "the thinking of women must never become unmoored from the embodied reality of women and men."

5. Virginia Held, *The Ethics of Care: Personal, Political and Global* (New York: Oxford University Press, 2006), p. 48.

6. Diana Tietjens Meyers, "Agency," *A Companion to Feminist Philosophy*, in Alison M. Jaggar and Iris Marion Young, eds., (Oxford: Blackwell Publishers Ltd., 1998), p. 382.

7. Ibid, p. 377.

8. Ibid, p. 378.

9. Ann Ferguson, "Can I Choose Who I Am? And How Would That Empower Me? Gender, Race, Identities and the Self," in Ann Garry, Marilyn Pearsall, eds., *Women, Knowledge, and Reality: Explorations in Feminist Philosophy* (New York: Routledge, 1996, Second Edition), p. 111.

10. Ibid, p. 112.

11. Although proponents of the ethics of care tend to prefer avoiding the language of rights because of its ties to individualistic liberal theories, a defense of rights is essential for feminist philosophy. As Carol Gould argues, "some conception of equal rights is both implicit in the critique of domination and essential to the justification of democracy" (Carol C. Gould, selection from "Feminism and Democratic Community Revisited," in John W. Chapman and Ian Shapiro, eds., *Democratic Community: NOMOS XXXV* (New York University Press, 1993), p. 327.)

12. Roger Gottlieb, "Embodied Love," *Hypatia* 17, no. 3 (2002): 229–30.

13. Martha Nussbaum, "Introduction to the Symposium on Eva Kittay's *Love's Labor: Essays on Women, Equality and Dependency,*" *Hypatia* 17, no. 3 (2002): 198.

14. Ibid, p. 197.

15. Of course, one has to separate the essential elements of Aristotelian anthropology from some of the problematic conclusions to which he arrived—regarding, for example, the inferiority of women and the existence of natural slaves. These conclusions are not necessary consequences of Aristotle's account of human nature, but simply a result of historical and cultural limitations, including an inadequate understanding of human biology.

16. For a more detailed discussion of the Aristotelian theory of action, see Antonio Malo, *Il Senso Antropoligco dell'Azione: Paradigmi e Prospettive* (Rome: Armando Editore, 2004).

17. Schwarzenbach offers an interesting critique of the Marxian concept of praxis in comparison with the Aristotelian concept. According to Schwarzenbach, Marx Wartofsky's Marxian conception of praxis oversimplifies Aristotelian notion by reducing it to "social interaction." Marxists have ignored the fundamental aspect of *praxis* as an activity in which the end lies within the action itself. Schwarzenbach argues that this misunderstanding of praxis led to Marx's failure to recognize the value of caring labor in the home and of caring relations in general. This insight could make an interesting contribution to the ethics of care (Sibyl A. Schwarzenbach, "The Marxian Concept of Praxis," in Carol C. Gould, ed., *Constructivism and Practice: Toward a Historical Epistemology* (Lanham, Maryland: Rowman and Littlefield Publishers, 2003), p. 209.)

18. Aristotle, *Nicomachean Ethics*, trans. H. Rackham, Loeb Classical Library (Cambridge: Harvard University Press, 1999), VI, 2, 1139b 4–5; see also Aristotle, *Metaphysics*, Books I–IX, trans.

Hugh Tredennick, Loeb Classical Library (Cambridge: Harvard University Press, 1996), IX, 1048b22.

19. Margaret Archer, *Being Human: The Problem of Agency* (Cambridge: Cambridge University Press, 2000), pp. 124–25.

20. Ibid, p. 124.

21. Ibid, p. 127.

22. Ibid, p. 128.

23. Ibid, p. 129.

24. Ibid, p. 130.

25. Ibid, p. 132.

26. Ibid, p. 132.

27. Ibid, cf. p. 133.

28. Ibid, cf. pp. 134–45.

29. Ibid, cf. pp. 135–36.

30. Ibid, p. 136.

31. Margaret Archer, *Structure, Agency and the Internal Conversation* (Cambridge: Cambridge University Press, 2003), p. 120.

32. Margaret Archer, *Being Human: The Problem of Agency* (Cambridge: Cambridge University Press, 2000), p. 137.

33. Ibid, pp. 141–42.

34. Ibid, cf. p. 142.

35. Ibid, cf. p. 143.

36. Ibid, cf. pp. 143–44.

37. Ibid, cf. p. 148.

38. Ibid, cf. pp. 149–50

39. Ibid, p. 163.

40. Ibid, cf. p. 164.

41. Ibid, p. 161.

42. Ibid, p. 249.

43. Ibid, p. 190.

44. Ibid, cf. p. 222.

45. Ibid, cf. p. 242.

46. Diana Tietjens Meyers, "Frontiers of Individuality:

Embodiment and Relationships in Cultural Context," *History and Theory* 42 (May, 2003): 285.

47. Alasdair MacIntyre, *Dependent Rational Animals: Why Human Beings Need the Virtues* (London: Duckworth, 1999), p. 8.

48. Ibid, p. 5.

49. Margaret Archer, *Being Human: The Problem of Agency* (Cambridge: Cambridge University Press, 2000), p. 122.

50. Alasdair MacIntyre, *Dependent Rational Animals: Why Human Beings Need the Virtues* (London: Duckworth, 1999), p. 82.

51. Ibid, p. 83.

52. Although here my focus is on the child's development of personal identity, rather than the qualities that parents and other caregivers must have in order to facilitate this development, it is interesting to note that MacIntyre believes parents must have the sort of unqualified commitment to the child that is exemplified by (good) parents of disabled children. This observation could contribute to discussions regarding of the ethics of care, particularly to the work of Eva Feder Kittay.

53. Alasdair MacIntyre, *Dependent Rational Animals: Why Human Beings Need the Virtues* (London: Duckworth, 1999), p. 85.

54. Ibid, p. 94.

55. Ibid, p. 95.

56. Margaret Archer, *Structure, Agency and the Internal Conversation* (Cambridge: Cambridge University Press, 2003), p. 298.

57. Ibid, p. 298.

58. Ibid, cf. pp. 167–68.

59. Ibid, cf. p. 210.

60. Ibid, p. 278.

61. Ibid, cf. pp. 298–99.

62. Ibid, p. 336.

63. Here I am not considering the case of those with extreme mental disabilities.

64. Diana Tietjens Meyers, "Frontiers of Individuality:

Embodiment and Relationships in Cultural Context," *History and Theory* 42 (May, 2003): 274–78.

65. Ibid, cf. p. 276.

66. Milton Diamond and H. K. Sigmundson, "Sex Reassignment at Birth: A Long Term Review and Clinical Implications," *Archives of Pediatric and Adolescent Medicine* 150 (1994): 298–304. Available on-line at: http://www.hawaii.edu/PCSS/online_artcls/intersex/mdfnl.html.

67. Ibid.

68. Larry Cahill, "His Brain, Her Brain," *Scientific American* 292, no. 5 (2005).

69. Other scientists have conducted experiments on monkeys rather than humans to avoid the problem of societal forces that shape sexually differentiated behavior. For example, research conducted on vervet monkeys found that, when presented with a selection of toys, the males tended to play with the more typically masculine toys such as trucks, while the females preferred playing with dolls. Both males and females demonstrated equal interest for typically gender-neutral toys, such as picture books.

70. J. Connellan, S. Baron-Cohen, S. Wheelwright, A. Ba'tki, and J. Ahluwalia, "Sex Differences in Human Neonatal Social Perception," *Infant Behavior and Development* 23, no. 1 (2000): 113–118.

71. Ibid.

72. Peter A. Lawrence, "Men, Women, and Ghosts in Science," *PLoS Biology* 4, no. 1 (2006): e19.

73. L.S. Allen, M. Hines, J. E. Shryne, and R. A. Gorski, "Two Sexually Dimorphic Cell Groups in the Human Brain," *Journal of Neuroscience* 9 (1989): 497–506.

74. Larry Cahill, "His Brain, Her Brain," *Scientific American* 292, no. 5 (2005).

75. Ibid.

76. Here I use the word "natural" to mean "spontaneous."

77. The comments and criticisms of Carol Gould, Michael Kimmel, Chris Beasley and Lucia Ruggerone during the discussion of my paper at the STI Gender Identity Experts Meeting were helpful in making me realize the need to articulate more clearly the distinctions between basic anatomical differences and the tendential differences that may be related to them. On this point I am also indebted to Ana Marta Gonzalez for her clarification of the difficulties involved in trying to draw ethical conclusions from reflection on biological facts.

78. Sarah Blaffer Hrdy, "The Past, Present and Future of the Human Family," in Grethe Peterson, ed., *The Tanner Lectures on Human Values* 23 (Salt Lake City: University of Utah Press, 2001), pp. 57–110; see also Craig Howard Kinsley and Kelly G. Lambert, "The Maternal Brain," *Scientific American* 294, no. 1 (2006); see also Shelley E. Taylor, Brian P. Lewis, Tara L. Gruenewald, Regan A. R. Gurung, John A. Updegraff, and Laura Cousino Klein, "Sex differences in biobehavioral responses to threat: Reply to Geary and Flinn," *Psychological Review* 109, no. 4 (2002): 751–53.

79. Susan J. Brison, "Outliving Oneself: Trauma, Memory and Personal Identity," in Diana T. Meyers and Alison Jaggar, eds., *Feminists Rethink the Self* (Boulder: Westview Press, 1997), p. 16.

80. Sylvia Hewlett, *Creating a Life: Professional Women and the Quest for Children* (New York: Hyperion, 2002).

81. Tina Chanter, "Postmodern Subjectivity," in Alison M. Jaggar and Iris Marion Young, eds., *A Companion to Feminist Philosophy* (Oxford: Blackwell Publishers Ltd., 1998), p. 268.

CHAPTER 5

1. A. Friedman, "Unintended Consequences of the Feminist Sex/Gender Distinction," in *Genders* (2006), p. 43.

2. N. Chodorow, *The Reproduction of Mothering. Psycho-*

analysis and the Sociology of Gender (University of California Press, Los Angeles, 1978).

3. C. Gilligan, *In a Different Voice* (Cambridge, MA: Harvard University Press, 1982).

4. L. Ruggerone, "Immagine del self e identità di genere: come si cresce nella società contemporanea," in E. Besozzi, ed., *Il genere come risorsa comunicativa* (Milano: FrancoAngeli, 2003), pp. 211–29.

5. E. Goffman, *Gender Advertisements* (Cambridge: Harvard University Press, 1979); see also E. Goffman, "The Arrangements Between the Sexes," in *Theory and Society* 4, no. 3 (1977): 301–32.

6. H. Garfinkel, *Studies in Ethnomethodology* (New York: Polity Press, 1967).

7. J. Butler, *Gender Trouble* (London: Routledge, 1990).

8. A. Fausto-Sterling, "The Five Sexes. Why Male and Female Are Not Enough," in *The Sciences* (March/April, 1993): 20–25.

9. In the article "The Five Sexes" Fausto-Sterling claims that, on the basis of her medical experience, in nature not 2 but at least 5 different sexes can be found.

10. Phenomenologists and ethnomethodologists have produced interesting work on this topic and sometimes shown radical examples of bodily impaired individuals, who were able to develop *extra-ordinary* body techniques, in order to find alternative ways of performing their agency with and through their *extra-ordinary* bodies.

11. M. Foucault, "Technologies of the self," in L. H. Martin, et al., *Technologies of the Self: A Seminar with Michel Foucault* (London: Tavistock, 1988), pp. 16–49.

12. M. Foucault, *Discipline and Punish: The Birth of the Prison* (New York: Random House, 1977).

13. This is probably true of non western societies as well: these more traditional systems have at least the merit of not trying to deny their foundation on women's subordination; on the con-

trary they struggle to preserve even the most visible symbols of women's inferior position (for example, the veil, the burka, the restricted access to public places etc…).

14. G. Rubin, "The Traffic in Women: Notes on the Political Economy of Sex," in R. Reiter, ed., *Toward an Anthropology of Women* (New York: Monthly Review Press, 1976), pp. 157–210.

15. S. Bartky, *Femininity and Domination: Studies in the Phenomenology of Oppression* (New York: Routledge, 1990).

16. S. Bordo, *Unbearable Weight: Feminism, Western Culture and The Body* (Berkeley: University of California Press, 1993).

17. S. Bartky, *Femininity and Domination: Studies in the Phenomenology of Oppression* (New York: Routledge, 1990), p. 64.

18. Ibid, p. 75.

19. On this issue see also S. Jeffreys, *Beauty and Misogyny* (London: Routledge, 2005).

20. M. Wittig, "The Category of Sex," in D. Leoard and L. Adkins, eds., *Sex in Question: French Materialist Feminism* (London: Taylor and Francis, 1996), p. 28.

21. E. Wilson, "These New Components of the Spectacle: Fashion and Postmodernism," in R. Boyne and A. Rattansi, eds., *Postmodernism and Society* (London: Macmillan Education, 1990); see also E. Wilson, *Adorned in Dreams* (London: IBTauris, 2003).

22. The idea that feminine beauty and fashion practices can be seen as playful fun rather than oppressive, echoes (and is probably directly inspired by) the theories of Judith Butler (1990) on "performativity." Her work has also inspired queer theorists and activists who argue that by "queering" the performance of gender (like, for example, in practices of cross-dressing or drag) they can actually unsettle mainstream narratives and thereby perform a revolutionary political act.

23. There is a whole school of feminist philosophy arguing that in order to gain their place as social subjects, women must create a new language and a new thought, since the language of theory and especially philosophy has been based on and has devel-

oped out of the exclusion of women and their bodies from discourse. Cfr. A. Cavarero, *Tu che mi guardi, tu che mi racconti* (Milano: Feltrinelli, 1997); see also M.L. Boccia, *La differenza politica* (Milano: Il Saggiatore, 2002).

24. J. Ussher, *Managing the Monstrous Feminine: Regulating the body, regulating woman* (London: Routledge, 2006).

25. Ibid, p. 1.

26. In the article "Fleshing out Gender: Crafting Gender Identity on Women's Bodies" in *Body and Society* 8, no. 2 (2002): 55–77, Valerie Fournier makes a similar point when she suggests that women are denied the materials necessary to make "something of oneself." If modern identity is a project of self-fulfilment (see M. Foucault, *Discipline and Punish: The Birth of the Prison* (Penguin, Harmondsworth, 1977), and M. Foucault, *The History of Sexuality. Volume 1* (Penguin, Harmondsworth, 1982), individuals need to be provided with materials to carry out this project, lest they just emerge as "other than," in this case, men.

27. R. Betterton, *Intimate Distance, Women, Artists and the Body* (London: Routledge, 1996).

28. Ibid.

29. Ibid, p. 135.

30. Ibid, p. 135.

31. L. Irigaray, "The Other Woman," in *I Love to You: Sketch for a Felicity Within History* (London: Routledge, 1996), pp.59–69.

32. S. de Beauvoir, *The Second Sex* (New York: Vintage Books, 1989).

33. J. P. Sartre, *Being and Nothingness* (New York: Washington Square Press, 1992).

34. T. Moi, *Sex, Gender and the Body* (Oxford, New York: Oxford University Press, 2005).

35. Cfr. E. Goffman, *Interaction rituals: essays on face-to-face behavior* (New York: Doubleday Anchor, 1967); see also E. Goffman, *Gender Advertisements* (Cambridge, MA: Harvard University Press, 1979).

36. D. Perpich, "Subjectivity and sexual difference: New figures of the feminine in Irigaray and Cavarero," *Continental Philosophy Review* 36, no. 4 (2003): 391–413.

37. T. Moi, *Sex, Gender and the Body* (Oxford, New York: Oxford University Press, 2005), pp. 62–63.

38. E. Goffman, *Interaction Rituals: Essays on face-to-face Behaviour* (New York: Doubleday Anchor, 1967).

39. T. Moi, *Sex, Gender and the Body* (Oxford, New York: Oxford University Press, 2005), p. 68.

40. Each woman's encounter with patriarchy obviously depends on a vast range of experiences: the socialization she had, her education, her family, the cultural context in which she was brought up, the place where she lives, etc; there are innumerable different ways of living with one's specific body potential as a woman.

41. D. Perpich, "Subjectivity and sexual difference: New figures of the feminine in Irigaray and Cavarero," *Continental Philosophy Review* 36, no. 4 (2003): 391–413.

CHAPTER 6

1. For some helpful historical reflections upon the relationships of modernity to the civilizing mission of colonialism see for instance, Paul Gilroy, *The Black Atlantic: Modernity and Double Consciousness* (Cambridge, MA: Harvard University Press, 1993); see also Mary Louise Pratt, *Imperial Eyes* (London and New York: Routledge, 1992); see also David Brion Davis, *The Problem of Slavery in Western Culture* (Ithica, NY: Cornell University Press, 1970); see also Robert Ross, ed., *Racism and Colonialism: Essays on Ideology and Social Structure* (The Hague: Martinus Nijhoff, 1982).

2. I explored how a Kantian ethical tradition was helped to shape a secularized Protestant tradition within modernity and ways that this encoded a dominant masculinity in *Kant, Respect*

and Injustice: The Limits of Liberal Moral Theory (London and New York: Routledge, 1986). At the time gender was a concern that was largely framed as a feminist concern with philosophy.

3. I was concerned to show how concerns to do with gender that were being framed separately needed to be brought into critical dialogue with traditions of philosophy and social theory in *Unreasonable Men: Masculinity and Social Theory* (London and New York: Routledge, 1994).

4. Feminist concerns about the relationship of power to consciouness were being explored in different ways. There are some helpful reflections in Sheila Rowbotham, *Dreams and Dilemmas* (London: Virago, 1983), which developed some of her earlier notions in *Woman's Consciousness, Man's World* (Harmondsworth: Penguin, 1972). For a useful later collection from the United States see Linda Nicholson, ed., *Feminism/Postmodernism* (New York: Routledge, 1990).

5. Carol Gilligan, *In a Different Voice: Psychological Theory and Women's Development* (Cambridge, MA: Harvard University Press, 1982) made a significant contribution to showing how gender relations of power worked to frame relationships of power and silence between different moral voices. Framed within the terms of development psychology it was keenest in its critique of assumptions underling Kohlberg's scales of moral development revealing relationships of gender where science was framed impartially and universally.

6. Some of Stanley's early philosophical work that had been through a sustained engagement with Wittgenstein and Austin was brought together in *Must We Mean What We Say? Modern Philosophical Essays in Morality, Religion, Drama, Music and Criticism* (New York: Charles Scribner's Sons, 1969). Cavell was also significant in creating possible bridges between analytic and continental traditions in philosophy. He has fostered this exchange in different ways, for example through a engaging with Derrida's readings of Austin.

7. Cavell was influenced in his philosophical writing through an engagement with Wittgenstein's later writings, particularly *Philosophical Investigations* (Oxford: Blackwells, 1958). Cavell's most sustained reading of Wittgenstein is to be found in *The Claim of Reason: Wittgenstein, Skepticism, Morality and Tragedy* (Oxford: The Clarendon Press, 1979).

8. Simone Weil explores the colonial encounter briefly as a theme in the *Need for Roots* (London: Routledge, 1972). But it was a longtime concern going back to her student days when early on she joined those who argued against colonial oppression. For a general introduction to the development of her thinking over time see Lawrence Blum, and Victor J. Seidler, *A Truer Liberty: Simone Weil and Marxism* (New York: Routledge, 1991). Partly due to the influence of Peter Winch and Rush Rhees there was a realization of the resonances between her thinking and that of Wittgenstein. This is a theme that is explored in Peter Winch, *A Just Balance: Reflections on the Philosophy of Simone Weil* (Cambridge: Cambridge University Press, 1989).

9. In a footnote to his paper on "The Availability of the Later Wittgenstein" Cavell recalls a review by Bernard Williams of Stuart Hampshire's *Thought and Action* in *Encounter* XV (November, 1960): 38–42 in which he "suggests on important fact about what I have, parochially, called "modern philosophy" (by which I mean the English and American academic traditions, beginning with Descartes and Locke and never domesticating Hegel and his successors) which, I think, is related to its unconcern with the knowledge of the person and in particular with self-knowledge: viz., its neglect of history as a form of human knowledge (fn p. 68, *Must We Mean What We Say?*). This is an insight that Williams holds and is made evident in his ability to appreciate the post-war work of Isaiah Berlin as a shift towards a different way of doing philosophy, rather than as an abandonment as Berlin himself was likely to think.

10. The place of feeling within philosophy and way that it has tended within a Kantian tradition to be identified with emotions and desires is a theme explored in Victor J. Seidler, *The Moral Limits of Modernity: Love, Inequality and Oppression* (Basingstoke: Macmillan, 1991). It is a concern that I may have picked up from attending Cavell's seminars on Wittgenstein's *Philosophical Investigations* in 1970 but also recognized it as a strength of a sexual politics that refused an easy distinction between reason and emotion.

11. For some interesting reflections drawn from anthropological work on the difficulties of understanding other cultures see for instance, Clifford Geertz, *The Interpretation of Cultures* (New York: Basic Books).

12. For a sense of the development of the notion of hegemonic masculinity see the work by R.W. Connell, *Gender and Power: Society, the Person and Sexual Politics* (Cambridge: Polity Press, 1987) and his more recent editions of *Masculinities* (Cambridge: Polity Press, 1995 and 2006). See also the challenges to generalizing notions of hegemonic masculinities in Victor J. Seidler, *Transforming Masculinities: Men, Cultures, Bodies, Power, Sex and Love* (London: Routledge, 2006).

13. Richard Sennett develops his ideas of the changing nature of identities within the new capitalism in his *The Corrosion of Character: The Personal Consequences of Work in the New Capitalism* (New York: W.W. Norton, 1998). As Richard Rorty comments "Sennett argues, convincingly, that the steadily increasing insecurity experienced by workers is making it impossible for them to achieve a moral identity."

14. There were different versions of "The Apprentice," with slightly different formats developed in different countries. It supposedly shows the reality of a regime of gender equality in which people are supposedly judged on the basis of their individual skills and abilities alone. But the continuing significance of gender is also made clear though it tends to operate at different levels.

15. For some interesting reflections upon the ways that bodies are shaped within different relational environments see, for instance Stanley Kelerman, *Myth and the Body*, a colloquia with Joseph Campbell (Berkeley, CA: Center Press, 1999). For a sense of the conceptual framework developed by Kelerman for the life of the body, see also his *Emotional Anatomy* and *Embodying Experience* also published by the Center Press.

16. For some exploration of how masculinities come to be embodied in different ways partly because of relational histories to do with family and culture, see for instance Victor J. Seidler, *Man Enough: Embodying Masculinities* (London: Sage), p. 19.

17. Some interesting papers that bring together work on men and masculinities in Scandinavia are provided by S. Ervo and T. Johansson, eds., *Among Men: Moulding Masculinities* and *Men's Bodies*, volumes 1 and 2 (Aldershot: Ashgate, 2002).

18. Lucy Rhoades' PhD work entitled "Commune Girls— Growing up in Utropia? Women reflecting back on childhoods in Intensional Community 1970–1985," Department of Sociology, Goldsmiths, University of London brings together extensive interviews with women reflecting back on their experiences and evaluating the impact their alternative histories had on decisions they are making about family and relationships in the present.

19. Ulrich Beck work *Risk Society* translated by Mark Ritter London: Sage 1992, has been influential in shaping the ways social life has changed towards risk and uncertainty in different spheres of life in what he frames as second modernity. See also the helpful reflections upon the changing character of work in Jeremy Rifkin, *The End of Work* (New York: Putnam, 1995), and Scott Lash and John Urry, *The End of Organised Capitalism* (Madison, WI: University of Wisconsin Press, 1987).

20. For some helpful reflections upon the changing nature of love and intimate relations under the pressure of the new capitalism see, for instance, Ulrik Beck and E. Beck-Gersheim, *The Normal Chaos of Love* (Cambridge: Polity Press, 1995).

21. The theme of a fear of intimacy that was associated with men in particular but that seems to have become a concern that has crossed boundaries of gender was a central concern in Victor J. Seidler, *Rediscovering Masculinity: Reason, Language and Sexuality* (London: Routledge, 1987).

22. For helpful discussions about the social nature of time see, for instance, Barbara Adam, *Time and Social Theory* (Philadelphia: Temple University Press, 1990). See also Lotte Bailyn, *Breaking the Mould: Men, Women, and Time in the New Workplace* (New York: Free Press, 1993).

23. Committed to Change Working Together to Stop HIV/Aids Produced by the Guardian in association with Concern Worldwide Saturday, 12/08/06, p.2.

24. Different reflections upon the experience of working around gender issues with men in different contexts of development in the South are explored in Ian Bannon and Maria C. Correia, eds., *The Other Half of Gender: Men's Issues in Development* (Washington: The World Bank, 2006); see also Sandie Ruxton, ed., *Gender Equality and Men: Learning from Practice* (Oxford: Oxfam UK, 2004).

25. For a discussion that draws upon the experiences of young men in different cultural settings and which explores the need to relate to cultural issues in ways that question prevailing Anglophone notions of hegemonic masculinities see for instance, Victor J. Seidler, *Young Men and Masculinities: Global Cultures* and *Intimate Lives* (London: Zed Books, 2006).

Acknowledgement: Themes developed in this piece of work took preliminary form in a co-authored conference paper: Chris Beasley and Juanita Elias, "Situating Masculinities in Global Politics," Refereed Conference Proceedings, *Oceanic Conference on International Studies*, 5–7 July 2006, University of Melbourne, Australia. The conference paper contained two distinct sections, drawing upon the somewhat different areas of expertise of the co-authors. To give due acknowledgement, I have specifically designated those points contributed by my co-author, Juanita Elias, rather than simply noting joint authorship.

CHAPTER 7

1. This paper was prepared for "Gender Identity in a Globalized Society," Experts Meeting of the Social Trends Institute (STI), Barcelona, Spain, 13–14 October, 2006, and was subsequently revised to take note of contributions arising from other papers and in discussion.

2. Such an approach draws upon the initiating impact of feminist analysis, as Kimmel and Clatterbaugh among others have pointed out. Michael Kimmel, "Men and Gender Equality: Resistance or Support?" UNESCO, Seminar within the Capacity Development and Training Programme in Gender Mainstreaming, 16 May, 2006, http://portal.unesco.org/en/ev.php; see also Kenneth Clatterbaugh, *Contemporary Perspectives on Masculinity: Men, Women, and Politics in Modern Society* (Boulder & Oxford: Westview Press, 1990), p. 1. My thanks to Virginia Held for her contribution to the STI discussion on this point.

3. Michael Kimmel, "Integrating Men into the Curriculum," *Duke Journal of Gender, Law and Policy* 4 (March 20, 2006) http://www.law.duke.edu/journals/djglp/articles/gen4p181.htm,; see also Judith K. Gardiner, "Men, Masculinities, and Feminist Theory," in Michael Kimmel, Jeff Hearn, and R. W. Connell, eds., Handbook of Studies on Men & Masculinities, (Thousand Oaks & London: Sage, 2005).

4. Jim McKay, et al., "Gentlemen, the Lunchbox has Landed: Representations of Masculinities and Men's Bodies in the Popular Media," in Kimmel et al., *Handbook*, p. 270.

5. Michael Kimmel, "Invisible Masculinity," *Society* (September/October, 1993): 30; see also Michael Kimmel, "Foreword,"

in Frances Cleaver, ed., *Masculinities Matter!: Men, Gender and Development* (London & N. Y., Zed books, 2003), p. xi.

6. R. W. Connell, *Masculinities* (Sydney: Allen & Unwin, 1995, 2005, 2nd edition), p. xxi.

7. Ibid, pp. 254–55.

8. Ibid, pp. xx–xxi.

9. R. W. Connell, Jeff Hearn, and Michael Kimmel, "Introduction," in Kimmel et al., *Handbook*, p. 9.

10. R. W. Connell, *Masculinities* (2nd edition), p. xxiv.

11. R. W. Connell, et al., "Introduction," in Kimmel et al., *Handbook*, p. 9.

12. R. W. Connell, *Masculinities* (2nd edition), p. xviii; R. W. Connell and James Messerschmidt, "Hegemonic Masculinity: Rethinking the Concept," *Gender & Society* 19, no. 6 (December, 2005): 829–30.

13. William Connolly, *The Terms of Political Discourse*, (Oxford: Martin Robertson, 1974, 1983, 2nd edition), p. 21. My thanks to Carol Bacchi for this point.

14. George Lakoff and Mark Johnson, *Metaphors We Live By* (Chicago & London: University of Chicago Press, 1980), p. 3.

15. Chris Beasley and Carol Bacchi, "Envisioning a New Politics for an Ethical Future: Beyond Trust, Care and Generosity Towards an Ethic of Social Flesh," *Feminist Theory* 8, no. 3 (2007); see also Carol Bacchi, *The Politics of Affirmative Action:'Women,' Equality and Category Politics* (London: Sage, 1996), chapter 1.

16. Jeff Hearn, "From Hegemonic Masculinity to the Hegemony of Men," *Feminist Theory* 5, no. 1 (April, 2004); see also R. W. Connell, "Men's Bodies," in R. W. Connell, *Which Way is Up?* (London & Boston, MA: Allen & Unwin, 1979, 1983); see also Chris Beasley, *Gender & Sexuality: Critical Theories, Critical Thinkers* (Thousand Oaks & London: Sage, 2005), p. 192.

17. Michael Kimmel, "Integrating Men into the Curriculum," *Duke Journal of Gender, Law and Policy* 4 (1997).

18. Robert van Kriekan, et al., *Sociology: Themes and Perspectives*, (Sydney: Pearson Education Australia, 2000, 2nd edition), p. 413.

19. Michael Flood, "Between Men and Masculinity: An Assessment of the Term 'Masculinity' in Recent Scholarship on Men," in Sharyn Pearce and Vivienne Muller, eds., *Manning the next Millennium: Studies in Masculinities* (Perth: Black Swan Press, 2002).

20. Hearn notes this distinction between powerful and widespread in his analysis of notions of dominant or pre-eminent masculinity. Jeff Hearn, "The Swimsuit Issue and Sport: Hegemonic Masculinity in 'Sports Illustrated,'" *The American Journal of Sociology* 103, no. 6 (May, 1998).

21. For a more detailed account of how this slippage occurs, see first section—on hegemonic masculinity—by Chris Beasley, in Chris Beasley and Juanita Elias, "Situating Masculinities in Global Politics," Refereed Conference Proceedings, *Oceanic Conference on International Studies*, 5–7 July 2006, University of Melbourne, Australia.

22. Michael Flood, "Between Men and Masculinity: An Assessment of the Term 'Masculinity' in Recent Scholarship on Men," in Sharyn Pearce and Vivienne Muller, eds., *Manning the next Millennium: Studies in Masculinities* (Perth: Black Swan Press, 2002).

23. In 2006, R. W. Connell took up a transgender positioning. However, I refer to Connell in this paper as "he," because the works which I discuss were written when the masculine pronoun was appropriate.

24. R. W. Connell, *The Men and the Boys* (Cambridge: Polity Press, 2000), p. 30; Connell and Messerschmidt, "Hegemonic Masculinity," pp. 838, 846; see also Chris Beasley, *Gender & Sexuality*: 229; see also Patricia Y. Martin, "Why can't a Man be more like a Woman? Reflections on Connell's Masculinities," *Gender & Society* 12 (1998): 473.

25. R. W. Connell, "Reply," *Gender & Society* 12 (1998): 476.

26. Connell and Messerschmidt, "Hegemonic Masculinity," pp. 846, 852–53.

27. Ibid, p. 846, emphasis added.

28. Michael Flood, "Between Men and Masculinity: An Assessment of the Term 'Masculinity' in Recent Scholarship on Men," in Sharyn Pearce and Vivienne Muller, eds., *Manning the next Millennium: Studies in Masculinities* (Perth: Black Swan Press, 2002.)

29. Ken Plummer, "Male Sexualities," in Kimmel et al., *Handbook*, pp. 181–82, Michael Kimmel, *The Gender of Desire: Essays on Male Sexuality* (Albany, NY: SUNY Press, 2005), p. 71; see also Michael Kimmel, "Mars and Venus, or Planet Earth: Women and Men at Work in the 21st Century," Lecture for the European Professional Women's Network, 25 May 2005, Paris, http://www.europeanwn.net/tht_career/articles_indiv_career/m_kimmel_wom_men.html; see also Cliff Cheng, "Marginalized Masculinities and Hegemonic Masculinity: Introduction," The Journal of Men's Studies 7, no. 3 (Spring, 1999); see also Geert Hofstede, Culture's Consequences (Beverly Hills, CA.: Sage, 1984).

30. Kenneth Clatterbaugh, "What is Problematic about Masculinities?" *Men and Masculinities* 1 (July, 1998): 33.

31. Website, http://www.kpmg.com.au, 20 March, 2006.

32. Connell and Messerschmidt, "Hegemonic Masculinity," p. 838.

33. The utility is a peculiarly Australian vehicle, broadly similar to the American "pickup truck." However, it has a single body, with two seat front compartment and open tray with sides at the back.

34. The female character is not, however, simply marked by her clothing. Her bodily "repertoire" is also telling, signaling not only a hyper-feminine display, but importantly heterosexual availability. She appears in the front seat of the utility beside the male character with her body turned towards his, head slightly tilted to

one side, smiling seductively, eyes wide, concentrating on his face, and one hand playing with her long hair. Such a bodily presentation stands in as normative code for heterosexual masculine fantasy, and by this means she confirms the cross-class legitimacy of his manhood as an appropriate ideal. (For discussion of gendered bodily display, see Lucia Ruggerone, "Bodies Between Genders: In Search of New Forms of Identity," "Gender Identity in a Globalized Society," Experts Meeting of the Social Trends Institute (STI), Barcelona, Spain, 13–14 October, 2006.

35. The former TV host in question is Suzie Wilks. When questioned about the advertisement, she asserted that complaints about it showed a lack of a sense of humor and that she was a role model for women. Steve Connolly, "Greer Smear Rejected," *The Advertiser*, 10 March, 2006.

36. Greg Stolz, "Mellow Greer Less Fiery on Feminism," *The Courier-Mail*, March 9, 2006; Connolly, "Greer smear rejected"; see also Katherine Kizilos, "Greer's Spray on Ads Hits a Nerve in Objects and Subjects," *The Age*, March 10, 2006.

37. For use of the term, "mateship," by Prime Minister John Howard, leader of the conservative Liberal Party, see Carol Johnson, "Shaping the Culture: Howard's 'Values' and Australian Identity," paper presented at Politics Discipline seminar series, University of Adelaide, 20 March, 2006; see also Judith Brett, *Australian Liberals and the Moral Middle Class: From Alfred Deakin to John Howard* (Melbourne: Cambridge Univeristy Press, 2003), pp. 183–216.

38. Matt Price, "Mateship Misses the Mark," *The Australian*, Tuesday, 26 September, 2006; "Latham's Latest: Revenge of nerds prompts new book," *Advertiser*, Tuesday, 26 September, 2006, p. 27; see also Catherine McGrath, "Latham says US Alliance Makes Australia More of a Terrorist Target," *AM*, ABC Radio transcript, Monday 19 September, 2005, http://www.abc.net.au/am/content/2005/s1463058.htm. Other examples of the importance of

working class inflected manhood in Australia include the iconic status of singers such as Jimmie Barnes, who became known internationally for his song "Working Class Man," and the box-office success of Paul Hogan in the Crocodile Dundee films, a comic actor strongly identified by Australian audiences with his working class origins. For ethnographic work on related models of manhood amongst Australian teenagers, see Martino, Wayne, "'Cool Boys,' 'Party Animals,' 'Squids,' and 'Poofters': Interrogating the Dynamics and Politics of Adolescent Masculinities in School," British Journal of Sociology of Education 20, no. 2 (1999).

39. Bethan Benwell, "Introduction," in Bethan Benwell, ed., *Masculinities and Men's Lifestyle Magazines* (Oxford: Blackwell, 2003), p. 13. Michael Kimmel has suggested that the valorizing of working class inflected masculinity may also be relevant to the United States. In discussion at the STI Experts Meeting ("Gender Identity in a Globalized Society," Barcelona, Spain, 13–14 October, 2006), he postulated that the presumed hyper-masculinity of working class men speaks to a sense of emasculation amongst middle class white men. Hence, the latter "buy" both literally and metaphorically the restorative power of an idealized image of working class manhood by consuming products that reference the hard "purity" of manual labor and the untainted physicality of the cowboy, such as can be found in Timberland boots, Stetson cologne and Chaps denim shirts. I thank also Carol Gould and Nira Yuval-Davis for their contributions to this discussion.

40. Connell et al., "Introduction," in Michael Kimmel, et al eds., *Handbook of Studies on Men & Masculinities* (Thousand Oaks & London: Sage, 2005), p. 9.

41. Michael Kimmel, "Globalization and its Mal(e)contents: 'The Gendered Moral and Political Economy of Terrorism,'" in Kimmel et al., *Handbook*, p. 415.

42. R.W. Connell, *The Men and the Boys* (Cambridge: Polity Press, 2000), p. 46.

43. Interestingly, here Connell makes plain, by employing Altman's analysis, that hegemonic masculinity in the global gender order is not necessarily marked by homophobia, nor does this global form necessarily have the same sexual relation to women. Given that homophobia and heterosexuality marked by gender hierarchy are taken as central to his earlier (local/national/western) account of hegemonic masculinity (as is also the case for most Masculinity Studies writers—for example, Plummer), it is odd that this presumably highly important shift does not produce a discussion which might involve some reconsideration of the term integrating earlier and more recent global accounts. At the very least the global analysis suggests that Connell (and others) might need to rethink earlier assumptions about the fit between Gender and Sexuality as axes of social structuring. At most, the shift suggests a rethinking of hegemonic masculinity as supposedly precisely about upholding gender hierarchy. Dennis Altman, *Global Sex* (Chicago: University of Chicago Press, 2001); see also Connell, *Masculinities* (2nd edition), pp. 78–79; see also R. W. Connell and Julian Wood, "Globalization and Business Masculinities," *Men and Masculinities* 7, no. 4 (April, 2005): 359; Plummer, "Male Sexualities."

44. Connell, *Masculinities* (2nd edition), p. xxiii, pp. 255–56; R. W. Connell, "Globalization, Imperialism, and Masculinities," in Kimmel et al., *Handbook*, p. 77.

45. Even Connell's own critique of globalization literature as the view from the metropole, a projection from "the centre," involving erasure of the non-metropolitan world seems only somewhat integrated into his analysis of hegemonic masculinity, which for the most part appears schematic and from the vantage point of considering the spread of that which he associates with the hegemonic. North Atlantic, white, class-privileged, heterosexual men remain centre stage in the analysis. The non-metropolitan and those cast as peripheral tend to remain in the shadows. R. W. Con-

nell, "The Northern Theory of Globalization," paper delivered at the Sociology Seminar Series, Flinders University, South Australia, 7/10/2005; see also Beasley, *Gender & Sexuality*, p. 215; Judith Newton, "White Guys," *Feminist Studies* 24, no. 3 (Fall, 1998).

46. See for example, Paul Hirst, and Grahame Thompson, *Globalization in Question: The International Economy and the Possibilities of Governance* (Cambridge: Polity Press, 1999, 2nd edition), chapter 2, pp. 19–42; see also Michael Mann, "Globalization and September 11," *New Left Review* 12 (November/December, 2001): 51–72; see also for an uneven and pluralized account of economics within globalizing processes, V. Spike Peterson, "Plural Processes, Patterned Connections," *Globalizations* 1, no. 1 (September 2004).

47. Connell, *Masculinities* (2nd edition), pp. 86, 185–203; Connell, *The Men and the Boys*, pp. 40–56.

48. Kate Hughes, Review of *The Men and the Boys*, *Arena Magazine* (April, 2001): 46.

49. The analysis of Connell's linkage between gender and class is developed further in Beasley, *Gender & Sexuality*, for example, pp. 226–28; see also Newton, "White Guys."

50. Connell and Messerschmidt, "Hegemonic Masculinity," p. 837; see also Harry Brod, "Some thoughts on some histories of some masculinities: Jews and other Others," in Harry Brod and Michael Kaufman, eds., *Theorizing Masculinities* (London & Thousand Oaks, CA: Sage, 1994), pp. 85, 87 (quoting Michael Kimmel), and 89.

51. See second section—on feminist analyses of gender and globalisation—by Juanita Elias, in Beasley and Elias, "Situating Masculinities."

52. For example, Kimmel, "Globalization and its Mal(e)contents," pp. 414–17.

53. Connell, "Globalization, Imperialism, and Masculinities," p. 73.

54. There are indeed few analyses which show *how* legitimating processes actually work in relation to masculinity. Some directions for investigating their operation may be found in Michael Kimmel, "Globalization and its Mal(e)contents: The Gendered Moral and Political Economy of the Extreme Right," "Gender Identity in a Globalized Society," Experts Meeting of the Social Trends Institute (STI), Barcelona, Spain, 13–14 October, 2006.

55. For a discussion of the issues at stake in clarifying the meaning of terms, see Chris Beasley, "Speaking of feminism . . . what are we arguing about?: difference and the politics of meaning," in Lynda Burns, ed., *Feminist Alliances* (Amsterdam & New York: Rudopi, 2006,) and Chris Beasley, "Negotiating difference: debatable feminism," in Carol Bacchi and Paul Nursey-Bray, eds., *Left Directions: Is There a Third Way?* (Perth: University of Western Australia Press, 2001).

56. See endnote above regarding definitional matters.

57. The study of socially dominant men may perhaps be conceptualized following Donaldson's terminology of "the masculinity of the hegemonic," but once again I am uncertain about the use of the word hegemonic. "The masculinity of the dominant" seems to me a more accurate way to describe what Donaldson wants to highlight. Mike Donaldson, "What is Hegemonic Masculinity?" *Theory and Society* 22 (1993).

58. Working class models of manhood that I have identified in relation to Australia and elsewhere are clearly culture-specific and do not necessarily resonate as mobilizing ideals in other sites. For an account of male identity construction located in Italy that demonstrates this point, see Emanuela Mora, "Clothing as Men's Identity Resources. The Case of the Italian Fashion Industry," "Gender Identity in a Globalized Society," Experts Meeting of the Social Trends Institute (STI), Barcelona, Spain, 13–14 October, 2006.

59. R. W. Connell, *Masculinities* (2nd edition), pp. xviii–xix, 72–73; see also Connell, *Gender* (Oxford: Polity, 2002), p. 71; see also Connell, *The Men and the Boys* (2000), pp. 20–21; see also Hearn, "The Swimsuit Issue," Jeff Hearn, "Is Masculinity dead? A critical account of the concept of masculinity/masculinities," in Máirtín Mac an Ghaill ed., *Understanding Masculinities—Social Relations and Cultural Arenas*, Milton Keynes: Open UP, 1996; see also Jeff Hearn, and David Collinson, "Theorizing unities and differences between men and masculinities," in Brod and Kaufman, *Theorizing Masculinities*; Clatterbaugh, "What is problematic about Masculinities?"

60. Connell and Messerschmidt, "Hegemonic Masculinity," pp. 831, 838, 841.

61. Ibid, p. 842, emphasis added.

62. Connell, *Gender* (2002), p. 71; Connell, *The Men and the Boys* (2000), pp. 1–20.

63. Connell, *Masculinities* (2nd edition), p. xix.

64. Connell and Messerschmidt, p. 846

65. For example, if dominant and hegemonic masculinities are not equated, this has a significant impact on the focus of political work to achieve gender equality—on the development of counter-hegemonic strategies—and hence has important implications for the constitution of what Carol Gould has designated as resistant "network solidarities" at both national and global levels. Carol Gould, "Women's Human Rights in a Culturally Diverse World," "Gender Identity in a Globalized Society," Experts Meeting of the Social Trends Institute (STI), Barcelona, Spain, 13–14 October, 2006.

66. Fred Block, *Post-Industrial Possibilities: A Critique of Economic Discourse* (University of California Press, 1990).

67. Points regarding critical globalization scholarship within the paper were developed by Juanita Elias, in Beasley and Elias, "Situating Masculinities."

68. Connell and Messerschmidt, "Hegemonic Masculinity," pp. 840–41, 845.

69. Ibid, p. 850.

70. Ibid, p.845.

71. Annamarie Jagose, Interview with Judith Halberstam, "Masculinity without Men," *Genders* 29 (1999). This taxonomical impulse is developed in relation to Queer theorizing and "female masculinity" in Halberstam's work (see for example Judith Halberstam, *Female Masculinity* (Durham, NC & London: Duke UP, 1998).)

72. These terms are intended to extend the existing concern in Masculinity Studies with relations between masculinities to hegemonic masculinity. Nevertheless, the distinction between supra and sub hegemonic masculinities requires further clarification and empirical research. As I have indicated in relation to Connell's work, more analysis is required regarding how legitimization occurs, and thus why one masculinity may be more critical to it and more overarching in mobilizing solidarity across a wide range of masculinities. With regard to clarifying the meaning of these terms as against other commonly used languages such as "hyper" and "hypo" masculinity, it is worth noting that the latter terms refer not so much to political legitimization as to the degree of particular characteristics that at any one time may be associated with normative manliness. Thus it is possible for an individual or group to exhibit what is deemed hyper-masculinity but not to be constituted as an ideal, not to mobilize legitimization. For example, bike gang members in Australia epitomize a hyper-masculinity but do not widely mobilize political legitimization and hence do not invoke sub, let alone supra, hegemonic status.

73. A recent television advertisement in the United States for an SUV, a vehicle named the Hummer (tinyurl.com/mea23), invoked a similar form of beefy working class masculinity to that which I have outlined in relation to the Holden Rodeo advertise-

ment in Australia (see "Extreme Dining," *The Guardian*, Wednesday August 23, 2006, http://www.guardian.co.uk/g2/story/ 0,,1856005,00.html). My thanks to Juanita Elias for this reference. For a related analysis of the Land Rover "Himba" advertisement screened in South Africa, see Jeanne Van Eeden, "Land Rover and Colonial-Style Adventure: the 'Himba' Advertisement," *International Feminist Journal of Politics* 8, no. 3 (September 2006).

74. Randall Germain, "Introduction: Globalization and its Critics" in Randall D. Germain, ed., *Globalization and its Critics: Perspectives from Political Economy* (Basingstoke: MacMillan, 2000), pp. xiii–xx.

75. This analysis draws upon the work of Juanita Elias, in Beasley and Elias, "Situating Masculinities."

76. Bob Pease, "Moving beyond Mateship: Reconstructing Australian Men's Practices," in Bob Pease and Keith Pringle, eds., *A Man's World?: Changing Men's Practices in a Globalized World* (London & New York: Zed Books, 2001); see also endnote 42 for further discussion of the ways in which Connell's depiction of a monolithic global hegemonic masculinity may not capture sufficiently the particular relationships between metropolitan centre and local periphery that characterize sites like Australia.

77. Anna Johnston and Alan Lawson, "Settler Colonies," in Henry Schwarz and Sangeeta Ray, eds., *A Companion to Postcolonial Studies* (Oxford: Blackwell, 2000), p. 361; Brian Kiernan, "Australia's Postcoloniality," *Antipodes 11* 14, no. 1 (June, 2000): 12.

78. Connell, *Masculinities* (2nd edition), p. xviii.

CHAPTER 8

1. Barrington Moore, *The Social Origins of Democracy and Dictatorship: Lord and Peasant in the Making of the Modern World* (Boston: Beacon, 1966), p. 505.

2. R. W. Connell, "Masculinities and Globalization" in *Men and Masculinities* 1, no. 1 (1998).

3. M. Sinha, *Colonial Masculinity: The Manly Englishman and the Effeminate Bengali in the Late Nineteenth Century* (Manchester: Manchester University Press, 1995).

4. R. W. Connell, "Masculinities and Globalization" in *Men and Masculinities* 1, no.1, (1998): 14.

5. Ibid, p. 15.

6. Ibid.

7. Mark, Juergensmeyer, *The New Cold War? Religious Nationalism Confronts the Secular State* (Berkeley: University of California Press, 1993); see also Mark Juergensmeyer, *Terror in the Mind of God: The Global Rise of Religious Violence* (Berkeley: University of California Press, 2000); see also B. Barber, *MacDonalds and Jihad* (New York: Simon and Schuster, 1992).

8. M. Kimmel, *Manhood in America: A Cultural History* (New York: Free Press, 1996); see also M. Kimmel, *The Politics of Manhood* (Philadelphia: Temple University Press, 1996); see also M. Messner, *Politics of Masculinities: Men and Movements* (Newbury Park: Pine Forge, 1998).

9. B. Ehrenreich, "The Making of McVeigh," *The Progressive*, July, 2001.

10. R. Barro, "The Myth that Poverty Breeds Terrorism," *Business Week*, June 10, 2002, p. 26; see also N. Kristof, "What Does and Doesn't Fuel Terrorism," *The International Herald Tribune*, May 8, 2002, p. 13; see also N. Kristof, "All-American Osamas," *The New York Times*, June 7, 2002, p. A–27.

11. Let me make clear that I explore here only the terrorism of social movements, such as Al Qaeda, and not the systematic terrorism of states, where terror is a matter of political strategy or military opportunity. My analysis, however, may well apply to social movements in the former Yugoslavia, as well as other cases.

12. J. Hearn, *Men in the Public Eye* (London: Routledge, 1996); see also J. Hearn, *The Violences of Men* (London: Routledge, 1997).

13. R. W. Connell, *Masculinities* (Berkeley: University of California Press, 1995), pp. 109–112.

14. Ibid, p. 109.

15. This section is based on collaborative work with Abby Ferber, and appears in Kimmel and Ferber, 2000.

16. *Intelligence Report*, Spring, 2002.

17. J. Kramer, "The Patriot," *The New Yorker*, May 6, 2002, p. 104.

18. Ibid, p. 119.

19. K. Blee, *Inside Organized Racism: Women in the Hate Movement* (Berkeley: University of California Press, 2002).

20. Quoted in Citizens Project, 3.

21. B. Dobratz, and S. Shanks-Meile, *The White Separatist Movement in the United States: White Power! White Pride!* (Baltimore: Johns Hopkins University Press, 2001), p. 10.

22. L. Rubin, *Families on the Fault Line* (New York: Harper-Collins, 1994), p. 186.

23. B. Dobratz, and S. Shanks-Meile, *The White Separatist Movement in the United States: White Power! White Pride!* (Baltimore: Johns Hopkins University Press, 2001), p. 115.

24. J. Coplon, "The Roots of Skinhead Violence: Dim Economic Prospects for Young Men," *Utne Reader* (May/June, 1989): 84.

25. B. Dobratz and S. Shanks-Meile, *The White Separatist Movement in the United States: White Power! White Pride!* (Baltimore: Johns Hopkins University Press, 2001), p. 160.

26. W.A.R. 8 (2), 1989, p. 11.

27. A. L. Ferber, *White Man Falling: Race, Gender and White Supremacy* (Lanham, MD: Rowman and Littlefield, 1998), p. 81.

28. Ibid, p. 76.

29. Ibid, p. 91.

30. Of course, there is a well-developed literature on the "gendered" elements of Nazism that underlies my work here. See especially K. Theweleit, *Male Fantasies*, volumes I and II, trans. Stephen Conway, Erica Carter, and Chris Turner (Minneapolis: University of Minnesota Press, 1987, 1989).

31. A. L. Ferber, *White Man Falling: Race, Gender and White Supremacy* (Lanham, MD: Rowman and Littlefield, 1998), p. 140.

32. *Racial Loyalty* 72 (1991): 3.

33. W. Pierce, *The Turner Diaries* (Hillsboro, VA: National Vanguard Books, 1978), p. 42.

34. A. L. Ferber, *White Man Falling: Race, Gender and White Supremacy* (Lanham, MD: Rowman and Littlefield, 1998), pp. 125–26.

35. Ibid, p. 127.

36. W. Pierce, *The Turner Diaries* (Hillsboro, VA: National Vanguard Books, 1978), p. 33.

37. A. L. Ferber, *White Man Falling: Race, Gender and White Supremacy* (Lanham, MD: Rowman and Littlefield, 1998), p. 136.

38. R. Blazak, "White Boys to Terrorist Men: Target Recruitment of Nazi Skinheads," *American Behavioral Scientist* 44, no. 6 (February, 2001): 991.

39. A. L. Ferber, *White Man Falling: Race, Gender and White Supremacy* (Lanham, MD: Rowman and Littlefield, 1998), p. 139.

40. Katrine Fangen, "Pride and Power: a Sociological Interpretation of the Norwegian Radical Nationalist Underground Movement," Ph.D. dissertation, Department of Sociology and Human Geography, University of Oslo, 1999, p. 36.

41. Katrine Fangen, "On the Margins of Life: Life Stories of Radical Nationalists," *Acta Sociologica* 42 (1999): 359–63.

42. This downward mobility marks these racist skinheads from their British counterparts, who have been embedded within working class culture. These young Nordic lower-middle class boys

do not participate in a violent, racist counter-culture as preparation for their working lives on the shop floor. Rather, like their American counterparts, they see *no* future in the labor market. They do not yearn nostalgically for the collective solidarity of the shop floor; for them that life was already gone.

43. Katrine Fangen, "Pride and Power: a Sociological Interpretation of the Norwegian Radical Nationalist Underground Movement," Ph.D. dissertation, Department of Sociology and Human Geography, University of Oslo, 1999, p. 84.

44. Katrine Fangen, "Death Mask of Masculinity," in Soren Ervo, ed., *Images of Masculinities: Moulding Masculinities*, (London: Ashgate, 1999), p. 2.

45. Katrine Fangen, "Living Out our Ethnic Instincts: Ideological Beliefs among Rightist Activists in Norway," in Jeffrey Kaplan and Tore Bjorgo, eds., *Nation and Race: The Developing Euro-American Racist Subculture*, (Boston: Northeastern University Press, 1998), p. 214.

46. I have changed the names of individual interviewees and changed a few details so they would not be recognizable. Names of staff at Exit and other names have not been changed. All quotes are from interviews, except as noted.

47. Karl-Olov Arnstberg and Jonas Hallen, *Smaka Kanga: Intervjuer med avhoppade nynazister* (Stockholm: Fryhusset, 2000), p. 9.

48. EXIT, *EXIT: A Way Through: Facing NeoNazism and Racism among Youth*, published by EXIT (2000), p. 5.

49. Ibid, pp. 3–4.

50. Katja Wahlstrom, *The Way Out of Racism and Nazism* (Stockholm: Save the Children Foundation, 2001), pp. 13–14.

51. EXIT, *EXIT: A Way Through: Facing NeoNazism and Racism among Youth*, published by EXIT (2000), p. 6.

52. Karl-Olov Arnstberg, and Jonas Hallen, *Smaka Kanga: Intervjuer med avhoppade nynazister* (Stockholm: Fryhusset, 2000).

53. Ibid, p. 13.

54. Les Back, "Wagner and Power Chords: Skinheadism, White Power Music, and the Internet," in Vron Ware and Les Back, eds., *Our of Whiteness: Color, Politics and Culture*, (Chicago: University of Chicago Press, 2002), p. 114.

55. Karl-Olov Arnstberg and Jonas Hallen, *Smaka Kanga: Intervjuer med avhoppade nynazister* (Stockholm: Fryhusset, 2000), p. 23.

56. T. Bjorgo, *Racist and Right-Wing Violence in Scandinavia: Patterns, Perpetrators, and Responses* (Leiden: University of Leiden, 1997), p. 234.

57. Karl-Olov Arnstberg and Jonas Hallen, *Smaka Kanga: Intervjuer med avhoppade nynazister* (Stockholm: Fryhusset, 2000), p. 7.

58. EXIT, *EXIT: A Way Through: Facing NeoNazism and Racism among Youth*, published by EXIT (2000), p. 3.

59. The difference with the American White Supremacists could not be starker. In a page that feels torn from the recent book *What's the Matter with Kansas*, the American men would happily sign away all mineral extraction and environmental protection to the very corporations that are undercutting their artisanal ways of life.

60. EXIT, *EXIT: A Way Through: Facing NeoNazism and Racism among Youth*, published by EXIT (2000), p. 7.

61. Karl-Olov Arnstberg and Jonas Hallen, *Smaka Kanga: Intervjuer med avhoppade nynazister* (Stockholm: Fryhusset, 2000), p. 31.

62. Katrine Fangen, "Death Mask of Masculinity," in Soren Ervo, ed., *Images of Masculinities: Moulding Masculinities* (London: Ashgate, 1999), p. 36.

63. T. Bjorgo, *Racist and Right-Wing Violence in Scandinavia: Patterns, Perpetrators, and Responses* (Leiden: University of Leiden, 1997), p. 136.

64. Martin Durham, "Women and the Extreme Right: A Comment," *Terrorism and Political Violence* 9 (1997): 165–68.

65. Ibid.

66. Helene, Loow, "Racist Youth Culture in Sweden: Ideology, Mythology, and Lifestyle," in C. Westin, ed., *Racism, Ideology and Political Organisation* (Stockholm: CEIFO Publications, University of Stockholm, 1998), p. 134.

67. In that sense, these groups are similar to British groups such as Blood and Soil, and the Patriotic Vegetarian and Vegan Society.

68. P. Marsden, *The Taliban: War and Religion in Afghanistan* (London: Zed, 2002), pp. 29–31.

69. "Who They Are," 2002, *Newsweek,* April 15.

70. Nasra Hassan, "An Arsenal of Believers," *The New Yorker,* 19 November, 2001, p. 36.

71. Tony Judt, "America and the War," *The New York Review of Books* 48, no. 18, www.nybooks.com/articles/14760, November 15, 2001.

72. B. Crossette, "Living in a World Without Women," *The New York Times,* 4 October, 2001, p. 1.

73. B. Ehrenreich, "The Making of McVeigh," *The Progressive,* July, 2001.

74. P. Marsden, *The Taliban: War and Religion in Afghanistan* (London: Zed, 2002), p. 99.

75. *The New York Times Magazine,* 7 October.

76. All unattributed quotes come from a fascinating portrait of Atta in J. Yardley, "A Portrait of the Terrorist: From Shy Child to Single-Minded Killer," *The New York Times,* 10 October, 2001.

77. CNN, 2 October, 2001.

78. *Intelligence Report,* Winter, 2001.

79. J. Ridgeway, "Osama's New Recruits," *The Village Voice,* 6 November, 2001, p. 41.

CHAPTER 9

1. N. McKendrick, J. Brewer and J.H. Plumb, *The Birth of a Consumer Society: The Commercialization of Eighteenth-Century England* (Indiana University Press, Bloomington, Indiana, 1982); see also R. Bowlby, *Just Looking: Consumer Culture in Dreiser, Gissing & Zola* (London: Routledge, 1985).

2. V. De Grazia, E. Furlough, eds., *The Sex of Things. Gender and Consumption in Historical Perspective* (Berkeley: University of California Press, 1996).

3. P. Bourdieu, *La distinzione. Critica sociale del gusto* (Bologna: Il Mulino, 1983, 1979).

4. S. Bellassai, *La mascolinità contemporanea* (Rome: Carocci, 2004), p. 11.

5. J. Berger, *Questione di sguardi* (Milano: Il Saggiatore, 2002, original edition 1972).

6. P. Hirsch, "Processing Fads and Fashions: An Organizational-Set Analysis of Cultural Industry Systems," *American Journal of Sociology* LXXVII (1972): 639–59.

7. E. Rouse, *Understanding Fashion* (London: Blackwell, 1989).

8. D. Crane, *Questioni di moda. Classe, genere, identità nell'abbigliamento* (Milano: FrancoAngeli, 2004, 2000).

9. L. Boltanski, *Stati di pace. Una sociologia dell'amore* (Milano: Vita & Pensiero, 2005, 1990); see also M. Foucault, *L'archeologia del sapere. Una metodologia per la storia della cultura* (Milano: Rizzoli, 1980, original edition 1969).

10. G. Vattimo, *Il soggetto e la maschera. Nietsche e il problema della liberazione* (Milano, Bompiani, 1974).

11. P. Bourdieu, *Il Dominio Maschile* (Milano: Feltrinelli, 1998, original edition 1998).

12. J. C. Fluegel, *Psicologia dell'abbigliamento* (Milano: FrancoAngeli, 2000, 1930); see also T. Veblen, *La teoria della classe agiata* (Turin: Edizioni di Comunità, 1999, 1899).

13. G. Deleuze, Guattari F., *L'anti-edipo. Capitalismo e schizofrenia* (Turin: Einaudi, 1975, 1972); see also R. Rorty, *La Filosofia e lo specchio della natura* (Milano: Bompiani, 1986, original edition 1979).

14. V. Marchetti, *Fissazioni e transizioni*, in Bellassai and Malatesta (2000), p. 103.

15. I. Kopytoff, *La biografia culturale degli oggetti: La mercificazione come processo*, in E. Mora (2005), pp. 101–102.

16. E. Rouse, *Understanding Fashion* (London: Blackwell, 1989).

17. W. Sombart, *Dal lusso al capitalismo* (Roma: Armando, 2003, 1922); see also A. Ghirardi, *Strategie dell'apparire. Ritratti d'amore e di morte nell'Italia Moderna* (Belfanti and Giusberti, 2003), pp. 149–83.

18. D. Roche, *Il linguaggio della moda. Alle origini del'industria dell'abbigliamento* (Turin: Einaudi, 1991, 1989), p. 90.

19. Ibid.

20. C. Campbell, *L'etica romantica e lo spirito del consumismo moderno* (Roma: Edizioni Lavoro, 1992, 1987).

21. E. Morini, *Storia della moda. XVIII—XX secolo* (Milano: Skira, 2000).

22. A. Ferrara, *Autenticità riflessiva. Il progetto della modernità dopo la svolta lingüistica* (Milano: Feltrinelli, 1998), pp. 27–28.

23. J. MacInnes, *The End of Masculinity* (Buckingham: Oxford University Press).

24. Ibid, (1998), p. 2.

25. L. Boltanski, *Stati di Pace. Una sociologia dell'amore* (Milano: Vita & Pensiero, 2005, original edition 1990), p. 25.

26. Ibid, p. 25.

27. J. C. Fluegel, *Psicologia dell'Abbigliamento* (Milano: FrancoAngeli, 2000, original edition 1930).

28. P. Bollon, *Elogio dell'apparenza. Gli stili di vita dai merveilleux ai punk* (Costa & Genoa Nolan, 1991, 1990); see also D.

Hebdige, *Sottocultura. Il fascino di uno stile innaturale* (Costa & Genoa Nolan, 1990, 1979).

29. E. Moers, *Storia inimitabile del dandy* (Milano: Rizzoli, 1965, 1960), pp. 40–41; see also D. Hebdige, *Subculture. The Meaning of Style* (London: Routledge, 1979).

30. J. C. Fluegel, *Psicologia dell'abbigliamento* (Milano: FrancoAngeli, 2000, 1930), p. 123.

31. Ibid, pp. 124–25.

32. E. Moers, *Storia inimitabile del dandy* (Milano: Rizzoli, 1965, 1960).

33. C. Breward, *The Dandy Laid Bare: Embodying Practices and Fashion for Men* (Bruzi and Church Gibson, 2000), pp. 221–38.

34. R. Dellamora, *Homosexual Scandal and Compulsory Heterosexuality in the 1890's* (Pyckett, 1996), p. 82.

35. C. Breward, *The Dandy Laid Bare: Embodying Practices and Fashion for Men* (Bruzi and Church Gibson, 2000), p. 231.

36. Ibid, p. 225.

37. S. Fillin-Yeh, *Introduction: New Strategies for a Theory of Dandies* (2001), pp. 1-2.

38. S. Bellassai, *La mascolinità contemporanea* (Roma: Carocci, 2004); see also S. M. Whitehead and F. J. Barrett, eds., *The Masculinities Reader* (London: Polity Press, 2001).

39. R. W. Connell, *Maschilità. Identità e trasformazioni del maschio occidentale* (London: Feltrinelli, 1996, 1995).

40. S. Bellassai, *La mascolinità contemporanea* (Roma: Carocci, 2004), pp. 12-13.

41. S. Bellassai and Malatesta M., eds., *Genere e mascolinità. Uno sguardo storico* (Roma: Bulzoni, 2000), pp. 269, 275.

42. F. La Cecla, "Modi bruschi. Come si fanno gli uomini," in Malossi G., ed., *Uomo oggetto. Mitologie, spettacolo e mode della maschilità* (Bergamo: Edizioni Bolis, 2000), pp. 34-43; see also T. Polhemus, "L'uomo invisibile. Stile e corpo maschile," in Malossi (2000), p. 47.

43. Polhemus, "L'uomo invisibile. Stile e corpo maschile," in Malossi (2000), p. 47.

44. M. Kimmel, *The Gendered Society* (New York and Oxford: Oxford University Press, 2000), pp. 5-8.

45. F. La Cecla, "Modi bruschi. Come si fanno gli uomini," in Malossi (2000), p. 36.

46. P. Bourdieu, *Il senso pratico* (Roma: Armando Editore, 2005, original edition 1980), p. 105.

47. M. Kimmel, "Maschilità e omofobia. paura, vergogna e silenzio nella costruzione dell'identità di genere," in Leccardi (2002), p. 191.

48. S. M. Whitehead and F. J. Barrett, eds., *The Masculinities Reader* (London: Polity Press, 2001), pp. 351-365.

49. T. W. Adorno, et al., *La Personalità Autoritaria* (Milano: Edizioni di Comunità, 1973, 1950).

50. H. Brod, *The Making of Masculinities: The New Men's Studies* (Boston: Allen & Unwin, 1987).

51. M. Kimmel, *The Gendered Society* (New York and Oxford: Oxford University Press, 2000), pp. 289-294.

52. M. A. Messner, *Friendship, Intimacy and Sexuality* (Whitehead and Barrett, 2001), pp. 253-265.

53. F. Mort, *Cultures of Consumption. Masculinities and Social Space in Late Twentieth-Century Britain* (London: Routledge, 1996), p. 18; see also F. Boni, "Men's Help," *Sociologia dei periodici maschili* (Roma: Meltemi, 2004).

54. F. Mort, *Cultures of Consumption. Masculinities and Social Space in Late Twentieth-Century Britain* (London: Routledge, 1996), p. 16.

55. S. Nixon, "Exibiting Masculinity," in Hall (1997), pp. 293, 295.

56. Ibid, p. 308.

57. Ibid, p. 314.

58. G. Vergani, *Sarti d'Abruzzo* (Milano: Skira, 2004), pp. 13–23.

59. N. White, *Reconstructing Italian Fashion. America and the Development of the Italian Fashion Industry* (Oxford and New York: Berg, 2000).

60. A. Balestri and M. Ricchetti, "Il prezzo di essere uomini," in Malossi (2000), p. 57.

61. I. Paris, "La nascita della camera nazionale della moda italiana e il suo ruolo nello sviluppo del sistema italiano della moda," in *Balbi sei. Ricerche storiche Genovesi* (2004), pp. 32-77.

62. M. Naldini, *Uomini e moda. Mezzo secolo di abbigliamento maschile nel racconto di giuliano angeli* (Milano: Baldini Castaldi, 2005).

63. G. Maresca, "L'eleganza e' una virtu' che nasce dall'anima," *Monsieur* (March, 2003).

64. E. Goffman, *Stigma. L'identità negata* (Verona: Ombre Corte, 2003, 1963), p. 159.

65. D. Crane, *Questioni di moda. Classe, genere, identità nell'abbigliamento* (Milano: FrancoAngeli, 2004, original edition 2000).

66. P. Colaiacomo, *Fatto in Italia. La cultura del made in Italy (1960-2000)* (Roma: Meltemi, 2006), pp. 16-17.

67. S. Hall, *Notes on Deconstructing "the Popular,"* in R. Samuel, ed., *People's History and Socialist Theory* (London: Routledge and Paul Kegan, 1981).

68. J. Craik, *The Face of Fashion* (London: Routledge and Paul Kegan, 1994); see also V. Steele, "Uomini senza Stile," in Malossi (2000), pp. 78-83.

69. J. Reich, *Undressing the Latin Lover: Marcello Mastroianni, Fashion and La Dolce Vita* (Bruzzi: Church Gibson, 2000), pp. 209-220.

70. T. Polhemus, *StreetStyle* (London: Thames and Hudson, 1994), p. 45.

71. J. Berger, "The Suit and the Photograph," in C. Mukerji and M. Schudson, eds., *Rethinking Popular Culture* (Berkeley: University of California Press, 1991), p. 430.

72. E. Mora, "Globalizacion y cultura de la moda," in M. Codina and M. Herrero, eds., *Mirando la moda. Once reflexiones* (Madrid: Ediciones Internacionales Universitarias, 2004), pp. 105-124.

73. D. Crane, *Questioni di moda. Classe, genere, Identità nell'abbigliamento* (Milano: FrancoAngeli, 2004, original edition 2000).

I would like to thank the feminist scholars working on care in both Aalborg and Roskilde universities in Denmark for their hospitality and support when working on this paper. Their feedback and support were invaluable. I particularly want to thank Birte Siim, Hanne Marlene Dahl, Anne-Dorte Christensen and Annette Borchorst for their specific important bibliographic suggestions. An earlier version of this paper was published in the Danish Women's Studies journal *Kvinder Kon & Forskning*, nos. 2-3, (2007): 91-100.

CHAPTER 10

1. Thomas More, *Utopia* (1516, 1965), p. 103.

2. Nira Yuval-Davis and Marcel Stoetzler, "Imagined Borders and Boundaries: A Gendered Gaze," *European Journal of Women's Studies* (August, 2002); see also Nira Yuval-Davis, "Belonging: from the Indigene to the Diasporic," in Umut Ozkirimli, ed., *Nationalism and its Futures* (Basingstoke: Macmillan, 2003), pp. 127-144.

3. Stephen Castles and Mark J. Miller, *The Age of Migration* (Basingstoke: Macmillan, 2003).

4. Nira Yuval-Davis, "The Spaced-Out Citizen: Collectivity, Territoriality and the Gendered Construction of Difference," in E. Inis, ed., *Rights to the City: Citizenship, Democracy and Cities in a Global Age* (London: Routledge, 1999).

5. T. H. Marshall, *Citizenship and Social Class* (Cambridge: Cambridge University Press, 1950).

6. Nira Yuval-Davis, Floya Anthias, and Eleonore Kofman, "Secure Borders—White Haven: The White paper and the Gendered Politics of Migration and Belonging," in *Ethnic and Racial Studies* (2005).

7. David Blunkett, *Secure Borders, Safe Haven* (White paper, Home Office, 2002).

8. Georgie Wemyss, "The Power to Tolerate," *Patterns of Prejudice* 40, no. 3 (2006): 215-236.

9. Wendy Sarvasy and Patrizia Longo, "Kant's World Citizenship and Filipina Migrant Domestic Workers," *International Feminist Journal of Politics* 6, no. 3 (2004): 392-415.

10. Michael Ignatief, *Human Rights as Politics and Idolatry* (Princeton: Princeton University Press, 2001).

11. A. Favell, "To Belong or not to Belong: The Postnational Question," in A. Geddes and A. Favell, eds., *The Politics of Belonging: Migrants and Minorities in Contemporary Europe* (Aldershot: Ashgate, 1999), pp. 209-27.

12. Adrian Oldfield, *Citizenship and Community: Civic Republicanism and the Modern World* (London: Routledge, 1990); see also Amitai Etzioni, *The Spirit of Community* (New York: Crown Publishers, 1993); see also S. Avineri and A. Shalit, eds., *Communitarianism & Individualism* (Oxford: Oxford University Press, 1992).

13. Nira Yuval-Davis and Floya Anthias, eds., *Woman-Nation-State* (London: Macmillan, 1989); see also Nira Yuval-Davis, *Gender and Nation* (London: Sage, 1997).

14. Virginia Held, *The Ethics of Care* (Oxford: Oxford University Press, 2005); see also Arlie Russell Hochschild, *The Commercialization of Intimate Life: Notes from Home and Work* (Berkeley: University of California Press, 2003); see also Fiona Robinson, *Globalizing Care: Ethics, Feminist Theory and International Relations* (Boulder: Westview Press, 1999); see also Joan Tronto, "Care

as the Work of Citizens: A Modest Proposal" in Marilyn Friedman, ed., *Women and Citizenship* (Oxford: Oxford University Press, 2005), pp.130-148.

15. *Soundings*, special issue on *Regimes of Emotion* 20 (Autumn, 2001).

16. Joan Tronto, *Moral boundaries* (New York: Routledge, 1992); see also Arnlaug Leira, "Concepts of Care," *Social Service Review* 68, no. 2 (1994), pp. 185-201.

17. Carol Gilligan, *In a Different Voice* (Cambridge, MA: Harvard University Press, 1982).

18. Sara Ruddick, *Maternal Thinking* (London: The Women's Press, 1989).

19. Richard Dawkins, *The Selfish Gene* (Oxford: Oxford University Press, 1976).

20. Adam Curtis, *The Trap*, 3-part documentary series, BBC2, April, 2007.

21. John F. Nash, "Non Cooperative Games," *The Annals of Mathematics* 54, no. 2 (1951): 286-295.

22. Maxine Molineus, "Beyond the Domestic Labor Debate," *New Left Revie* I, no. 116 (July/August, 1979); see also Deborah Fahybrycesa and Ulla Vuorerla, "Outside the Domestic Labor Debate," *Review of Radical Political Economics* 16, nos. 2-3 (1984): 137-166.

23. Chiara Saraceno, "Family, Market and Community," *Social Policy Studies*, no. 21 (Paris: OECD, 1997).

24. Arlie Russell Hochschild, *The Commercialization of Intimate Life: Notes from Home and Work* (Berkeley: University of California Press, 2003).

25. Joan Tronto, "Care as the Work of Citizens: A Modest Proposal" in Marilyn Friedman, ed., *Women and Citizenship* (Oxford: Oxford University Press, 2005), pp. 130-148.

26. David Harvey, *The Condition of Post Modernity* (New York: Blackwell, 1990).

27. Joan Tronto, "Care as the Work of Citizens: A Modest Proposal" in Marilyn Friedman, ed., *Women and Citizenship* (Oxford: Oxford University Press, 2005), p. 130.

28. Ninna Nyberg Sorensen, "Narratives of Longing, Belonging and Caring in the Dominican Diaspora" in J. Besson & K.F. Olwig, eds., *Caribbean Narratives* (London: Macmillan, 2005).

29. B. Anderson, *Imagined Communities: Reflections on the Origins and Spread of Nationalism* (London: Verso, 1983).

30. L. Althusere, *Lenin and Philosophy and other Essays* (London: New Left Review, 1971); see also Ernest Gellner, *Nations and Nationalism* (Ithaca, NY: Cornell University Press, 1983); see also Eric Hobsbawm, *Nations and Nationalism since 1780* (Cambridge: Cambridge University Press, 1990).

31. Cynthia Enloe, "Womenandchildren: Making Feminist sense of the Persian Gulf Crisis," *The Village Voice*, 25 September, 1990.

32. Nira Yuval-Davis, "Front and Rear: Sexual Divisions of Labor in the Israeli Military," *Feminist Studies* 11, no. 3 (1985): 649-676; see also Nira Yuval-Davis, *Gender and Nation* (London: Sage, 1997).

33. G. Delanty, *Inventing Europe: Idea, Identity, Reality* (Basingstoke: Macmillan, 1995); see also Michael Savage, Gaynor Bagnall, and Brian Longhurst, *Globalization and Belonging* (London: Sage, 2004).

34. Michael Cohen, "Rooted Cosmopolitanism," *Dissent* (Fall, 1992): 478-483.

35. Sheldon Pollock, Homi K. Bhabha, Carol A. Breckenridge, and Dipesh Chakrabarty, "Cosmopolitanisms" in C.A. Breckenridge, S. Pollock, H. K. Bahbha, and D. Cahkrabarty, eds., *Cosmopolitanism* (Durham: Duke University Press, 2002).

36. Ulrike Vieten, (forthcoming), *Situated Cosmopolitanisms*, Ph.D. dissertation at the University of East London.

37. M. Castells, *The Power of Identity* (Oxford: Blackwell, 1997).

38. Zygmunt Bauman, *Wasted Lives* (Cambridge: Polity Press, 2004).

39. Sara Ahmed, *The Cultural politics of Emotions* (Edinburgh: Edinburgh University Press, 2004).

CHAPTER 11

1. The paper that Virginia Held gave at the STI conference in Barcelona was entitled "Gender Identity and The Ethics of Care in Globalized Society," appearing in Rebecca Whisnant and Peggy DesAutels, eds., *Global Feminist Ethics* (Lanham, MD: Rowman and Littlefield, 2008), pp. 43-57. The ideas for this paper emerged out of the discussion of her work and the illuminating conversations that we were able to have at the conference.

2. For some understanding of the development of Virginia Held's work and the ways that it has turned towards an appreciation of an ethics of care see for example, Virginia Held, *Feminist Morality: Transforming Culture, Society and Politics* (Chicago: University of Chicago Press, 1993), and her more recent *The Ethics of Care: Personal, Political, and Global* (New York: Oxford University Press, 2006).

3. n *Kant, Respect and Injustice: The Limits of Liberal Moral Theory* (London and New York: International Library of Philosophy, Routledge, 1986), I was concerned to questioned the rationalist assumptions that informed a Kantian ethical tradition and the ways emotions, feelings and desires, gathered by Kant as "inclinations" were discounted as sources of moral insight and self-understanding. I showed how the disavowal of emotions had its source in the radical distinction that Kant draws between reason and nature and the identification of morality with reason.

4. For some of Seyla Benhabib's reflections upon the uneasy relationship between feminism and postmodernism see, for

instance, "Feminism and Postmodernism: An Uneasy Alliance," in Linda Nicholson, ed., *Feminist Contentions: A Philosophical Exchange* (New York: Routledge, 1995).

5. I explore some of these tensions in relation to respect, power and equality particularly in relation to issues of dependency to do with class, "race," and gender within Rawls original theory of justice that he developed in *A Theory of Justice* (Cambridge, MA: Harvard University Press, 1970), in *Kant, Respect and Injustice: The Limits of Liberal Moral Theory* (London and New York: Routledge, 1986).

6. For some reflections upon embodiment and forms of knowledge within feminist theory that Held draws from see Nancy Hartsock, "Experience, Embodiment and Epistemologies," *Hypatia* 21, no. 2 (Spring, 2006).

7. For some helpful reflections upon the changing relationships that characterize work within the new capitalism see, for instance, Richard Sennett, *The Corrosion of Character: The Personal Consequences of Work in the New Capitalism* (New York: W.W. Norton and Co, 1998). See also Jeremy Rifkin, *The End of Work* (New York: Putnam, 1995); see also Bennett Harrison, *Lean and Mean* (New York: Basic Books, 1993), and Eileen Applebaum and Rosemary Batt, *The New American Workplace* (Ithaca, NY: Cornell University Press, 1993).

8. I have explored some of these connections between Marxism, feminism and Wittgenstein's later philosophy as they flowed as influences into each other in the 1970s and 80s in *Recovering the Self: Morality and Social Theory* (London and New York: Routledge, 1994). In their different ways they helped to produce a different sensibility to the post-structuralism that was for a time to be so influential within social and political theory.

9. For Stanley Cavell's reading of Wittgenstein that helped potentially to make connections with the humanities and social sciences see *The Claim of Reason: Wittgenstein, Skepticism, Morality and Tragedy* (Oxford: The Clarendon Press, 1979).

10. For some sense of Althusser's reading of Marx and the ways it framed a break with humanistic traditions on the left see *For Marx*, trans. Ben Brewster (London: Verso Books, 1970), and *Essays on Self-Criticism* (London: New Left Books, 1972). For some critical engagement with Althusserian Marxism and the influence that it had in shaping an intellectual sensibility on the left that was antagonistic to personal and emotional life, see Ted Benton, *The Rise and Fall of Structuralist Marxism* (London: Routledge, 1984) and S. Clarke, T. Lovell, K. Robins and V.J. Seidler, *One Dimensional Marxism: Althusser and the Politics of Culture* (London: Allison and Busby, 1980), and the diverse reflections gathered in Dave Morley and Kuan-Hsing Chen, eds., *Stuart Hall: Critical Dialogues in Cultural Studied*, (London and New York: Routledge, 1996).

11. For a sense of the development of Carol Gilligan's work on an ethics of care see *In a Different Voice: Psychological Theory and Women's Development* (Cambridge, MA: Harvard University Press, 1982); see also Lyn Mikel Brown and Carol Gilligan, *Meeting at the Crossroads: Women's Psychology and Girls' Development* (Cambridge, MA: Harvard University Press, 1992), and more recently Carol Gilligan, *The Birth of Pleasure: A New Map of Love* (New York: Vintage Books, Random House, 2003). For a sense of Nell Nodding's work see, for instance, *Caring: A Feminist Approach to Ethics and Moral Education* (Berkeley: University of California Press, 1984).

12. Simone Weil's essay "Human Personality" is to be found in R. Rees, ed., *Selected Essays 1934-43* (Oxford: Oxford University Press, 1962). For a discussion of Weil's different conceptions of justice see Lawrence Blum and Victor J. Seidler, *A Truer Liberty: Simone Weil and Marxism* (New York: Routledge, 1991).

13. For a fuller exploration of Virginia Held's thinking about an ethics of care see *The Ethics of Care: Personal, Political and Global* (New York: Oxford University Press, 2006.)

14. For an exploration of cultural masculinities and ways they have traditionally inscribed distinctions between reason and emo-

tion that help to shape discrete moral traditions see, for instance, Victor J. Seidler, *Man Enough: Embodying Masculinities* (London: Sage, 1999), and more recently *Transforming Masculinities: Men, Cultures, Bodies, Power, Sex and Love* (London and New York: Routledge, 2006).

15. I explore some connections between men, masculinities and an ethics of care in *Unreasonable Men: Masculinity and Social Theory* (London and New York: Routledge, 1994).

16. See the paper presented by Shelly Wilcox at the STI conference in Barcelona entitled "Who pays for Gender De-Institutionalization?" that appears in this collection.

17. For some interesting reflections upon the relationship between feminism, globalization, and human rights see, for instance, Julie Peters and Andrea Wolper, eds., *Women's Rights, Human Rights* (London: Routledge, 1995); see also Marianne H. Marchand, and Anne Sisson Runyon, eds., *Gender and Global Restructuring* (London: Routledge, 2000); see also Robin Cooke, ed., *The Human Rights of Women* (Philadelphia: University of Pennsylvania Press, 1994).

18. For a sense of the development of Carol Gould's work see, for instance, *Rethinking Democracy* (Cambridge: Cambridge University Press, 1988); see also *Globalising Democracy and Human Rights* (Cambridge: Cambridge University Press, 2004), and the special issue of the *Journal of Social Philosophy* 37, no. 1 (Spring, 2006), on Carol Gould and Alistair Macleod, eds., *Democracy and Globalization*.